COMPARATIVE GOVERNMENT AND POLITICS
Series Editor: **Vincent Wright**

Published

Rod Hague and Martin Harrop
Comparative Government and Politics
(2nd edition)

Joni Lovenduski and Jean Woodall
Politics and Society in Eastern Europe

Neill Nugent
The Government and Politics of the European Community

Stephen White, John Gardner and George Schöpflin
Communist Political Systems: An Introduction
(2nd edition)

Forthcoming

Rudy Andeweg and Galen A. Irwin
Dutch Politics

Nigel Bowles
American Government and Politics

Robert Leonardi
Government and Politics in Italy

Douglas Webber
The Government and Politics of Germany: Policy and Politics in the FRG

COMPARATIVE GOVERNMENT AND POLITICS
Series Editor: Vincent Wright

Published

Rod Hague and Martin Harrop
Comparative Government and Politics
(2nd edition)

Tom Bottomore and Ivan Woodall
Politics and Society in Eastern Europe

Neil Nugent
The Government and Politics of the European
Community

Stephen White, John Gardner and George Schöpflin
Communist Political Systems:
An Introduction
(2nd edition)

Forthcoming

Rudy Andeweg and Galen A. Irwin
Dutch Politics

Nigel Bowles
American Government and Politics

Robert Leonardi
Government and Politics in Italy

Douglas Webber
The Government and Politics of Germany: Policy and
Politics in the FRG

The Government and Politics of the European Community

Neill Nugent

MACMILLAN

First published 1989

Published by
MACMILLAN EDUCATION LTD
Houndmills, Basingstoke, Hampshire RG21 2XS
and London
Companies and representatives
throughout the world

Typeset by Vine & Gorfin Ltd, Exmouth, Devon

Printed in the People's Republic of China

British Library Cataloguing in Publication Data
Nugent, Neill
The Government and Politics of the European
Community
1. European Community
I. Title
341.24'22
ISBN 0–333–42896–X (hardcover)
ISBN 0–333–42897–8 (paperback)

Series Standing Order

If you would like to receive future titles in this series as they are
published, you can make use of our standing order facility. To place a
standing order please contact your bookseller or, in case of difficulty,
write to us at the address below with your name and address and the
name of the series. Please state with which title you wish to begin your
standing order. (If you live outside the United Kingdom we may not
have the rights for your area, in which case we will forward your order
to the publisher concerned.)

Customer Services Department, Macmillan Distribution Ltd,
Houndmills, Basingstoke, Hampshire RG21 2XS, England.

Contents

v

vi *Contents*

List of Tables, Figures, Exhibits, and Documents

Tables

Figures

Exhibits

vii

Documents

Preface

The aim of this book is to provide an introduction to the government and politics of the European Community. I hope it will serve both as a useful text for students and as a readily understandable guide for the general reader.

The book is divided into three parts. In Part One the historical evolution of the Community is explored: from pre-Second World War tensions and hostilities between the states of Western Europe to present-day co-operation and integration. Part Two focuses on the institutional structure, and the associated political actors, of the Community. In Part Three, the policy output of the Community, and the processes which produce that output, are considered. It is hoped that, having read all three parts, plus the conclusion, the reader will have a good understanding of why and how the Community has developed, how it works, and what it does.

Many people working in the institutions of the Community, and in national capitals, provided information and advice without which I would have been unable to write this book. To them I express my genuine thanks. For their detailed comments on the manuscript I am extremely grateful to Simon Bulmer, John Gibbons, and Vincent Wright. For his encouragement and helpful advice I must also express my debt to Steven Kennedy of Macmillan.

Acknowledgement is extended to the *Journal of European Integration* for permission to reproduce Figure 10.2.

Finally, I would like to thank my family. My daughters Helen and Rachael were often patience personified, and endured endless requests to 'keep the noise down' when I was writing. My wife Maureen, in addition to suffering the added domestic burdens which fell to her because of my involvement with the book, did a superbly efficient job in typing the manuscript.

Any responsibility for errors in the book remains, of course, mine.

November 1988   NEILL NUGENT

List of Abbreviations

ACP	African, Caribbean, and Pacific Countries
BEUC	European Bureau of Consumers' Associations
BRITE	Basic Research in Industrial Technologies for Europe
CAP	Common Agricultural Policy
CCP	Common Commercial Policy
CCT	Common Customs Tariff
CDU/CSU	German Christian Democratic Union/Christian Social Union
CET	Common External Tariff
CFP	Common Fisheries Policy
COPA	Committee of Professional Agricultural Organisations
COREPER	Committee of Permanent Representatives
CSP	Confederation of the Socialist Parties of the European Community
DC	Italian Christian Democratic Party
DG	Directorate General
DRIVE	Dedicated Road Infrastructure for Vehicle Safety in Europe
EAGGF	European Agricultural Guidance and Guarantee Fund
EC	European Community
ECOFIN	Council of Economic and Finance Ministers
ECSC	European Coal and Steel Community
Ecu	European Currency Unit
EDC	European Defence Community
EEB	European Environmental Bureau
EEC	European Economic Community
EFTA	European Free Trade Association
EIB	European Investment Bank

x

EMS	European Monetary System
EP	European Parliament
EPC	European Political Co-operation
EPP	European People's Party – Federation of the Christian Democratic Parties of the European Community
ERDF	European Regional Development Fund
ESC	Economic and Social Committee
ESF	European Social Fund
ESPRIT	European Strategic Programme for Research and Development in Information Technology
ETUC	European Trade Union Confederation
Euratom	European Atomic Energy Community
EUROFER	European Confederation of Iron and Steel Industries
EUREKA	European Programme for High Technology Research and Development
FDP	German Free Democratic Party
GATT	General Agreement on Tariffs and Trade
GDP	Gross Domestic Product
GNP	Gross National Product
IEA	International Energy Agency
IMF	International Monetary Fund
IMP	Integrated Mediterranean Programme
JET	Joint European Torus
LDP	Federation of Liberal and Democratic Parties of the European Community
MCA	Monetary Compensation Amount
MEP	Member of the European Parliament
NATO	North Atlantic Treaty Organisation
NCI	New Community Instrument
OECD	Organisation for Economic Co-operation and Development
OEEC	Organisation for European Economic Co-operation.
OJ	*Official Journal of the European Communities*
PCF	French Communist Party
PCI	Italian Communist Party
PDB	Preliminary Draft Budget
RACE	Research and Development in Advanced Communications Technologies for Europe

SCA	Special Committee on Agriculture
SEA	Single European Act
UK	United Kingdom
UN	United Nations
UNCTAD	United Nations Conference on Trade and Development
UNICE	Union of Industries of the European Community
USA	United States of America
VAT	Value Added Tax
WEU	Western European Union

Member States of the European Community

Founding Members (1952 ECSC; 1958 EEC and Euratom)

First enlargement (1973)

Second enlargement (1981)

Third enlargement (1986)

PART ONE

The Historical Evolution

Introduction

No political system or organisation can properly be understood unless it is set in its historical and operational contexts. The structure and functioning of government institutions, the nature and dynamics of political forces, and the concerns and conduct of those who exercise power do not happen as a matter of chance. They are shaped and are constantly being remoulded by evolving forces and events.

Though a relatively new organisation, the European Community (EC) is no less subject to these dictates than are long-established nation states and, like them, its nature cannot be appreciated without reference to its historical sources or to the world in which it functions. Thus, the Community is often criticised for being weak in structure and quarrelsome in nature, with far too much bickering over matters such as the price of butter and not enough visionary thinking and united action to tackle unemployment, regional imbalances, and other major problems. Unquestionably there is much in these criticisms, but that the Community should find harmonious collective policy-making difficult is not surprising to anyone with a historical perspective. For, before they became members of the Community the now twelve member states made decisions for themselves on most matters. It is not easy, especially for those which, until relatively recently, have been great powers or which believe themselves to be different or to have special interests, to have to cede sovereignty by transferring decision-making responsibilities to a multinational organisation in which other voices may prevail. An explanation and understanding of what the EC is, and what it has and has not achieved, must recognise this. The Community must, in other words, be seen in the context of the forces that have made it, and are still making it. Some of these forces, notably ones of increasing economic interdependence, have served to push the states together. Others, and long-established assumptions regarding the importance of national independence and sovereignty are very much amongst these, have resulted in progress towards co-operation and integration being slow, difficult, and far from continuous.

The sovereignty issue may also be used to give another, rather different, example of the importance of both historical background and contemporary operational context in explaining and evaluating the EC. Many of the Community's opponents and critics subscribe to the view that the nation state, not an international organisation, is the 'natural' supreme political unit. They argue that insofar as transferences of power to Brussels, Luxembourg and Strasbourg – the three main seats of the Community's institutions – undermine national sovereignty, they should be resisted. But what proponents of this view all too often fail to recognise is that the states of Western Europe saw their sovereignties being steadily eroded long before the EC was established, and since it was established have seen them further eroded by forces that are not a consequence of the Community membership. Whether it is because of movements in financial markets, transfers of capital within multinational corporations, changing trade patterns, or superpower military dominance, virtually all West European states have become increasingly affected by, and at the mercy of, international developments they cannot control. This loss of power may not have involved legal transfers of sovereignty, but it has had a similar effect to that of EC membership: in an ever expanding range of policy and decision-making sectors states have not been able to act in isolation but have had to adjust and adapt so as to fit in with an array of external influences. The Community should not, therefore, be viewed as a unique threat to the sovereignties of the states of Western Europe. On the contrary, it is in some ways an attempt to meet this threat by providing a means by which the states, if not able to regain their sovereignty, can at least reassert control over aspects of decision-making by co-operating together at levels and in ways which match post-war internationalism.

The purpose of Part One is thus to trace the evolution of the Community and to place it in its historical settings.

In Chapter 1 the sharp divide between pre-war and post-war West European inter-state relations is examined. The factors which explain what amounted to a post-war transformation in those relations are analysed. And the EC is placed in the context of other organisational developments that also occurred in the 1940s and 1950s.

Chapter 2 analyses the development of the three Communities

which make up what is now usually referred to in the singular as the European Community: the European Coal and Steel Community which was founded by the Treaty of Paris in 1951, and the European Atomic Energy Community (Euratom) and the European Economic Community (EEC) both of which were established in March 1957 with the signing of the Treaties of Rome.

1

The Post-war Transformation

Historical Divisions

Since the late 1940s Europe has been divided into two halves, East and West. The line of division has little to do with geography but is drawn according to whether countries fall within the Soviet or the Western spheres of influence. Only a few states are not readily classifiable in this way. Finland and Yugoslavia are obvious examples, with both, for a mixture of political and geographical reasons, seeking to look to the East and the West without ever getting too close to either. And then there are those countries – of which Austria, Sweden and Switzerland are the most important – which affirm their neutrality, which are not militarily allied to either 'side', but which are clearly Western orientated in most political, economic and social respects.

Division in Europe is not new. Even if attention is just restricted to that part of Europe which is of most interest to us in this book, the peoples and the states of Western Europe have long differed and been divided in many ways.

Language has been perhaps the obvious divisive force. Linguists may identify structural similarities between European languages, but the fact is that most peoples have not been able to, and still cannot, directly converse with one another. Religion has been another source of division, with the northern countries (except Ireland) being mainly Protestant, and the southern countries (including France but excluding Orthodox Greece) being predominantly Catholic.

Contrasting cultural traditions and historical experiences have further served to develop distinct identifications – and feelings of 'us' and 'them' – across the map of Europe.

Such differences have helped to bind some peoples together, but they have also served to separate others from one another. Along with the legacies of power struggles and wars they help to explain why Western Europe has been divided into so many states, each with its own identity and loyalties. Some of these states – France, Spain and the United Kingdom for example – have existed in much their present geographical form for centuries. Others – including Germany, Italy and Ireland – have been constituted only comparatively recently, mostly in the nineteenth and early twentieth centuries, as nationalism flourished and as force was used to bring nation and state into closer alignment.

Until at least the Second World War, and in some cases well beyond, linguistic, religious and cultural divisions between the West European states were exacerbated by political and economic divisions.

The political divisions took the form of varying systems of government and competing ideological orientations. In the nineteenth and early twentieth centuries autocracies contrasted with emerging, and more liberal, parliamentary democracies. Between the two world wars parliamentary democracy found itself under attack and in some cases was overthrown: in Italy in 1922 by Fascism, in Germany in 1933 by Nazism, and in Spain after the 1936–9 civil war by conservative authoritarianism. It was not until the mid-1970s – following the collapse of the dictatorships of the Iberian peninsula and the overthrow of the military regime in Greece – that parliamentary democracy finally became general throughout Western Europe.

Economic divisions were no less marked. From the beginnings of the Industrial Revolution until the middle of the nineteenth century Britain was industrially and commercially dominant. Gradually it was challenged, particularly by Germany, but also by Belgium, France and others, so that by the early years of the twentieth century competition between these countries for overseas markets was fierce. At the same time, the economies of the northern countries were increasingly differentiated from those of the south, in that the former mostly had substantial industrial bases while the latter remained predominantly agricultural and underdeveloped.

Western Europe was thus long divided and many of these divisions provided sources for tensions, hostilities and wars. Finding their expression in economic and ideological competition, in drives for national power and prestige, and in territorial disputes, and compounded by dangerous mixtures of assertive/weak/incompetent leaderships, the divisions ensured that until after the Second World War rivalry and distrust governed the relationships between most of the states most of the time.

In the twentieth century alone two devastatingly destructive world wars, both of which began as European wars, have been fought. The first (1914–18) saw the countries of the Triple Entente – Britain, France and Russia – plus Italy from 1915, fighting against Germany and Austria – Hungary. The second (1939–45) saw Germany, assisted from 1940 by Italy, attempting to impose itself by force on virtually the whole of Europe outside the Iberian peninsula.

The background to the Second World War is worth outlining briefly because it puts in perspective how dramatically different, and how suddenly found, were the more co-operative relationships between the states in the post–1945 era. In short, the period between the wars was characterised by particularly sharp and fluid interstate relations. There was no stable alliance system and no clear balance of power. For the most part the states regarded one another with, at best, suspicion. Though multilateral and bilateral treaties, agreements and pacts abounded there was little overall pattern to them and few had any lasting effect. States came together in varying combinations on different issues in a manner which, far from indicating mutual confidence, was increasingly suggestive of fear.

From time to time in the inter-war period proposals for greater co-operation between the states were advanced but little came of them. The international climate – characterised by national rivalries and clashing interests – was not favourable, and most of the leading advocates of closer linkages were seen as having, as indeed they did have, specific national purposes in mind. Aristide Briand, for example, who was French Foreign Minister from 1925–32, supported European co-operation but clearly had as his prime aim a stable European political system which would preserve the peace settlement that had been imposed on Germany in 1919. Gustav Stresmann, by contrast, who was the German Foreign Minister from 1923–9, saw European co-operation as a way in which Germany could loosen the grip of Versailles and regain its position as a major power.

The lack of any real interest in European co-operation before the Second World War is revealed in the functioning of the League of Nations. Established in 1919 to provide for international collective security it was, in practice, dominated by the Europeans and had some potential as a forum for developing understandings and improving relationships between the European states. It failed, and did so for three main reasons. First, its aims were rather vague and were interpreted in different ways. Second, it was intergovernmental in its structure and therefore dependent on the agreement of all member states before any action could be taken. Third, and most importantly, the states wanted different things from it: some – notably France, most of the medium-sized central European countries which had been constituted in 1918–19 out of the collapsed Austria–Hungarian Empire, and to some extent Britain – saw it as a means of preserving the Versailles *status quo*; others – particularly Germany and Italy – wanted to use it to change the 1919 settlement and were prepared to leave or ignore it if it did not serve that purpose.

Inter-war Europe thus experienced rising tensions as national rivalries remained unharnessed and, above all, as German territorial and power ambitions could not be satisfied. When war did finally break out the Axis powers (Germany and Italy) gained control over virtually the whole of the Continent from the Atlantic to deep inside the Soviet Union. In Western Europe only Britain and those countries which remained neutral (Ireland, Portugal, Spain, Sweden and Switzerland) were not occupied. By May 1945, when German government representatives agreed to unconditional surrender, Nazism and Fascism had been defeated, but economies and political systems throughout Europe had been severely shaken, cities and towns had been destroyed, and millions had been killed.

The Post-War Transformation

Since the Second World War the relations between the Western European states have been transformed. There are three principal aspects to this:

Over Forty Years of Peace

The states have lived peacefully with one another since 1945 and armed confrontation between any two does not now appear to be even remotely possible. As Altiero Spinelli, one of the great advocates and architects of European integration, observed in 1985 shortly before his death:

> [a] major transformation ... has occurred in the political consciousness of Europeans, something which is completely new in their history. For centuries, neighbouring countries were seen as potential enemies against whom it was necessary to be on one's guard and ready to fight. Now, after the end of the most terrible of wars in Europe, these neighbours are perceived as friendly nations sharing a common destiny.

The belief in a common destiny is perhaps questionable, but the reality and importance of the transformation from hostile to friendly relations is not. Certainly the states continue to compete against one another in many arenas, and this does sometimes lead to strains and tensions, but these disagreements are mostly on issues where military conflict is just not relevant to the resolution of differences. In any event, such friction as there is occurs within a context in which all the states share roughly similar views as to who are basically friends and who are real or potential enemies, and within a context too where most are full or part members of the same military alliance: the North Atlantic Treaty Organisation (NATO).

A Transformed Agenda

Throughout the international system the subject matter of discussions and negotiations between states has become more varied. Whilst, as superpowers relations and regional conflicts show, the case should not be overstated, international agendas have undoubtedly become less centred upon traditional or 'high policy' issues and have increasingly focused on 'low policy' issues. That is to say policies concerned with the existence and preservation of the state (such as defence policy and balance of power manoeuvrings), have been joined by policies concerned more with the wealth and welfare of populations (such as policies on trade, monetary stability, environmental protection, and airline safety).

This change in the content of agendas has been particularly marked in Western Europe, and above all in the EC where a transformation can be said to have occurred. Classic 'power politics' have not, of course, disappeared, but they are just not as dominating or as prominent as they were formerly. When representatives of the twelve European Community states meet it is normally to consider topics which a generation or two ago would not have been regarded as proper subjects for international negotiations. For instance: what constitutes 'fair' economic competition, how might research information be pooled to the general advantage, should farmers be given a 5 or 7 per cent increase in their incomes, and what should be the maximum weight of lorries permitted on roads?

New Channels and Processes

Paralleling, and partly occasioned by, the increasingly diverse international agenda has been a transformation in the ways in which states interrelate with one another. The traditional diplomatic means of interstate communications have declined in importance as new channels and processes have become established. Governments, especially governments of the developed world and governments between whom friendly relations exist, are frequently in touch with one another on all sorts of matters and in all sorts of ways.

As with changing agendas, changing forms of interstate communications have been taken further in Western Europe, and particularly in the EC, than anywhere else. Whereas before 1945 relations between the states were largely the responsibilities of Ministries of Foreign Affairs and embassies, there are now few significant parts of any state's machinery that do not have some involvement in managing external relations with European neighbours. Written communications, telephone conversations, telex messages, bilateral and multilateral meetings, have all become ever more numerous. Contacts range from the *ad hoc* and informal to the regularised and highly structured. They may have as their purpose the taking of binding decisions, the exploration of possible advantageous policy co-ordination, or merely the exchanging of views and information.

In the Community, governmental representatives of different sorts meet with one another every working day. At the lower end of the seniority scale junior and middle-ranking officials, working often from tightly drawn negotiating briefs and with their actions subject to later approval from national capitals, convene in committees over months or even years to try and hammer out detailed agreements on proposed legislation. At the other end of the scale, Heads of Government regularly meet, for what are usually wide-ranging and relatively unstructured discussions, in a number of forums: in the twice-yearly European Councils where all twelve Community states are represented; in bilateral meetings, which in the case of the British Prime Minister, the French President, the German Chancellor, and the Italian Prime Minister, are fixed on an at least annual basis; and in the broader setting of the annual Western economic summits which bring together the political leaders of Britain, France, Germany, Italy, Canada, Japan and the United States, plus the President of the European Commission and the head of government of the member state which is currently chairing the Community's Council of Ministers if he is not already present.

Explanations for the Post-war Transformation

In seeking to explain post-war co-operation and integration in Western Europe – which includes locating the foundations of, and reasons for the development of, the European Community – observers have often highlighted different factors, and sometimes indeed have looked in rather different directions. Among the questions that have caused difficulties are these: to what extent do the developments have deep historical roots and to what extent have they been a reaction to specifically post-1945 circumstances: what has been the balance between political and economic factors; what has been the role of general international influences as opposed to more narrowly based West European ones; and has there been a constant underlying movement in an integrationist direction or just a series of specific, and not very well co-ordinated, responses to specific problems?

In looking at the ways in which questions of this sort have been answered four broad explanatory themes can be found in the literature. For analytical purposes they will be considered here separately, but it should be recognised that, in practice, they are by no means mutually exclusive but rather complement, overlap and reinforce one another. It should be recognised, too, that their usefulness as explanations is not constant, but varies over time. So, for example, while political ideals and utopian visions of a united Europe may have had at least some part to play in the early post-war years, more recently they have counted for little, and it has been hard-headed national calculations of economic and political advantages and disadvantages that have been the principal determinants of progress.

The Deep Roots of Integration

Some have found the roots of post-war developments in the distant past. Supporters and advocates of European integration have been especially prominent in this regard. They have suggested that Europe is, and has long been, a unique and identifiable entity. As evidence of this it is often argued that Europe was the cradle of modern civilisation and that there have long been European values and a European culture, art and literature. Walter Hallstein, the first President of the Commission of the EEC, typifies this sort of view:

> Europe is no creation. It is a rediscovery. The main difference between the formation of the United States of Europe and that of the United States of America is not that America did not have to merge a number of firmly established nation-states, but that for more than a thousand years the idea of a unified Europe was never quite forgotten . . . [The advocates of a European federation] know that Europe shares a sense of values: of what is good and bad; of what a man's rights should be and what are his duties; of how society should be ordered; of what is happiness and what disaster. Europe shares many things: its memories that we call history; achievements it can take pride in and events that are shameful; its joys and its sufferings; and not least its tomorrows. (Hallstein, 1972)

Clearly there is much idealism in this. People such as Hallstein are suggesting that transcending the differences, divergences and conflicts between peoples and states there has long been a certain commonality and identity of interest in Europe based on inter-relationships between geography and historical, political, economic, social and cultural developments. It is a contentious view and certainly not one to which many historians would attach much importance. Division and dissension, they would contend, have been more prominent than identity of interest or shared values and experiences. Such limited commonality as has existed has largely been a consequence of geographical proximity.

But if the 'idealistic' interpretation does not now find much favour, there are still those who would wish to stress the importance of the historical dimension of Western European integration. Interstate relations in the nineteenth century are sometimes seen as foreshadowing post-1945 developments insofar as peace endured for much of the century and did so, in part at least, as a result of understandings and agreements between the major powers. The problem with this view, however, is that it rather overstates the extent to which the nineteenth century was a century of peace and it exaggerates, too, the extent to which the states did co-operate. Arguably, the so-called concert of nations represented an embryonic attempt to exercise strategic control through diplomacy and summitry, but that was at a time when conservative autocracies ruled much of Europe, when many of today's states did not even exist in their present forms. And in any event, the system lasted at best only from 1815 to the Crimean War. It then gave way to the wars of mid-century and later to the balance of power – which was hardly based on European trust and co-operation – as the means of seeking to preserve the peace.

It is perhaps in the field of economic history that the most fertile ground for identifying long-term influences and explanations is to be found. From about the late eighteenth century *national* economic integration began to occur, as barriers to economic activity *within* states were dismantled. This helped to promote, and in turn was encouraged by, national political integration which manifested itself in nationalism and in the elevation of the sovereign state to the status of the supreme collective unit. From about the middle of the century the achievement and successes of this internal economic and political integration, allied with an increasing interconnectedness in Europe which followed from technological changes and economic advance, resulted in increasing interstate co-operation to promote trade, competition and growth. For some economic historians an embryonic European economy was being established. Pollard, for example, has written of the mid-nineteenth century:

> Europe's industrialisation proceeded relatively smoothly among other reasons precisely because it took place within what was in many essentials a single integrated economy, with a fair amount of movement for labour, a greater amount of freedom for the movement of goods, and the greatest freedom of all for the movement of technology, know-how and capital. (Pollard, 1981)

But, unlike the customary pattern within nation states, there was nothing inevitable about European economic integration. Nor was there a clear and developing relationship between it and political integration. On the contrary, from the last quarter of the nineteenth century, states, for a variety of reasons, moved increasingly in the direction of economic protectionism and at the same time developed national identities and consciousness such as had not been seen before. In the first part of the twentieth century, and especially between the wars, the European free trading system virtually disappeared, as states sought to protect themselves at the expense of others and as national economies were increasingly reshaped along autarkic lines. Alongside these increasingly closed economic systems developed the ever sharper political tensions and rivalries between the states that were noted earlier.

The European historical experience thus emphasises the extremely important, but often overlooked fact, that although industrialisation and economic liberalisation provide potential bases for the furtherance of interconnections, agreements, and harmonious relations between states, they do not ensure or guarantee them. The powers of Europe went to war with their principal trading partners in 1914. Furthermore, between the wars, economic linkages did little to bring the nations together or to act as a restraint on governments when divergences developed in their aims and strategies. This must be borne in mind when, later in this chapter, attention is turned to modernisation and interdependence as explanations for post-war political and economic integration. Doubtless they have both been extremely important, but, as pre-1939 European history shows, they do not have an inevitable integrationist logic attached to them. Much depends on their relationship to the circumstances of the time, and as will now be shown, these were very different in the post-1945 world to what they had been before the war.

The Impact of the Second World War

The Second World War unquestionably marks a turning point in the West European state system. Within a few years of its ending states were co-operating, and in some instances and in some respects were even integrating, in a manner that would have been inconceivable before the war. Fundamental to this transformation were a number of factors resultant upon the war that combined to bring about radical changes in both the climate of opinion and the perceptions of requirements. They can be grouped under two broad headings:

Political factors. These may be subdivided:

(1) The Second World War produced a greater realisation than had existed ever before that unfettered and uninhibited nationalism was a recipe for war, which in the post-1945 world was increasingly seen as meaning mass destruction. At the international level this thinking was reflected in calls for a larger and more powerful body than the pre-war League of Nations, and it played an important part in the establishment of the United Nations in 1944. But the fact that the two world wars had begun as European wars, and that Germany was generally seen as having been the prime cause of those wars, also brought forth demands and moves for specifically European arrangements. Among the strongest advocates of this view were many of those who had been associated with the Resistance movements of Continental Europe which, from 1943 onwards, had come to be linked via liaising networks and from which ideas and proposals had been generated looking forward to a post-war world that would be based more on co-operation and less on confrontation.

There was thus a widely shared optimism that if the states could work together in joint schemes and organisations barriers of mistrust could be broken down. On this basis, over 750 prominent Europeans came together at the Hague in May 1948 and from their Congress issued a call to the nations of Europe to create a political and economic union. This stimulated discussions at governmental levels, and in May 1949 the Statute of the Council of Europe was signed by representatives of ten states. Article 1 of the Statute states:

> The aim of the Council of Europe is to achieve a greater unity between its Members for the purposes of safeguarding and realising the ideals and principles which are their common heritage and facilitating their economic and social progress.

> This aim shall be pursued through the organs of the Council by discussions of questions of common concern and by agreements and common action in economic, social, cultural, scientific, legal and administrative matters and in the maintenance and further realisation of human rights and fundamental freedoms.

Despite these grandiose ambitions, however, the Council of Europe was to be a disappointment to those who hoped that it might serve as the basis for a new West European state system. In part, the problem was that its aims were just too vague; in part, that its decision-making structure was essentially intergovernmental and therefore weak; but mainly that some of its members, notably the UK, were not much interested in anything that went beyond limited and voluntary co-operation. (Ernest Bevin, British Foreign Secretary, commented on proposals for a really effective Council of Europe thus: 'Once you open that Pandora's box, you'll find it full of Trojan horses'). That all said, the weaknesses of the Council should not be overstated. It was to perform, and continues to perform, certain useful functions – notably in the human rights field through its European Convention of Human Rights, and as a forum for the discussion of matters of common interest. (This latter function is valuable today not least because, with a current membership of twenty-one states, it is the largest West European regional grouping.)

(2) Although it was not immediately apparent when hostilities ceased in 1945, the Second World War was to result in a fundamental redrawing of the political map of Europe. Most obviously, by the late 1940s it was clear that the legacy of war had left the Continent, and with it Germany, divided in two. In Winston Churchill's phrase an 'Iron Curtain' divided East from West.

In the West there was no question of the victorious powers – Britain and the United States – seeking or being able to impose anything like a Soviet style straightjacket on the liberated countries. None the less, if Western Europe did not quite take on the form of a bloc, liberal democratic systems were soon established, and not wholly dissimilar political ideas were soon prevailing, in most of the states. Inevitably this facilitated intergovernmental relations.

Perhaps the most important idea shared by the governments was one which stemmed directly from the East–West division: a determination to preserve Western Europe from Communism. Not only had the Soviet Union extended its influence far into the European heartland, but in France and Italy domestic Communist parties were commanding considerable support and from 1947 were engaging in what looked to many like revolutionary activities. The United States shared this anti-Communist concern, and the encouragement and assistance which it gave to the West European states after the war to co-operate was partly with this mind. In March 1947 President Truman, stimulated by the events in Greece (where the Communists were trying to overthrow the government), outlined what became known as the Truman doctrine which amounted to a political guarantee of support to 'free peoples who are resisting attempted subjugation by armed minorities or by outside pressures'. This political commitment was quickly followed up in 1948 by economic assistance in the form of Marshall Aid, and in 1949 by military protection with the foundation of NATO and a guarantee to the then ten West European member states (Canada and the US brought the founding membership to twelve) of US military protection against a Soviet attack.

The influence of the United States on the West European states at this time should not be seen as having been unwelcome, or be exaggerated. Contrary to the impression that is sometimes given, it was not unwillingly or insidiously imposed but was actively sought by the states themselves. Furthermore, the US wanted much more West European interstate integration than was to be achieved. But it is undeniable, that by its political, economic, and military interventions and assistance, the US did exert pressures and did, at the least, help to make a number of developments possible.

(3) With the post-war division of Europe, with the moving of the international power balance from European state relations to United States – Soviet relations, and with the onset of the Cold War from 1947–8 producing the possibility of Europe being the battleground between East and West, there was a sense from the late 1940s of Western Europe beginning to look like an identifiable political entity in a way in which it had not done before. Not all states or politicians shared this perspective, but among many of those who did it produced a desire that the voice of Western Europe should be heard on the world stage and that this could be achieved only through unity and by speaking with one voice. For some of the smaller European states, which had rarely exercised much international influence and whose very existence had periodically been threatened by larger neighbours, the prospects of such co-operation were particularly attractive.

(4) The future of Germany naturally loomed large in the minds of those who had to deal with post-war reconstruction. Three times in seventy years, and twice in the twentieth century, Germany had occupied much of Europe. Rightly or wrongly it had come to be seen as innately aggressive. As a consequence, the initial inclination of most governments after the war was to try to contain it in some way. Just how this should be done, however, divided the wartime allies, with the consequence that matters drifted until what was initially intended as an interim division of Germany into zones gave way, as the Cold War developed, into a *de jure* division: the Federal Republic of Germany (West Germany) and the German Democratic Republic (East Germany) were both formally constituted in 1949.

By this time the Soviet Union was replacing Germany as the

perceived principal threat to democracy and stability in Western Europe. As this occurred those who were already arguing that a conciliatory approach towards Germany ought to be tried (since a policy of punitive containment had demonstrably failed between the wars), saw their hands strengthened by a growing feeling that attempts must be made to avoid the development of a political vacuum in Germany which the Communists might attempt to exploit. Furthermore, and the United States government played an important role in pressing this view from the early 1950s, use of Germany's power and wealth could help to reduce the contributions that other countries were making to the defence of Europe. The 'incorporation' of the Federal Republic into Western Europe thus had a number of political aspects to it.

Economic factors. Just as pre-war and wartime experiences helped to produce the United Nations, so did they stimulate an interest in the creation of new international economic and financial arrangements. The first fruits of this were realised at the Bretton Woods Conference in 1944 where the representatives of forty-four countries, with the UK and the USA playing the leading roles, agreed to the establishment of two new bodies. The first was the International Monetary Fund (IMF), which was to alleviate problems of currency instability by creating facilities for countries with temporary balance of payments difficulties to have access to short-term credit facilities. The second was the International Bank for Reconstruction and Development (the 'World Bank'), which was to provide long-term loans for schemes which necessitated a major investment. In 1947, at much the same time as the IMF and the World Bank became operative, international economic co-operation was taken a stage further when twenty-three countries negotiated the General Agreement on Tariffs and Trade (GATT) which had as its purpose the facilitating of trade through the lowering of international trade barriers.

Although West European governments (or, more usually, national representatives, since governments on the Continent were not properly restored until 1945–6) played their part in helping to create the new international economic arrangements, it was felt in many quarters that there should also be specifically West European based economic initiatives and organisations. In 1947–8 these feelings were given a focus, an impetus, and an urgency when the rapid post-war economic recovery that most states were able to engineer by the adoption of expansionist policies created massive balance of payments deficits and dollar shortages in particular. Governments were faced with major currency problems, with not being able to pay for their imports, and with the prospect of their economic recoveries coming to a sudden and premature end. In these circumstances, and for reasons that were not altogether altruistic – a strong Western Europe was in its political, security and economic interests too – the United States stepped in with the offer of Marshall Aid. But it was an offer that had attached to it the condition that the recipient states must endeavour to seek greater economic co-operation between themselves. As a result, the first major post-war Western European organisation, the Organisation for European Economic Co-operation (OEEC), was established, with sixteen founding member states in April 1948. Its task, in the short term, was to manage the aid, encourage joint economic policies, and discourage barriers to trade; in the longer term, its stated aim was to build 'a sound European economy through the co-operation of its members'. In the event, though the OEEC did some valuable work, the most notable perhaps being in establishing payments schemes which in the 1940s and 1950s did much to further trade between member countries, it never made much progress with its grander ambitions. Rather like the Council of Europe, its large and somewhat heterogeneous membership, coupled with the strictly intergovernmental nature of its decision-making structure, meant that ambitious proposals were always successfully opposed. Partly as a result of this, and partly in recognition of growing interdependence between all industrialised countries, the OEEC gave way, in 1961, to the Organisation for Economic Co-operation and Development (OECD) whose membership was to be open to non-European countries and which was to have broader objectives reflecting wider and changing interests.

The OEEC thus stemmed from post-war circumstances that mixed the general with the particular. That is to say, attitudes coming out of the war that favoured economic co-operation between West European states were given a direction by particular requirements that were related to the war and its immediate aftermath. Only three years later, in a way that is described in the next chapter, a similar mixture of underlying and triggering factors combined to produce the first of the European Communities: the European Coal and Steel Community (ECSC).

It might be argued that the effect of some of the political and economic factors that have just been considered, such as the existence of Resistance leaders in governments, were essentially short term. It might be argued, too, that other factors, such as the increased need and willingness of the states to co-operate with one another economically, were not so much caused by the war as given a push by it. But what can hardly be disputed is that the factors taken together produced a set of circumstances that enabled Western European co-operation and integration to get off the ground in the 1940s and 1950s.

States, of course, differed in the particulars and the perceptions of their post-war situations. As a result, there was no general agreement as to just exactly what the new spirit of co-operation should attempt to achieve. Many different schemes were advanced and many different organisations were established to tackle particular issues, problems and requirements. The war did not thus produce anything remotely like a united West European movement between the states. But it did produce new realities and changed attitudes which enabled, or forced, virtually all the states to recognise at least some commonalities and shared interests. As a consequence, it became possible for new interstate European organisations to be established. Of these organisations, those that were able to offer clear advantages and benefits to members were able to act as a base for further development. As the ECSC in particular was quickly to demonstrate, co-operation and integration can breed more of the same.

Interdependence

It has become customary to suggest that while both political and economic factors were crucial to Western European co-operation and integration in the formative post-war years, the former have now declined in relation to the latter. The impact of modernisation is generally agreed to be a key reason for this. It has broadened the international agenda from its traditional power and security concerns to embrace a range of economic and social issues, and at the same time it has produced an interconnectedness and interrelatedness between states, especially on economic matters, that amounts to interdependence.

Economic interdependence arises particularly from three features of the post-1945 world: the enormously increased volume of world

TABLE 1.1

Membership of Western and Western European organisations

	Western Organisations			Western European Organisations			
	NATO	OECD	Council of Europe	European Community	EFTA	WEU	Nordic Council
Australia		√(1971)					
Austria		√(F)	√(1956)		√(F)		
Belgium	√(F)	√(F)	√(F)	√(F)		√(F)	
Canada	√(F)	√(F)					
Cyprus			√(1961)				
Denmark	√(F)	√(F)	√(F)	√(1973)	Withdrew in 1972 on joining EC		√(F)
Finland		√(1969)			√(1961)		√(F)
France	S (Since 1966)(F)	√(F)	√(F)	√(F)		√(F)	
Germany	√(1955)	√(F)	√(1951)	√(F)		√(F)	
Greece	√(1952)	√(F)	√(1949)	√(1981)			
Iceland	√(F)	√(F)	√(1950)		√(1970)		√(F)
Ireland		√(F)	√(F)	√(1973)			
Italy	√(F)	√(F)	√(F)	√(F)		√(F)	
Japan		√(1964)					
Liechtenstein			√(1978)				
Luxembourg	√(F)	√(F)	√(F)	√(F)		√(F)	
Malta			√(1965)				
Netherlands	√(F)	√(F)	√(F)	√(F)		√(F)	
New Zealand		√(1973)					
Norway	√(F)	√(F)	√(F)		√(F)		√(F)
Portugal	√(F)	√(F)	√(1976)	√(1986)	Withdrew in 1985 on joining EC	√(1988)	
Spain	S(1982)	√(F)	√(1977)	√(1986)		√(1988)	
Sweden		√(F)	√(F)		√(F)		√(F)
Switzerland		√(F)	√(1962)		√(F)		
Turkey	√(1952)	√(F)	√(1949)				
United Kingdom	√(F)	√(F)	√(F)	√(1973)	Withdrew in 1972 on joining EC	√(F)	
United States	√(F)	√(F)					
Yugoslavia		S					

Note: Dates in brackets refer to when membership of post foundation members came into effect.
KEY √ Full member
    S Special status or associate member
    (F) Founding member

trade; the internationalisation of production – in which multinational corporations have played a prominent part; and – especially since the early 1970s – the fluctuations and uncertainties associated with currency exchange rates and international monetary arrangements. As a result of interdependence a wide variety of economic and financial issues can no longer be limited to, and indeed in some respects do not even bear much relationship to, national boundaries. States are increasingly vulnerable to outside events and are increasingly unable to act in isolation. They must consult, co-operate and, some would argue, integrate with one another in the interests of international and national economic stability and growth.

When the nature of the problem has been seen to require a truly international economic effort most West European states have been prepared to try solutions at this level: in the IMF, in the Bank for International Settlements, in Western economic summits, and elsewhere. Where a regional response has seemed to be more appropriate or more practical, West European-based arrangements have been sought. The most obvious examples of such arrangements are those associated with the European Community. For instance: the Community's internal and external trading agreements are rooted in the belief that successful trade development is dependent on co-ordinated, ordered, stable, and open commercial rules and relations; the European Monetary System stemmed from the external stimulus of the withdrawal by the US in the 1970s from its management of the international monetary system; and the gradual movement of the Community into advanced research is a response to an increasing belief that the Western European states must show a greater willingness to pool their scientific and technological resources and knowledge if they are to compete successfully in world markets against the Americans, the Japanese, and other competitors.

Economic interdependence is not the only feature of modern interdependence. Advances in communications and travel have necessarily placed on the international and European agendas issues which a generation or two ago either did not exist or were seen as being of purely domestic concern. Now, it is commonly accepted that if they are to be tackled with any prospect of success they must be dealt with at an interstate level. Governments thus discuss, and in Western Europe have adopted understandings and made decisions on, matters as diverse as trans-frontier television arrangements, data protection, action against drug traffickers, and football hooliganism.

But despite all the attention that is now given to interdependence, and especially economic interdependence, as the motor of West European integrative processes, and despite, too, the associated assertion that economic factors now far outweigh political factors in determining the relations between the West European, and particularly the EC, states, the case should not be overstated. First, because political factors have not withered as much as is sometimes suggested. Indeed, the continuing decline in the power and weight of the individual West European states in the international system that has been apparent since at least 1945 has meant that it has become more important than ever for them to try and speak as one if they are to exert any significant influence on world political events. Most of the Community states do wish to exert such an influence and so, since the early 1970s, there has been a gradual strengthening of the Community's European Political Co-operation machinery which provides for extensive policy consultations between the member states and encourages the adoption of joint positions on key international issues. Second, because the continuing perception of the Soviet Union as Western Europe's main political enemy, allied with the inability of any single West European state to offer by itself a wholly credible defence capability, has necessitated continuing military co-operation in the context of both the Western Alliance and associated Western European groupings. Since the early 1980s the latter have even been given increased attention as a result of uncertainties and misgivings about the depth of the American commitment to the defence of Western Europe.

Of course, there is a sense in which these political and security inducements to co-operation might also be viewed as an aspect of interdependence: the states have to co-operate because by themselves they cannot hope to be very effective. But if political and security co-operation is to be regarded as stemming from an underlying interdependence it is clearly a different type of interdependence to that which arises from post-war modernisation. One reason for this is that its roots are different – lying in the East-West division and in the diminished significance of the West European states in the age of the superpowers. Another reason is that whereas economic interdependence is inescapable, political and security interdependence is more a matter of choice: states tending to have rather more control over their political and security policy instruments than they do over their economic policy instruments.

National Considerations

While most Western European states since 1945 have paid at least lip service to the idea of a united Western Europe there has never been any consensus between them on what this is to mean in practice. The rhetoric has often been grand, but discussions on specific proposals have usually revealed considerable variations in ambitions, motives, intentions and perceptions. Most crucially of all, states have differed in their assessments of the consequences for them, in terms of gains and losses, of forging closer relations with their neighbours. As a result, some states have been prepared, and have been able, to go further than others, or have been prepared to do so at an earlier time. There has not, therefore, been a coherent and ordered movement towards West European unity. In the late 1940s and 1950s most states were willing to be associated with intergovernmental organisations that made few demands on them – and hence joined the newly created OEEC and the Council of Europe – but there was no similar breadth of support when organisations were proposed that went beyond intergovernmental co-operation into supranational integration. Consequently, the more ambitious post-war schemes – for the ECSC, for a European Defence Community (EDC, which in the event was never established), and for the EEC and Euratom – initially involved only a restricted membership. It was not until circumstances and attitudes in other states changed, and until an obstacle that emerged among the founding states themselves was removed, that the Community's membership opened out in the 1970s and 1980s to include eventually most, though still not all, West European states.

So although all states have long been touched by at least some of the factors that have been examined on the last few pages, the differences between the states have been such that their interest in, and enthusiasm for, co-operation and integration processes have varied, both with regard to nature and timing. Three broad categories of states can be identified:

The six founding members of the European Community. Belgium, France, Germany, Italy, Luxembourg and the Netherlands – the six states which, in 1951, signed the Treaty of Paris to found the ECSC and in 1957 signed the Treaties of Rome to found the EEC and Euratom – were the first to show a willingness to go beyond the essentially intergovernmental organisations which were established in Western

Europe in the late 1940s. Cautiously, tentatively, and not without reservations, each took the view that the benefits of integration, as opposed to just co-operation, would outweigh what looked to be the major disadvantage – some loss of sovereignty. Some of their perceptions of the advantages of creating organisations with supranational characteristics were generally shared. But there were also more nationally-based hopes and ambitions.

● For the three Benelux countries, the experience of the war had re-emphasised their vulnerability to hostile and more powerful neighbours and the particular desirability of being on good terms with Germany and France. Related to this, their size – Belgium and the Netherlands were only middle-ranking European powers while Luxembourg was an almost insignificant one – meant that their only real prospect of being able to exercise any sort of influence in Europe, let alone the world, was through a more unified interstate system. As for economic considerations, the idea of integration was perhaps more acceptable to them than it was to most other states since their own Benelux economic agreements and arrangements pre-dated the war, and negotiations to relaunch and deepen these were under way well before the war ended. Finally, and perhaps most crucially of all, none of the Benelux states was in a strong enough position to ignore Franco-German led economic initiatives.

● Italy, too, had a number of particular reasons for welcoming close relations with other West European states. First, after over twenty years of Fascist rule followed by military defeat, they offered the opportunity of a new start, and from a basis of respectability. Second, in May 1947, as also occurred in France, the Communist Party left government and for some years thereafter seemed to be intent on fermenting internal revolution. The clear anti-Communist tenor of other West European governments looked comforting, and a possible basis of assistance, to Italy's nervous Christian Democratic-led governments. Third, Italy faced economic difficulties on all fronts: with unemployment, inflation, balance of payments, currency stability, and – especially in the south – poverty. Almost any scheme which offered the possibility of finding new markets and generating economic growth was to be welcomed.

● Integration helped French Governments to deal with two of their key post-war policy goals: the containment of Germany and economic growth. The ECSC was especially important in this regard, offering the opportunity to break down age old barriers and hostilities on the one hand, and giving France access to vital German raw materials and markets on the other. Later, in the 1950s, when 'the German problem' was seen to be no longer so pressing, but when German economic competition looked to be an increasing threat, France took steps to ensure that as part of the price of continued integration certain French interests would be given special treatment (see below).

● For Konrad Adenauer, the German Chancellor from 1949 to 1963, it was to be primarily in and through West European unification that Germany would re-establish itself in the international mainstream and thereby regain its self-respect. Western Europe would also, along with the Atlantic Alliance, provide a much needed buttress against the perceived threat from the East. At more specific levels, the ECSC was a means by which Germany could rid itself of Allied restrictions and interference, while the more open markets of the EEC offered immense opportunities for what, in the 1950s, quickly became the fastest growing economy in Western Europe.

The six post-foundation members of the European Community. Although all were to make approaches to the European Community between 1961–3 for either full or associated membership, and although all were to become full members by 1986, Denmark, Greece, Ireland, Portugal, Spain and the United Kingdom kept and/or were kept to the fringes of the integrative developments of the 1950s and did not become Community members. There were a number of reasons for this.

● In the case of Spain and Portugal, political and economic circumstances were unfavourable. The policial circumstances were that both countries were authoritarian dictatorships to which the democratic governments of the founding six did not wish to be too closely attached. The economic circumstances were that both were predominantly agricultural and underdeveloped, and both were pursuing essentially autarkic economic policies until the end of the 1950s: factors which hardly made them suitable candidates for the ECSC, and which had the knock-on effect of excluding them from the EEC negotiations which the founding six opened up only to the UK.

● The Greek economy was similarly unsuitable for ECSC or EEC membership , being predominantly peasant based. Additionally, Greece's history, culture and geographical position all rather put it ouside the West European mainstream.

● Ireland and Denmark were also heavily dependent on agriculture and thus had little interest in the ECSC and many reasons to doubt that the EEC would be to their benefit. The most important of these reasons was that both had strong economic and historical links elsewhere: in Denmark's case with the other Scandinavian countries and with the UK; in Ireland's case with the UK. And the UK did not wish to join the integrative ventures of the six.

● Three factors were especially important in governing the UK's attitude. First, Britain saw itself as operating within what Churchill described as three overlapping and interlocking relationships: the Empire and Commonwealth; the Atlantic Alliance and the 'special relationship' with the United States; and Western Europe. Until the early 1960s Western Europe was seen as being the least important of these. Second, British governments were not prepared to accept the loss of sovereignty that integration implied. There were several reasons for this, in particular: Britain's long-established parliamentary tradition; the record, in which there was considerable pride, of not having been invaded or controlled by foreign powers in modern times; a generally held view that cessation of sovereignty was neither desirable nor necessary, since Britain was still a world power of the first rank; and a certain distaste with the idea of being dependent on the not altogether highly regarded governments and countries of 'the Continent'. Third, Britain's circumstances were such that three of the four main integrationist organisations to be proposed in the 1950s had few attractions in terms of their specific areas of concern: the restrictions entailed in the ECSC looked very unappealing to a country whose coal and steel capacity far exceeded that of any of the six; the EDC would have limited manoeuvrability and options at a time when Britain's defences were already stretched by the attempt to maintain a world role; and Euratom looked as though it would involve sharing secrets with less advanced nuclear powers. Only the EEC seemed to have much to offer, but it carried with it the problems of its proposed supranationalism. From 1955 to 1958 attempts were made to persuade the six not to be so ambitious and to restrict their attention to the construction of a West European free trade area, but with no success. As a result, and with a view also to increasing its bargaining power with the six, Britain looked elsewhere: to other non-signatories of the Treaty of Rome. This led, in January 1960, to the Stockholm Convention which established the European Free Trade Association (EFTA). Its founding members were Austria, Denmark, Norway, Portugal, Sweden, Switzerland and the UK.

The reasons why the six non-founding states were later to turn to the Community are considered in Chapter 2.

Non-members of the European Community. Six significant West European states remain which are neither founding nor post-foundation members of the European Community: Austria, Finland, Iceland, Norway, Sweden and Switzerland. Their non-membership should not be taken as an indication of a narrow nationalism or of an unwillingness to work within West European settings for, on the contrary, each has shown an interest in, and a willingness to be part of, intergovernmental organisations. So, with the exception of Finland, all are members of the OECD and of the Council of Europe. (Finland is a member of the OECD only.) Finland, Iceland, Norway and Sweden, plus Denmark, together constitute the Nordic Council. This organisation was established by a treaty signed in 1953 which specified the aims as being the development of co-operation in the fields of legislation, of cultural, social and economic policies, and of transport and communications. Its achievements, in practice, have perhaps not wholly lived up to these rather ambitious aims but, at a minimum, it does provide a useful forum for joint discussions between ministers, parliamentarians and civil servants on matters of mutual interest and potential co-operation. Most importantly of all, the six non-Community states make up the membership of EFTA – 'Little Europe' as it is sometimes called. When it was constituted in 1960 (with Denmark, Portugal and the UK then also as members, but not, at that stage, Finland or Iceland) EFTA had two principal objectives: first, the establishment of free trade in industrial products between the member countries; second, making Western Europe a free trade area for industrial goods. Both of these objectives have been broadly achieved: the first with the removal of virtually all internal industrial tariffs by the end of 1966; the second with the entry into force in 1973 of a Special Relations Agreement between the EC and EFTA providing for industrial free trade between the countries of the two organisations.

There are a number of reasons why these six countries are not members of the Community.

● Austrian, Swedish and Swiss neutrality are major obstacles to Community accession. There was some doubt about this in the 1960s, and Austria and Sweden considered the possibility of applying for full membership, but uncertainties were removed in 1970 when the Community's Council of Ministers agreed that full membership could be granted only to those countries which accepted all of the Community's aims, obligations and rights, including the declared objectives of economic and monetary union and also political union.

● Finland's special position in relation to the Soviet Union, which forces it to be neutral, means that Community membership cannot be considered.

● Iceland did consider the possibility of Community membership at the time of the first enlargement, but in the event concluded that there were too many policy difficulties. In particular, the EC's fishing policy would oblige Iceland to grant the fleets of other member countries access to its territorial waters.

● Alone of the EFTA six, Norway has applied for full Community membership: in 1962, 1967 and 1969 when it linked its applications with those from the UK. On the third occasion, terms of entry were agreed but were then rejected by the Norwegian people in a referendum, following a campaign in which suspicions about the implications for agriculture, fishing and national sovereignty all played prominent parts.

Geographical proximity and the Community–EFTA free trade area ensure that relations between 'the twelve' and 'the six' are close. The relations are not, however, balanced. The main reason for this is that the twelve are collectively stronger, but important contributory reasons are the much weaker institutional structure of EFTA, and the fact that the free trade arrangements are negotiated between the Community and each individual EFTA state, rather than between the Community and EFTA *en bloc*. The EFTA countries do attempt to co-ordinate their actions, but there is often very little they can do when they are presented by the Community with what are virtually *de facto* situations – as, for example, is often the case when the Community lays down product specifications. This problem, of having to accept trading rules which they have played no part in helping to formulate, may, in the future, encourage some EFTA countries – Norway and Austria are the most likely candidates – to seek full Community membership.

Concluding Comments

Since the Second World War the way in which West European governments relate and communicate with one another has been transformed. As part of this transformation a key role has been played by new international governmental organisations. Some of these are worldwide in their composition, others are regionally based; some have sweeping but vaguely defined responsibilities, others have specific sectoral briefs; some are purely intergovernmental in structure, others are overlain with supranational powers. At a minimum all provide frameworks in which national representatives meet with one another to discuss matters of mutual interest.

At the West European level the European Community is by far the most important and the best known organisation. But it is not the only one, and its three constituent communities were not the first organisations to be established. The reality is that, since the war, many proposals have been advanced, and many arrangements have been developed, involving co-operation and integration between the states. The more ambitious of these have sought to bring the whole of Western Europe together in some sort of federal union. The more cautious, and, it may be thought, the more realistic, have limited themselves to modest aims for only some of the states.

So, although the logic of circumstances and of political and economic changes have brought the states much more closely together, there can hardly be said to have been a common and coherent integrationist force at work in Western Europe in the post-war years. The states have not been bound together in a common mission. This is not to say that there have not been those who have dreamed of a United States of Europe, or that there have not been many who have participated in new interstate arrangements entertaining hopes that they would constitute a basis for further, more ambitious, developments. But it is to say that, for the most part, attitudes and actions have been governed less by the visionary and more by the many differing perceptions of the necessary.

2

The Development of the Community

The European Coal and Steel Community

Much of the early impetus behind the first of the European Communities, the ECSC, emanated from two Frenchmen. Jean Monnet, who had pioneered France's successful post-war experiment with indicative economic planning, provided much of the technical and administrative initiative and behind-the-scenes drive. Robert Schuman, the French Foreign Minister from 1948 to early 1953, acted as the political advocate. Both were ardent supporters of European unity; both believed that the OEEC and the Council of Europe – where anyone could be exempted from a decision – could not provide the impetus that was required; and both came to the conclusion that, in Monnet's words: 'A start would have to be made by doing something both more practical and more ambitious. National sovereignty would have to be tackled more boldly and on a narrower front.'

Many of those who were attracted to the ECSC saw it in very restrictive terms: as an organisation that might further certain limited and carefully defined purposes. Certainly it would not have been established had it not offered to potential member states, and in particular to its two main pillars, France and Germany, the possibility that it might act as a means of satisfying specific and pressing national interests and needs (see previous chapter). But for some, not least Monnet and Schuman, the interest was much more ambitious and long term. In launching his plan in May 1950,

31

Schuman (in what subsequently became known as the Schuman Declaration) was quite explicit that his proposals were intended to be but the first step in the realisation of a vision; a vision of a united Europe which would have Franco-German reconciliation at its heart. But, he warned: 'Europe will not be made all at once or according to a single general plan. It will be built through concrete achievements, which first create a *de facto* solidarity.' In similar vein, Monnet informed governments during the negotiations:

> The Schuman proposals provide a basis for the building of a new Europe through the concrete achievement of a supranational regime within a limited but controlling area of economic effort . . . The indispensable first principle of these proposals is the abnegation of sovereignty in a limited but decisive field

Konrad Adenauer agreed with this. Addressing the Bundestag in June 1950 he stated:

> Let me make a point of declaring in so many words and in full agreement, not only with the French Government but also with M. Jean Monnet, that the importance of this project is above all political and not economic.

Schuman made it clear in his Declaration that while he hoped other countries would also participate, France and Germany were going to proceed with the plan in any event, Germany having already agreed privately in principle. Italy, Belgium, Luxembourg and the Netherlands took up the invitation, and in April 1951 the six countries signed the Treaty of Paris which established the ECSC. It came into operation in July 1952.

The Treaty broke new ground in two principal ways. First, its policy aims were extremely ambitious, entailing not just the creation of a free trade area but the laying of the foundations of a common market in some of the basic materials of any industrialised society: coal, coke, iron ore, steel and scrap. This, it was hoped, would ensure orderly supplies to all member states, would produce a rational expansion and modernisation of production, and would improve the conditions and lifestyles of those working in the industries. Second, it was the first of the European interstate organisations to display significant supranational characteristics. These were found in the new central institutions that were established with powers, among other things, to: see to the abolition and prohibition of internal tariff barriers, state subsidies and special charges, and restrictive practices; fix prices under certain conditions; harmonise external commercial policy by, for example, setting minimum and maximum rates of customs duties on coal and steel imports from third countries; and impose levies on coal and steel production to finance the ECSC's activities. Four main institutions were created:

The High Authority was charged 'To ensure that the objectives set out in this Treaty are attained in accordance with the provisions thereof' (Article 8 ECSC Treaty). To enable it to perform its task the High Authority could issue, either on its own initiative or after receiving the assent of the Council of Ministers: decisions (which were to be binding in all respects in the member states); recommendations (which were to be binding in their objectives); opinions (which were not to have binding force). Matters on which it was granted decision-making autonomy included the prohibition of subsidies and aids, decisions on whether agreements between undertakings were permissible or not, action against restrictive practices, the promotion of research, and the control of prices under certain conditions. It could impose fines on those who disregarded its decisions.

The High Authority thus had a formidable array of powers at its disposal and this, when taken in conjunction with its membership, gave it a clear supranational character. There were to be nine members, including at least one from each member state, and, crucially, all were to be 'completely independent in the performance of their duties'. In other words, none was to be, or to regard him or herself as being, a national delegate or representative.

In a number of respects the High Authority's powers were stronger than those which were to be given to the High Authority's equivalent, the Commission, under the Treaties of Rome. This has meant that since the institutions of the three Communities were merged in 1967, the Commission – which assumed the High Authority's powers – has had rather more room for independent manoeuvre when acting under the Treaty of Paris than it has when acting under the Treaties of Rome. In practice, however, it has not always been possible for these greater powers to be used to the full: from the earliest days of the ECSC political realities have dictated that the High Authority/ Commission be sensitive to governmental opinions and policies.

The Council of Ministers was set up mainly as a result of Benelux concern that if the High Authority had too much power, and there was no forum through which the states could exercise some control, the ECSC might be too Franco-German dominated. Ministers from the national governments were to constitute the membership of the Council, each state having one representative.

'The Council shall exercise its powers in the cases provided for and in the manner set out in this Treaty, in particular in order to harmonise the actions of the High Authority and that of the Governments, which are responsible for the general economic policies of their countries' (Article 26 ECSC Treaty). More specifically, the Treaty gave the Council formal control over some, but very far from all, of the High Authority's actions: it had, for instance, to give its assent to the declaration of a manifest crisis which opened the door to production quotas. Decision-making procedures in the Council were to depend on the matter under consideration: sometimes a unanimous vote would be required, sometimes a qualified majority, sometimes a simple majority.

Practice has shown the Council to be not altogether consistent in the manner in which it has exercised its role under the ECSC Treaty. On the one hand, a general reluctance of the states to lose too much power over their domestic industries has resulted in the Council seeking to take most major decisions itself. Since decision-making in the Council has customarily proceeded on the basis of consensus, and since the states have often been unable to agree when difficult decisions have been called for, this has frequently led to no, or to very weak, decision-making. On the other hand, when practicalities and political convenience have combined to suggest a less Council-centred decision-making approach, as they did with steel from the late 1970s, then the Council has been prepared to allow the High Authority/Commission a considerable measure of independence.

The Common Assembly's role was to provide a democratic input into ECSC decision-making. In practice it can hardly be said to have done so in the early years: members were not elected but were chosen by national parliaments, and the Assembly's powers – notwithstanding an ability to pass a motion of censure on the High Authoirty – were essentially only advisory. However, the expansion of the remit of the Assembly under the Rome Treaties to cover all three Communities, plus developments in the 1970s and 1980s such as the introduction of direct elections and more streamlined procedures, have increasingly made for a more effective Assembly (or European Parliament as it is now called).

The Court of Justice was created to settle conflicts between the states, between the organs of the Community, and between the states and the organs. Its judgements were to be enforceable within the territory of the member states. In similar fashion to the Assembly, but not the High Authority or Council of Ministers which remained separate until 1967, the Court assumed responsibility for all three Communities in 1958.

In addition to these four main institutions a Consultative Committee, made up of producers, workers and other interested parties, was also created. Its role was to be, and has been, purely advisory.

In its early years the ECSC was judged to be an economic success. Customs tariffs and quotas were abolished, progress was made in removing non-tariff barriers to trade, the restructuring of the industries was assisted, politicians and civil servants from the member states developed the practice of working with one another, and, above all, output and interstate trade rapidly increased. (Although many economists would now query whether the increases were *because* of the ECSC.) As a result the ECSC helped to pave the way for further integration.

However, the success of the early years was soon checked. In 1958–9, when cheap oil imports and a fall in energy consumption combined to produce an overcapacity in coal production, the ECSC was faced with its first major crisis – and failed the test. The member states rejected the High Authority's proposals for a Community solution and sought their own, unco-ordinated, protective measures. The coal crisis thus revealed that the High Authority was not as powerful as many had believed and that it was not in a position to impose a general policy on the states if they were resolved to resist.

This relative weakness of the High Authority/Commission to press policies right through is one of the principal reasons why truly integrated West European coal and steel industries, in which prices and distributive decisions are a consequence of an open and free market, have not emerged. Many barriers to trade still remain. Some of these, such as restrictive practices and national subsidies, the High Authority/Commission has tried to remove, but with only limited success. Others, particularly in the steel sector (see Chapter 9), have been formulated and utilised by the Commission itself as its task has switched from encouraging expansion to managing contraction.

But arguably the major problem with the ECSC has been that as coal and steel have declined in importance in relation to other energy sources, what has increasingly been required is not so much policies for coal and steel in isolation, but a co-ordinated and effective Community energy policy. National differences have prevented any such policy being possible.

From the ECSC to the EEC

In addition to the impetus that came from the ECSC there was another institutional development in the 1950s which played a particularly important role in paving the way for the creation of the two further European Communities that were to be created in 1957. This was the projected European Defence Community.

In the early 1950s, to the background of the Cold War and the outbreak of the Korean War, many Western politicians and military strategists took the view that there was a need for greater Western European co-operation in the field of defence. As part of this there was seen to be a pressing need to integrate Germany – which was not a member of NATO – into the Western Alliance. The problem was that some European Governments, especially the French, were not yet ready for German rearmament, while the Germans, though willing to rearm, were not willing to do so on the basis of the tightly controlled and restricted conditions that other countries appeared to have in mind for it. In these circumstances the French Prime Minister, René Pleven, launched proposals in October 1950 which offered a possible way forward. In announcing his plan to the National Assembly he stated that the French government 'proposes the creation, for common defence, of a European Army under the authority of the political institutions of a united Europe'. By the end of 1951 the same six governments which were in the process of establishing the ECSC had agreed to establish an EDC. Its institutional structure was to be similar to the ECSC: a Joint Defence Commission, a Council of Ministers, an advisory Assembly and a Court of Justice. In May 1952 a draft EDC Treaty was signed.

But, in the event, the EDC, and the European Political Community which increasingly came to be associated with it, were not established. Ratification problems arose in France and in Italy, and in August 1954 the French National Assembly rejected it by 319 votes to 264 with 43 abstentions. There were a number of reasons why it did so: continuing unease at the thought of re-arming Germany; concern that French governments would not have sole control of their military forces; doubts about the efficiency of an integrated force; disquiet that the strongest European military power (the UK) was not participating; and a feeling that, with the end of the Korean War and the death of Stalin, it was not as necessary as it had seemed when initially proposed.

Following the collapse of the EDC, an alternative, and altogether less demanding, approach was taken to the still outstanding question of Germany's contribution to the defence of the West. This took the form of a revival and extension of the Brussels Treaty 'for collaboration in economic, social and cultural matters and for collective defence' that had been signed in 1948 by the three Benelux countries, France and the UK. At a conference in London in the autumn of 1954 Germany and Italy agreed to accede to the Brussels Treaty, and all seven countries agreed that the new arrangements should be incorporated into a Western European Union (WEU). The WEU came into effect in May 1955 as a loosely structured, essentially consultative, primarily defence-orientated, organisation that, among other things, permitted German rearmament subject to various constraints. It also enabled Germany to become a member of NATO.

The failure of the EDC, especially when set alongside the 'success' of the WEU, highlighted the difficulties involved in pressing ahead too quickly with integrationist proposals. In particular, it showed that quasi-federalist approaches in politically sensitive areas would meet with resistance. But, at the same time, the fact that such an ambitious scheme had come so close to adoption demonstrated that alternative initiatives, especially perhaps if they were based on the original Schuman view that political union was best achieved through economic integration, might well be successful. It was partly with this in mind that the Foreign Ministers of the ECSC six met at Messina in June 1955 to discuss proposals which had been made by the three Benelux countries for further economic integration. At their Conference the Ministers agreed on a resolution which included the following:

The governments of Belgium, France, the Federal Republic of Germany, Italy, Luxembourg and the Netherlands consider that the moment has arrived to initiate a new phase on the path of constructing Europe. They believe that this has to be done principally in the economic sphere, and regard it as necessary to continue the creation of a united Europe through an expansion of joint institutions, the gradual fusion of national economies, the creation of a common market, and the gradual co-ordination of social policies. Such a policy seems to them indispensable if Europe is to maintain her position in the world, regain her influence, and achieve a steady increase in the living standards of her population.

To give effect to the Messina Resolution a committee of governmental representatives and experts was established under the chairmanship of the Belgian Foreign Minister, Paul-Henri Spaak. The UK was invited to participate and did so until November 1955 when it became apparent that hopes of limiting developments to the establishment of a loose free trade area were not acceptable to the six. In April 1956 the Foreign Ministers accepted the report of the Spaak Committee and used it as the basis for the negotiations that, in 1957, produced the two Treaties of Rome: the more important of these established the EEC, the other created Euratom.

Both before and after April 1956 negotiations between governments were extensive and intense. In very broad terms it can be said that clear provisions were made in the Treaties for those areas on which the governments were able to reach agreement, while where there were divisions matters were largely left aside for further negotiations and were either omitted from the Treaties altogether or were referred to only in a general way. So, in the EEC Treaty, the future rules on trade were set out fairly clearly, but only guiding principles were laid down for social policy and for agricultural policy.

The inclusion of topics such as social policy and agricultural policy highlights the fact that the content of the Treaties reflected a series of compromises between the six, especially between the two strongest countries, France and Germany. France feared that Germany was likely to be the main beneficiary of the more open markets of the proposed customs union and so looked for compensation elsewhere. This took a number of forms. For instance: insisting on special protection for agriculture – the French farmer had historically been well protected from foreign competition and around one-fifth of the French population still earned their living from the land; pressing the case of an atomic energy Community which would help guarantee France greater independence in energy through joint use of resources; and seeking privileged relations with the six for France's overseas dependencies.

Eventually the negotiations were completed, and, on 25 March 1957, the two Treaties were signed. Only in France and Italy were there any problems with ratification: the French Chamber of Deputies voted 342 for and 239 against, and the Italian Chamber of Deputies voted 311 for and 144 against. In both countries the largest bloc opposition came from the Communists.

The Treaties came into effect on 1 January 1958.

The Constitution of the European Community

The European Community thus has three founding treaties: the Treaty of Paris, which was examined above; the Treaty of Rome establishing Euratom; and the Treaty of Rome establishing the EEC. These Treaties have been subsequently supplemented and amended by other treaties and acts. Taken together, these all constitute elements of what may be regarded as the constitution of the Community, that is to say they provide the fundamental legal framework on which the Community is based.

Of the two Rome Treaties the EEC Treaty is by far the most important. Article 2 of the Treaty lays down the following broad objectives:

> The Community shall have as its task, by establishing a common market and progressively approximating the economic policies of Member States, to promote throughout the Community a harmonious development of economic activities, a continuous and balanced expansion, an increase in stability, an accelerated raising of the standard of living and closer relations between the States belonging to it.

Many of the subsequent Treaty articles are concerned with following up these broad objectives with fuller, though still often rather general, guidelines for policy development. These policy guidelines can be grouped under two broad headings:

Policy guidelines concerned with the establishment of a common market. The common market was to be based on:

(a) The removal of all tariffs and quantitative restrictions on internal trade. This would make the Community a free trade area.

(b)   The erection of a Common External Tariff (CET). This would mean that goods entering the Community would do so on the same basis no matter what their point of entry. No member state would therefore be in a position to gain a competitive advantage by, say, reducing the external tariffs on vital raw materials. The CET would take the Community beyond being a mere free trade area and would make it a customs union. It would also serve as the base for the development of a Common Commercial Policy (CCP).

(c)   The prohibition of a range of practices having as their effect the distortion or prevention of competition between the member states.

(d)   Measures to allow not only for the free movement of goods between the member states but also the free movement of persons, services and capital.

Policy guidelines concerned with making the Community more than just a common market. Making it exactly what, however, was left unclear, as it had to be given the uncertainties, disagreements and compromises which formed the background to the signing of the Treaty. There was certainly the implication of a movement towards some sort of general economic integration, and references were made to the 'co-ordination' of economic and monetary policies, but they were vague and implicitly long term. Such references as there were to specific sectoral policies – as, for example, the provisions for 'the adoption of a common policy in the sphere of agriculture', and the statement that the objectives of the Treaty 'shall . . . be pursued by Member States within the framework of a common transport policy' – were also couched in fairly general terms.

The EEC Treaty is thus very different in character from the constitutions of nation states. Whereas the latter have little, if anything, to say about policy, the EEC Treaty has policy as its main concern. The nature of that concern is such that many have suggested that the policy framework indicated and outlined in the Treaty is guided by a clear philosophy or ideology: that of free market, liberal, non-interventionist capitalism. Unquestionably there is much in this view: on the one hand, the market mechanism and the need to prevent abuses to competition are accorded a high priority; on the other hand, there are few references to ways in which joint activities and intervention should be promoted for non-market based purposes. But

DOCUMENT 2.1
Treaty establishing the European Economic Community: contents

[1]Under the Single European Act a new Chapter 1 is inserted: 'Cooperation in economic and monetary policy (Economic and Monetary Union)'. It is made up of a new Article 102a. Chapters 1, 2 and 3 above become Chapters 2, 3 and 4 respectively.
[2]Under the Single European Act three new Titles are added here:
Economic and Social Cohesion (Articles 130A to Article 130E).
Research and Technological Development (Articles 130F to 130Q).
Environmental (Articles 130R to 130T).

the case should not be overstated. First, because competition itself is seen as requiring considerable intervention and management from the centre. Second, because there are some provisions for non-market policies: in the proposed common policy for agriculture, for example, which was given a special place in the Treaty precisely because of (mainly French) fears of what would happen should agriculture be exposed to a totally free market; in the proposed social policy which was intended to help soften unacceptable market consequences; and in the proposed common transport policy where specific allowance was to be made for aids 'if they meet the needs of co-ordination of transport or if they represent reimbursement for the discharge of certain obligations inherent in the concept of a public service'. Third, because much of the Treaty is so vague, so general, and so dependent on the future co-operation of the states for successful policy development, that there was never any question (let alone preference given the Christian Democratic and Social Democratic principles of most of the founders) of an immediate abandonment of national economic controls and a remorseless and inevitable drive towards uninhibited free market capitalism.

The policy concerns of the Euratom Treaty are naturally confined to the atomic energy field. Chapters of the Treaty cover many vitally important areas of activity – promotion of research, dissemination of information, health and safety, supplies, a nuclear common market, etc. However, and probably even more than with the EEC Treaty, differences between the states on key points resulted in the apparent force of many of the provisions of these chapters being watered down by exceptions and loopholes. For example, under Article 52 an Agency is established with 'exclusive right to conclude contracts relating to the supply of ores, scarce materials and special fissile materials coming from inside the Community or from outside'. Article 66, however, sets out circumstances in which states may buy on the world markets provided Commission approval is obtained. Similarly, Treaty provisions aimed at a pooling and sharing of technical information and knowledge are greatly weakened – and were so largely at French insistence – by provisions which allow for secrecy where national security is involved.

Where the EEC and Euratom Treaties are most similar to national constitutions is in those articles which identify the main institutions of the Communities (principally 137–98 in the EEC, 107–70 in Euratom), and those articles which specify the powers and some of the procedures of the institutions (spread throughout the Treaties). The ECSC served as the institutional model, but with certain modifications which had as their effect a tilting away from supranationalism towards intergovernmentalism. As with the ECSC, both the EEC and Euratom were to have four principal institutions:

1. An appointed Commission would assume the role exercised by the High Authority under the ECSC. That is to say, it would be the principal policy initiator, it would have some decision-making power of its own, and it would carry certain responsibilities for policy implementation. But it would have less power than the High Authority to impose decisions on member states.

2. A Council of Ministers, with greater powers than its equivalent under the ECSC, would be the principal decision-making body. Circumstances in which it must take its decisions unanimously, and circumstances in which majority and qualified majority votes were permissible, were specified.

3. An Assembly would exercise advisory and (limited) supervisory powers. In the first instance it would be composed of delegates from national parliaments but after appropriate arrangements were made it was to be elected 'by direct universal suffrage in accordance with a uniform procedure in all Member States'.

4. A Court of Justice was charged with the duty of ensuring that 'in the interpretation and application of this Treaty the law is observed'.

A Convention, which was also signed on 25 March 1957, specified that the Assembly and the Court of Justice should be common to all three Communities.

These institutional arrangements were rather more inter-governmental in character than those who dreamed of political integration would have liked. In particular, the Council of Ministers was judged to have been given too much power and there was also disappointment that most of the key decisions in the Council would have to be made unanimously. However, there was hope for the future in that there were grounds for believing that the system could, and probably would, serve as a launching pad for a developing, a creeping, supranationalism. One of these grounds was provision in the EEC Treaty for increased use of majority voting in the Council as the Community became established. Another was the expectation that the Assembly would soon be elected by direct suffrage and that its power would thereby be increased. And a third was the seemingly reasonable assumption that if the Community proved to be a success the member states would become less concerned about their national rights and would increasingly cede greater powers to the central institutions.

Turning now to the Treaties and Constitutional Acts that have amended the three founding Treaties the most important have been the following.

The Treaty establishing a Single Council and a Single Commission of the European Communities. Signed in 1965, coming into force in 1967, and generally known as the Merger Treaty, this established a single Council of Ministers for all three Communities (though different individuals would attend different meetings), and merged into one Commission the High Authority of the ECSC, the Commission of Euratom and the EEC Commision. The powers exercised by these merged bodies were still to be based on the founding Treaties: in other words, the Treaties and the Communities themselves were not merged.

The Treaty amending Certain Budgetary Provisions of the Treaties (signed in 1970) and the *Treaty amending Certain Financial Provisions of the Treaties (signed in 1975).* Together, these two treaties laid down a budgetary procedure and allocated budgetary powers between the Community institutions. Of particular importance, given its relative weakness in most policy areas, were the powers allocated to the Parliament. The 1975 Treaty also established a Court of Auditors to examine the accounts of all revenue and expenditure of the Community.

The Act Concerning the election of the representatives of the Assembly by direct universal suffrage. Signed in 1976, but not finally ratified by all the member states until 1978, this Act provided the legal base for direct elections to the European Parliament, laid down certain rules for their conduct, but did not in any direct way increase the powers of the Parliament.

The Treaties of Accession. These have provided for the enlargement of the Community to include Denmark, Ireland and the United

Kingdom (signed in 1972 and taking effect on 1 January 1973), Greece (signed in 1979 and taking effect on 1 January 1981), and Spain and Portugal (signed in 1985 and taking effect on 1 January 1986).

The Single European Act (SEA). Signed in February 1986, but not coming into force until mid-1987 because of ratification difficulties in Ireland, the SEA is something of a mixed bag, containing tidying up constitutional provisions, provisions designed to give the Community a new impetus, and provisions which tinker with the Community's decision-making system. The main inclusions are:

1. Foreign policy co-operation, which had increasingly been practised since the early 1970s, but outside the Treaty framework, is put on a legal basis. (But not by Treaty incorporation.)
2. A number of policy areas not specifically mentioned in the EEC Treaty are formally incorporated and the capacity for decision making in these areas is thereby increased. These include, most notably, environment, research and technological development, and 'economic and social cohesion' (basically regional policy).
3. The completion of the internal market by 1992 is identified as a specific goal.
4. A qualified majority for a Council decision replaces the unanimity requirement in six articles of the EEC Treaty – the most important of these being Article 100 which is concerned with the approximation of laws 'which have as their object the establishment and functioning of the internal market'. This change is therefore closely linked with the completion of the internal market objective.
5. In those areas where the SEA provides for majority voting the European Parliament is given increased powers.

Since it began functioning in 1958 the Community has naturally developed in many ways. The most important of those can be grouped under the three headings which now follow.

Enlargement

The most obvious change since the Community's foundation has been the doubling in the size of its membership from six states to twelve.

The first enlargement could have occurred much earlier than it did had the French President, General de Gaulle, not opposed UK applications to join the Community which were made in 1961 and 1967 – applications to which separate applications from Denmark, Ireland and Norway were, in practice, attached. There has been much speculation about the reasons for the General's veto: he feared that the UK would rival and would attempt to thwart his desire to place France at the centre of the European stage; he believed UK membership would unsettle the developing Franco-German alliance – an alliance that was given symbolic force with the signing in 1963 of a Friendship Treaty between the two countries; he was suspicious of the UK's close links with the US and thought they would pave the way for American penetration and domination of Europe if the UK joined the Community. Whatever the explanation, the fact is the UK was barred from membership until after the resignation of de Gaulle in 1969 and the election as President of Georges Pompidou. A different view was then taken in Paris: the UK might serve as a useful counterweight to the increasingly strong and self-confident Germany; UK governments would lend support to the French opposition to pressures within the Community for increased supranationalism; and France would probably gain economically by virtue of having better access to UK markets and as a result of the UK being a net contributor to the Community budget.

The reasons for the UK's changed position on Europe were a mixture of the political and the economic. Politically, it was increasingly clear that the UK was no longer a world power of the first rank. The Suez débâcle underlined the decline, and the increasing tendency from 1960 for key world issues to be discussed between the USA and the USSR on a purely bilateral basis further confirmed it. Paralleling this decline the nature and status of the 'special relationship' with the USA weakened and became increasingly questionable. Further to all this the Empire was giving way to the Commonwealth, a very loose organisation and not one that was capable of providing the UK with much international political might.

On all the usual economic indicators, such as growth in trade, in investment, in gross national product, and in income, the member states of the EC were out-performing the UK. For example, between 1958–69 real earnings in Britain increased by about 38 per cent, whereas in the EC they increased on average by about 75 per cent. Quite simply the figures appeared to show that the Community was a success; all this at a time when the UK's pattern of trade, even when

not a Community member, was turning away from the Commonwealth and towards Europe. Moreover, the growing economic
strength of the EC seemed to be linked with a growing political status.

When Pompidou opened the door the Heath government thus
willingly took the UK in. It was joined by Denmark and Ireland, both
of which had traditional economic and cultural links with the UK and
which had consciously tied their applications to the Community with
those from the UK since the early 1960s.

The accession of Greece was also delayed longer than Greek
governments would have liked, but for very different reasons. The
initial problem, recognised on both sides when Greece made its first
approaches to Brussels soon after the EEC came into being, was the
underdeveloped nature of the Greek economy. A transition period
prior to membership was deemed to be necessary and this was
negotiated in the form of an Association Agreement that came into
force in 1962. The object of the Association was the 'continuous and
balanced strengthening of trade and economic relations between the
contracting parties, having particular regard to the need to secure an
accelerated development of the Greek economy'. Full incorporation
into the Community would follow when the Greek economy was
capable of sustaining the obligations imposed by membership.
However, from April 1967, when there was a military coup in Greece,
until June 1974, when civilian government was re-established, the
Association Agreement was virtually suspended. It might be thought
that the effect of this would have been to further delay full
membership. In fact, it had the opposite effect. After elections in
Greece in November 1974 the new government immediately made
clear its wish to become a full member of the Community. The
Commission issued a formal opinion that Greece was still not
economically ready and proposed a pre-accession period of unlimited
duration during wich economic reforms could be implemented. In
response the Greek government restated its wish for full membership
and, in so doing, particularly emphasised how Community
membership could help both to underpin Greek democracy and to
consolidate Greece's West European and Western Alliance bonds.
The Council of Ministers was sympathetic to these arguments,
rejected the Commission's Opinion, and membership negotiations
were opened in July 1976.

As with Greece, political considerations were also extremely important in governing the relations between the two Iberian states and the Community prior to their accession. Initially the influence was a negative one: had not both Spain and Portugal been governed by dictatorial political systems until the mid-1970s they would in all probability have been members of the Community long before they were. Not that there is anything in the Treaties specifying that Community members must be liberal democracies: Article 237 of the EEC Treaty says 'Any European State may apply to become a member of the Community.' To date, however, the assumption has been that a democratic political system is a necessary qualification for entry. (Quite what the Community would do should democracy be overthrown in a member state is uncertain.)

So, although both Spain and Portugal requested negotiations on an association with the Community as early as 1982, and Spain made it quite clear that its request was with a view to full membership at some future date, both countries were treated with caution by the Community states. Eventually they were granted preferential trade agreements – that for Spain coming into force in 1970, and for Portugal in 1973 as part of an agreement between the Community and all EFTA countries – but it was only with the overthrow of the Caetano regime in Portugal in 1974 and the death of General Franco in 1975 that full membership became a real possibility. Portugal applied in March 1977 and Spain in July 1977. The negotiations were protracted and difficult, covering, among many problems, the threat posed to other Mediterranean countries by Spanish agriculture, the size of the Spanish fishing fleet, and the implications of cheap Spanish and Portuguese labour moving north. As in the Greek negotiations political factors helped to overcome difficulties: member states wished to encourage political stability in southern Europe; there was the opportunity to widen and strengthen the political and economic base of the Community; and, by helping to link southern Europe to the north, there were seen to be strategic advantages for both Western Europe and NATO.

All three enlargements have inevitably affected and changed the Community in important ways. First, and most obviously, the Community has, simply by becoming bigger, become a more important international organisation. It now contains a population of over 320 million; its membership includes all the larger, and traditionally more influential, West European states; and it is the world's principal commercial power, accounting for around 22 per cent of world imports and 21 per cent of world exports (not counting commerce between the member states themselves).

Second, internal decision-making has become more complex, with twelve representatives sitting around the Council of Ministers' table rather than six, and with a much wider range of national and political interests wishing to be satisfied.

Third, and this is linked to the previous point, the Franco-German axis, which did so much to set the pace in the 1960s and early 1970s has been, if not undermined in its influence, less central and less dominating. More generally, as the number of smaller states have increased, it has not been quite so easy for the larger states to push their preferences through.

Fourth, the policy debates, concerns, and priorities of the Community have been affected as the new members have brought with them their own requirements and problems. So, for example, and of considerable importance for the future development of the Community, the growing influence, as a result of the second and third enlargements, of southern, less industrialised and poorer countries has produced pressures for a reorientation of the Common Agricultural Policy away from northern temperate products towards Mediterranean products, and also for more redistributive policies which will directly assist economic development in the south. (The North–South divide does not, of course, coincide completely with industrial/non-industrial or rich/poor divides: much of Spain is industrialised, most of Ireland is not; most of the UK outside southern England is relatively poor, much of northern Italy is relatively rich.)

Developments in Community Policy and Decision-making Processes

In general terms, it may be said that the Rome Treaties indicated a pattern of policy and decision-making in which the Commission would propose, the Parliament would advise, the Council would decide, and the Court would interpret. In many respects this is indeed how Community relationships and processes have worked in practice. But there have also been important additions and amendments to the projected pattern. The nature of these additions and amendments is examined in some detail in later chapters, but three are particularly worth noting at this stage.

First, the relationships between the four institutions themselves have altered in a number of ways. As the Community has evolved, all of the institutions have extended their interests and responsibilities and as this has happened they have increasingly become less compartmentalised and less self-contained within the Community system. A certain blurring has occurred as some of the lines of division over who does what have become less clear. The best example of this is the way in which the Council, by becoming progressively much more involved in policy initiating and setting the policy agenda, has usurped some of the Commission's proposing responsibilities.

Second, an increasing range and number of participants not associated with the four main institutions have become involved in Community policy and decision-making. The most important of these participants are the Heads of Government who, in the European Council, have come to assume a number of important responsibilities, some of which have had the effect of reducing the power and manoeuvrability of both the Council of Ministers and the Commission. Prominent among other actors who have inserted, or have attempted to insert, themselves into the Community's decision-making processes are the many national and transnational sectoral interests and pressures that have come to cluster around the Community institutions in order to monitor developments and, where possible, to advise or pressurise the formal decision-makers.

Third, Community processes have simply become more varied and more complex over the years as they have come to function in many different ways at many different levels. In addition to what occurs in the structured settings of Council and Commission meetings, Parliamentary plenaries and committees, and Court sittings, there is a mosaic of less formal channels in which representatives of the institutions, the states, and interests meet and interact to discuss and produce policy and decisions. Which processes and channels operate in particular cases, and what types of interactions occur therein, varies considerably from sector to sector, and can even do so from decision to decision.

Development of Policies

Along with its institutional structure and its decision-making processes the Community is most distinguished from other international organisations by the range and weight of its policy responsibilities and commitments. These have expanded steadily over the years, stimulated and encouraged by factors such as the provisions of the Treaties, the increasing internationalisation of economic forces, stiffening international economic competition, a growing recognition of the benefits of working together, integrationist pressures emanating from Community institutions, and the stimulus that policy development in one sphere often gives to developments in others.

At the heart of the Community's policy framework are what are often thought of as the 'Common Market' policies. That is to say, the policies which are designed, on the one hand, to promote the free movement of goods, people, services and capital between the member states, and, on the other hand, are designed to enable the Community to act jointly and present a common front in its economic relations with third countries. In addition to these 'Common Market' policies are a variety of other policies which include among their aims the furtherance of economic and monetary stability, protection against certain market consequences, and the promotion of political goals.

So extensive has the Community's policy framework become that it now incorporates initiatives and developments in virtually every sphere of public policy. No other combination of states has arrangements even remotely like those which apply in the Community where co-operation and integration are consciously practised across such a wide range of policy sectors, and where so many policy-making and policy-implementation responsibilities have been removed from the hands of individual states and given over to collective institutions. The nature of the Community's policy interests and responsibilities are examined at length in Part Three.

responsibilities and commitment. These have expanded steadily over the years established and maintained by factors such as the pressures of organisation, the increasing and sustained danger of unsociable forces, suffering recognition of trade-union conscription, a growing recognition of the benefits of working together, to some extent pressures, considerations (emphases, qualifications), and the premise that political development in any sphere or of a given and legal application without.

At the level of local community, a police framework are often sharp, often thought of as rather lost than May of policies, but rather say the policies which are designed, and in one hand, to enhance the free movement of goods, people, services and capital between the member states and, on the other hand, to encourage their peaceable Community econ-omic policy, but rests the expansion from trade through relations with third parties. In addition to these Combined shared policies are a series of other policies which include among them the influences of economic and monetary stability, a strategy against certain market circumstances, and the promotion of political action. So central is the Community's policy framework to economic and social integration and development, in virtually every sphere of public policy. One such consideration of major past arrangements, were entirely that those which apply to the Community, where co-operation and integration are conceivably been more or less well-informed policy projects, and whereas many policy-makers, and policy-makers past are clearly established, have been removed from the broad institutional stream and given over to collective institutions. By virtue of the Community's supra-national and administrative functions, described at length in Part Three.

PART TWO

The Institutions and Political Actors of the European Community

Introduction

As was indicated in Chapter 2 there are four main Community institutions: the Commission, the Council of Ministers, the European Parliament, and the Court of Justice. Chapters 3–6 consider each of these institutions, and the political actors that are associated with them. Chapter 6 has also been taken as the most appropriate place to examine the nature and status of Community Law.

In Chapter 7 the European Council is examined. As will be shown, these summits of Heads of Government, although given no place in the founding Treaties, have come to play an extremely significant role in the life of the Community.

Finally, Chapter 8 looks at those institutions and actors which, though not given a chapter in their own right because of pressures of space, none the less also exercise an important influence in the Community: the Economic and Social Committee, the European Investment Bank, the Court of Auditors, and Interests.

3

The Commission

Frequently portrayed as the civil service of the Community, the Commission is in reality both rather more, and rather less, than that: rather more in the sense that the Treaties, and political practice, have assigned to it much greater policy initiating and decision-making powers than national civil services, in theory at least, enjoy; rather less in that its role regarding policy implementation is greatly limited by virtue of the fact that it is the member states themselves which are charged with most of the Community's day-to-day administrative responsibilities.

Though much has been written in recent years about a decline in the power and influence of the Commission since the mid-1906s the fact is, that both directly and indirectly, it is still centrally involved in Community decision-making at all levels and on all fronts. With an array of power resources and policy instruments at its disposal – and strengthened by the frequent unwillingness or inability of the Council to provide clear leadership – the Commission is at the very heart of the Community system.

Appointment and Composition

Seated at the summit of the Commission are the individual Commissioners who are each in charge of particular policy areas and who meet collectively as the College of Commissioners. Originally, they numbered nine, but with the three Community enlargements their size has grown: to 13, to 14, and now to 17. Each of the five larger countries have two Commissioners (France, Germany, Italy, Spain, and the UK), and the remaining seven smaller countries each have one.

A new Commission is appointed every four years, with individual terms of office being renewable. According to Article 11 of the Merger Treaty, the method of appointment must be by 'common accord of the Governments of the Member States'. The thinking behind this procedure is that a collective appointment emphasises the Community, rather than the national, base of the Commission: Commissioners are not supposed to be national representatives. It is much the same sentiment that requires Commissioners, on taking up their appointment, to give a 'solemn undertaking' that they will serve the Community alone and will 'neither seek nor take instructions from any government or any other body'.

In practice, such a full and impartial 'Community consciousness' is neither achieved nor attempted. Although, in theory the Commissioners are collectively appointed they are, in fact, national nominees. It would, therefore, be quite unrealistic to expect them, on assuming office, suddenly to detach themselves from previous loyalties and develop a concern solely for 'the wider European interest' – not least since a factor in their appointment is likely to have been an expectation that they would keep an eye on the national interest. (A particularly graphic illustration of this latter point was seen in the way that the UK Commissioner, Lord Cockfield, was not reappointed by Mrs Thatcher to the Commission which took up office in January 1989. She believed he had been over-zealous in his support for aspects of the internal market programme for which he was responsible, and rather than looking to British interests had 'gone native'.)

The Treaty insistence on complete independence of Commissioners is therefore interpreted flexibly. Indeed, total neutrality is not even desirable since the work of the Commission is likely to be facilitated by Commissioners maintaining links with sources of influence throughout the Community and this they can most easily do in their own member states. But the requirements of the system and the necessities of the Community's institutional make-up are such that real problems arise if Commissioners try and force their own state's interests too hard. It is both legitimate and helpful to bring favoured national interests onto the agenda, to help clear national obstacles from the path, to explain to other Commissioners what is likely to be acceptable in 'my' national capital. But to go further and act consistently and blatantly as a national spokesman is to risk losing credibility with other Commissioners. It also makes it difficult for the Commission to function properly since clearly it cannot fulfil its set tasks if its divisions match those of the Council of Ministers. The Commission which was appointed to office in January 1985 under the Presidency of Jacques Delors soon ran into difficulties of this kind: the chauvinism of some of its members played an important part in limiting the ability of the Commission to act efficiently as a coherent team. Open criticisms by members of the German government of its two Commissioners for allegedly failing to defend their country's interests in Brussels, created further problems.

There are no rules or understandings as to what sort of people, with what sort of experience and background, member governments should nominate. In general, it would be fair to say that Commissioners tend to be former national politicians just short of the top rank. However, there are many who do not fully fit such a description. So, a significant – and increasing – number have held senior ministerial posts in their own countries, while others – now constituting a declining number – are best described as 'experts', 'technicians', or 'prominent national figures' of one kind or another.

Given the diverse political compositions of the Community's national governments there is naturally a range of political opinion represented in the Commission. The smaller countries tend to put forward somebody from, or associated with, their largest party. The five larger countries vary in what they do, but 'split representations' are common practice. Crucially, all governments have made it their custom to nominate people who are broadly pro-European and who have not been associated with any extremist party or any extreme of a mainstream party. So, while Commissions have certainly contained party political differences, these have usually been within a range that has permitted at least reasonable working relationships.

The most prestigious and potentially influential Commission post is that of the Presidency. The President is the principal representative of the Commission; he must try to encourage a sense of direction and a co-ordination of effort among his Commission colleagues; and he may take on specific policy portfolios of his own if he chooses. Inevitably, therefore, the states take care over the appointment. According to the Treaty they appoint from among the Commissioners but, in practice, extensive informal soundings are taken from an early stage and an appointment is agreed before the other members of the Commission are known. Reflecting the importance of the office the choices have tended to be people with senior ministerial experience and considerable political weight in their own countries. Although appointed for only a two-year term it has become customary to allow Presidents to remain in office for at least the full term of a Commission, that is four years.

To a marked extent the distribution of the policy portfolios among the other sixteen Commissioners is a matter of negotiation and political balance. The President's will is the most important single factor, but he cannot allocate posts simply in accordance with his own preferences: he is intensively lobbied, discussions – which may become heated – take place around the Commission table and in the President's private office, and certain constraints cannot be avoided. Among the constraints are:

1. Re-nominated Commissioners, of which there may well be around ten, normally expect senior positions.
2. National prestige cannot be ignored. All governments wish to see 'their' Commissioners in important positions, and the five states which have two Commissioners would certainly protest if both their nominees were to be allocated junior posts.
3. Governments do sometimes try to get 'their Commissioners into positions which are especially important from the national point of view. Mrs Thatcher's lobbying in 1981, which involved telephoning the new President, Gaston Thorn, to ensure Christopher Tugendhat retained his budget portfolio, was especially brazen in its form, but by no means unique in its intent.

With all these difficulties, it is not surprising that, unless a resignation, a death, or an enlargement enforces it, reshuffles are usually confined to the four-yearly terms of office.

To assist them in the performance of their duties – by, for example, keeping them informed of developments within and outside their allocated policy areas, and by liaising with other parts of the Commission and outside institutions and interests – Commissioners have personal *cabinets*. These consist of small teams of officials, normally numbering six. Mostly they are fellow nationals of the Commissioner, although at least one is supposed to be drawn from another member state. They are usually recruited either from national political parties or are seconded from domestic civil services or from some part of the Community's administration.

Below the Commissioners lies the Commission bureaucracy. This constitutes by far the biggest element of the whole Community administrative framework. Of a total Community administrative staff of almost 20,000, around 11,000 are employed by the Commission. Nearly 3000 of these are in administrative and executive grades, a similar number are engaged in research work (most of these being assigned to the Joint Research Centre's establishment at Ispra in Italy), about 2000 are engaged in the translation and interpretation work which arises from the Community's nine working languages (though most of the Commission's internal business is conducted in French), and the rest are in various executive, clerical and servicing posts. The majority of the Commission's non-research staff are based in and around the Commission's headquarters in the Berlaymont building in Brussels.

Most of the Commission employees are engaged on a permanent basis following open examinations, which, for the administrative grades in particular, are highly competitive. An internal career structure exists and most of the top jobs are filled by internal promotion. However, pure meritocratic principles are disturbed by a policy that tries to provide for a reasonable national balance among staff. All governments have watched this closely and have sought to ensure that their own nationals are well represented throughout the Community's administrative framework, especially in the policy-making 'A' grades. For the most senior posts something akin to an informal quota system operates.

This multinational staffing policy of the Commission, and indeed of the other Community institutions, has both advantages and disadvantages.

The main advantages are:
1. Staff have a wide range of experience and knowledge drawn from across all the member states.
2. The confidence of national governments and administrations in Community decision-making is helped by the knowledge that compatriots are involved in policy preparation and administration.
3. Those who have to deal with the Community, whether they be senior national civil servants or paid lobbyists, can often more easily do so by using their fellow nationals as access points. A two-way flow of information between the Community and the member states is thus facilitated.

The main disadvantages are:

1. Many senior personnel decisions are not made on the basis of objective organisational needs but result from national claims to posts and from lobbying activities which often become associated with this. The parachuting of outsiders into key jobs is less easy than it was – partly because staff and unions have pressed for a better internal career structure – but in the Commission's upper reaches promotion is still not based on pure meritocratic principles.

2. Senior officials can sometimes be less than wholly and completely Community-minded. For however impartial and even-handed they are supposed to be, they cannot, and usually do not wish to completely divest themselves of their national identifications and loyalties.

Organisation

The Directorates General

The work of the Commission is divided into separate policy areas in much the same way as national level governmental responsibilities are divided between ministries. Apart from specialised agencies and services – such as the Statistical Office and the Joint Research Centre – the Commission's basic units of organisation are its twenty-three Directorates General. Somewhat confusingly for those who do not know their way around the system these are customarily referred to by their number rather than by their policy responsibility. So, for example, External Relations is DGI, Agriculture is DGVI, and Energy is DGXVII (see Table 3.1).

The size and internal organisations of DGs varies. Most commonly, they have a staff of around 250 employees, divided into three or four directorates, which in turn are each divided into three or four divisions. However, policy importance, workloads, and specialisations within DGs produce many departures from this norm. DGXVIII (Credit and Investments), for example, has only two directorates and a grand total of five divisions, while the newly created (1986) DGXXII (Co-ordination of Structural Instruments), has no directorates and only three divisions. By contrast, DGI (External Relations) has nine directorates and twenty-four divisions,

TABLE 3.1

Directorates General and Special Units of the Commission

Directorates General	
DGI	External Relations
DGII	Economic and Financial Affairs
DGIII	Internal Market and Industrial Affairs
DGIV	Competition
DGV	Employment, Social Affairs and Education
DGVI	Agriculture
DGVII	Transport
DGVIII	Development
DGIX	Personnel and Administration
DGX	Information, Communication and Culture
DGXI	Environment, Consumer Protection and Nuclear Safety
DGXII	Science, Research and Development
DGXIII	Telecommunications, Information Industry and Innovation
DGXIV	Fisheries
DGXV	Financial Institutions and Company Law
DGXVI	Regional Policy
DGXVII	Energy
DGXVIII	Credit and Investments
DGXIX	Budgets
DGXX	Financial Control
DGXXI	Customs Union and Indirect Taxation
DGXXII	Co-ordination of Structural Instruments
DGXXIII	Enterprise

Special Units and Services
Secretariat General of the Commission
Legal Service
Spokesman's Service
Joint Interpreting and Conference Service
Statistical Office
Joint Research Centre
Euratom Supply Agency
Security Office
Office for Official Publications of the European Communities

while DGVI (Agriculture) has eight directorates (two of which are themselves subdivided) and thirty-two divisions. Behind these raw figures many further contrasts are to be found in the Commission's organisational structure. Thus, to take the size and nature of divisions, in DGVI they range from one with a staff of over 100 engaged in fairly general day-to-day administrative work in relation to the guidance section of the agriculture budget, to a number of small specialised teams such as the half dozen or so hormone experts.

The Hierarchical Structure

The hierarchical structure within the Commission is as follows:

● All important matters are channelled through the weekly meetings of the College of Commissioners. At these meetings decisions are taken unanimously if possible, but by majority vote if need be.

● In particular policy areas the Commissioner who is assigned the portfolio carries the main leadership responsibility.

● DGs are formally headed by directors general who are responsible to the appropriate Commissioner.

● Directorates are headed by directors who report to the director general or, in the case of large DGs, to an assistant director general.

● Divisions are headed by heads of division who report to the director responsible.

The structure thus appears to be quite clear. In practice, it is not completely so. At the topmost echelons in particular, lines of authority and accountability are sometimes blurred. One reason for this is that a poor match often exists between Commissioners' portfolios and the policy responsibilities of the DGs. Community enlargements and the consequent increasing size of the Commission over the years have allowed for greater policy specialisation on the part of individual Commissioners, and a better alignment with the responsibilities of individual DGs, but, even now, most Commissioners carry several portfolios, each of which may touch on the work of a number of DGs. Moreover, the content of portfolio responsibilities is changed from Commission to Commission. Some, such as Budget, Agriculture, or Regional Policy, are fixed, but others, of a broader and less specific kind, can be varied, or even created, depending on how a new President sees the role and tasks of the Commission and what pressures the Commissioners themselves exert.

Another problem that arises in relation to Commissioners is the curious half-way position in which they are placed. To use the British parallel, they are more than permanent secretaries but less than ministers. For while they are, on the one hand, the principal

Commission spokesmen in their assigned policy areas, they are not members of the Council of Ministers – the body which takes the final policy decisions on important matters.

These structural arrangements mean that any notion of individual responsibility, such as exists in most member states in relation to ministers – albeit usually only weakly and subject to the prevailing political currents – is difficult to apply to Commissioners. It might even be questioned whether it is reasonable that the Commission should be subject to collective responsibility, as it is by virtue of the Treaties which oblige it to resign if a motion of censure on its activities is passed in the EP by a two-thirds majority of the votes cast, representing a majority of all members. (No motion of censure has ever been passed.) Collective responsibility may be thought to be fair insofar as all Commission proposals and decisions are made collectively and not in the name of individual Commissioners, but, at the same time, it may be thought to be unfair insofar as much of the Commission's activity and the fortunes of its attempts to develop policy are dependent on the Council. Indeed, the Commission is at a theoretical risk of being dismissed by a Parliament frustrated by its inability to censure the Council.

Decision-making Mechanisms

The hierarchical structure that has just been described produces a 'model' route via which proposals for decisions make their way through the Commission machinery:

● An initial draft is drawn up at junior level in the appropriate DG. The parameters of the draft are likely to be determined by existing Community policy, or by guidelines that have been laid down at senior Commission and/or Council levels.

● The draft is passed upwards through superiors until the College of Commissioners is reached. During its passage the draft may be extensively revised.

● The College of Commissioners can do virtually what they like with the proposal. They may accept it, reject it, refer it back to the DG for redrafting, or defer taking a decision.

From this 'model' route all sorts of variations are possible, and in practice are commonplace. For example, where draft proposals are relatively uncontroversial, or where there is some urgency involved, procedures and devices can be employed which have as their purpose the prevention of logjams at the top and the expediting of business. One such procedure enables the College of Commissioners to authorise the most appropriate among their number to take decisions on their behalf. Another procedure is the so-called 'written procedure' by which proposals which seem to be straightforward are circulated among all Commissioners and are officially adopted if no objection is lodged within a specified time, usually a week. Urgent proposals can be adopted even more quickly by 'accelerated written procedure'.

Another set of circumstances producing departures from the 'model' route is where policy issues cut across the Community's administrative divisions – a common occurrence given the sectoral specialisations of the DGs. For example, a draft directive aimed at providing a framework in which alternative sources of energy might be researched and developed would probably originate in DGXVII (Energy), but would have direct implications too for DGXII (Research, Science and Education), DGXIX (Budgets), and perhaps DGIII (Internal Market and Industrial Affairs). Provision for liaison and co-ordination is thus essential if the Commission is to be effective and efficient. There are various procedures and mechanisms which attempt to provide this necessary co-ordination. Four of these are particularly worth noting.

First, the President of the Commission has an ill-defined, but generally expected, co-ordinating responsibility. A forceful personality may be able to achieve a great deal in forging a measure of collective identity out of the varied collection of people, from quite different national and political backgrounds, who sit around the Commission table. But it can only be done tactfully and with adroit use of social skills. Jacques Delors, who became President in January 1985, is a forceful personality, but he must take some of the blame for the lack of team spirit in his 1985–8 Commission: on assuming office he displayed clear policy preferences and interests of his own, he often tried to impose his will on fellow Commissioners, he criticised Commissioners in Commission meetings and occasionally in public, and he sometimes appeared to give more weight to the counsel of personal advisers than to that of Commissioners.

Second, the College of Commissioners is, in theory at least, in a strong position to co-ordinate activity and take a broad view of Commission affairs. Everything of importance is referred to the Commissioners' weekly meeting. At that meeting the whole sweep of

Commission interests is represented by the portfolios of those gathered around the table.

Commissioners' meetings are always preceded by preliminary meetings which have as their purpose the facilitation of effective Commission decision-making. Informal and *ad hoc* consultations may occur between those Commissioners particularly affected by a proposal. The Commissioners' agenda is always considered at the weekly meeting of the *chefs des cabinets* who try to resolve as many differences as possible. On a less formal basis, officials from the different *cabinets*, who are generally well known to one another and whose offices are grouped together on the upper floors of the Berlaymont Building, might exchange views on a proposal if it seems that problems might arise. (Normally *cabinets* do not become involved until a proposal has been formally launched by a DG, but earlier consultation sometimes occurs.)

Third, an increasing awareness of the co-ordination problem has resulted in the emergence of a number of practices and forums which have brought together people from different parts of the Commission below the level of the Commissioners themselves. So, in many policy areas, important co-ordinating functions are performed by a host of standing and *ad hoc* committees, task forces and project groups, and formal and informal meetings from Director General level downwards.

Fourth, the main institutional agency for promoting co-ordination is the Secretariat General of the Commission, which is specifically charged with ensuring that proper co-ordination and communication takes place across the Commission. In exercising this duty the Secretariat satisfies itself that all Commission interests have been consulted before a proposal is submitted to the College of Commissioners.

However, despite these various co-ordinating arrangements a feeling persists in many quarters that the Commission continues to function in too compartmentalised a manner, with insufficient attention paid to overall Community policy coherence. Among the problems are these:

1. The Commission has a rather rigid organisational framework. Despite the development of horizontal links of the kind that have just been noted, structural relationships, both between and within DGs, remain too vertical. Some encouragement has been given, principally via the President's office, to the creation of

agencies and teams which can plan on a broad front, but these are not sufficiently developed, and in any event they have had difficulties in asserting their authority in relation to the DGs – especially the larger and traditionally more independent ones. As for the President himself, he has no formal powers to direct the actions of the DGs, let alone the authority to dismiss or reassign the duties of those he judges to be incompetent or unco-operative.

2. Departmental and policy loyalties tend to discourage new and integrated approaches to problems and the pooling of ideas. Demarcation lines between spheres of responsibility are too tightly drawn, and policy competences are too jealously guarded.

3. Sheer workload has made it difficult for many Commissioners and senior officials to look much beyond their own immediate tasks. One of the duties of a Commissioner's *cabinet* is supposedly to keep him abreast of general policy developments, but it remains the case that the Commissioner holding the portfolio on, say, energy, can hardly be blamed if he has little to contribute to a Commission discussion on the milk market regime.

Responsibilities and Powers

Some of the Commissions's responsibilities and powers are prescribed in the three founding Treaties and in Community legislation. Others have not been formally laid down but have developed from practical necessities and the requirements of the Community system.

While recognising that there is, in practice, some overlap between the categories, the responsibilites and associated powers of the Commission may be grouped under six major headings: initiator and proposer of policies, executive functions, guardian of the legal framework, external representative and negotiator, mediator and conciliator, and the conscience of the Community.

Initiator and Proposer of Policies

The Commission is charged with the responsibility of proposing to the Council of Ministers measures which are likely to advance the development of Community policies. Article 155 of the EEC Treaty states this quite clearly: the Commission 'shall formulate recommendations or deliver opinions on matters dealt with in this Treaty, if it expressly so provides or if the Commission considers it necessary'.

What this means, in practice, is that the Council's legislative capacity is heavily dependent on the willingness and ability of the Commission to put proposals before it. The Council cannot initiate and draft legislation itself. Furthermore, if the Council wishes to amend a Commission proposal, Article 149 of the EEC Treaty states that it can only do so either with the Commission's agreement of by acting unanimously if the Commission disagrees. If neither of these two routes are open, the Council must accept the Commission's proposal as it stands, reject it, or refer it back to the Commission for reconsideration and resubmission at a later date.

In addition to these formal powers, political realities arising from the institutional structure of the Community also dictate that the Commission should have a major policy initiating role. The most important of these realities is that there is nothing like a Community Prime Minister, a Community Cabinet, or Community ministers capable of providing the Commission with clear and consistent policy direction. Senior Commission officials who have transferred from national civil services are often greatly surprised at the lack of political direction from above and at the amount of room for policy initiation that is available to them. Their duties are often only broadly defined and there can be considerable potential, especially for the more senior A-grade officials, to stimulate development in specific, and, if they wish, new and innovative, policy areas. An indication of the scale of this activity is seen in the fact that in an average year the Commission is likely to send the Council 700–800 proposals, recommendations, and drafts for Council instruments, and over 200 communications, memoranda and reports.

But, important though its role is, it must be emphasised that the Commission does not have a complete monopoly over policy initiation in the Community, nor does it have a totally free hand in what it does. As will be shown in later chapters all sorts of other institutions and actors – including member states, the Council of Ministers, the European Parliament, sectional groups, local authorities, and private firms, attempt to play a part too, by bringing policy options onto the political agenda and by exerting pressure directly on the Commission when that is possible. From its earliest deliberations the Commission is obliged to take note of many of these outside voices if its proposals are to produce legislation, and legislation that can be successfully implemented. It must concern itself not only with what is desirable but also with what is possible. The policy preferences of others must be recognised.

The Commission's advisory committee network. Extensive sounding and listening processes therefore precede and accompany Commission policy development. An important part in these processes, especially at the pre-proposal stage (that is, before the Commission has formally presented a proposal to the Council), is played by a vast network of advisory committees that have been established over the years. The committees are of two main types:

(a) *The expert committees.* These consist of officials, experts and specialists of various sorts nominated by national governments. Their concerns can be broad and wide ranging, such as the Regional Policy Committee, or highly technical and specialised, such as the Pharmaceutical Committee or some of the committees advising on programme management. These committees frequently include among their membership people who are also members of Council working groups – where formally submitted proposals from the Commission are examined.

(b) *The consultative committees.* These are composed of representatives of sectional interests and are organised and funded by the Commission without reference to the national governments. Members are normally appointed by the Commission from nominations made by representative Community level organisations: either umbrella groups such as the Union of Industries in the European Community (UNICE), the European Trade Union Confederation (ETUC), and the Committee of Professional Agricultural Organisations of the European Community (COPA), or more specialised sectoral organisations and liaison groups such as the Common Market Group of the International Union of Railways (IUR), or the Committee of Transport Unions in the Community (ITF—ICFTU). The effect of this appointments policy is that the consultative committees are made up overwhelmingly of full-time employees of associations and groups. The largest number of consultative committees are to be found in the agriculture sector, where there are some twenty committees for products covered by a

Community market regime, plus ten or so more general committees. Most of the agriculture committees have a membership of between thirty and fifty-five. (The Advisory Committee on Oils and Fats is the largest with sixty-eight members.)

In addition to these two types of committees there are many hybrids with mixed forms of membership.

Most of the advisory committees are chaired and serviced by the Commission. (A few are serviced by the Council and are, technically, Council committees.) Additionally, the Commission is entitled to observer status on all of the committees. Relevant Commission officials are thus fully aware of the views expressed in the committees and, where appropriate, take note of these in their policy proposals. However, not all the Community's policy spectrum is covered by committees. Three main factors determine their number and type: the importance of the policy; the dependence of the Commission on outside expertise and technical knowledge; and the preferences of the Directorates General – some incline towards the establishment of committees to provide them with advice, others prefer to do their listening in less structured ways.

The influence exercised by the advisory committees varies enormously. In general, the committees of national experts are better placed because not only can they, like the consultative committees, offer the Commission much needed technical knowledge, but they can also alert the Commission to probable governmental reactions to a proposal and, therefore, to possible problems that may arise at a future decision-making stage if certain views are not incorporated. They also have the advantage over consultative committees of tending to meet more regularly – often convening as necessary when something important is in the offing, whereas consultative committees gather on average no more than two or three times a year. Usually, consultative committees are at their most influential when they have high-ranking figures among their membership, when they are given the opportunity to discuss policy at an early stage of development, when the timetable for the enactment of a proposal is flexible, and when the matter under consideration is not too constrained by existing legislation.

Of the many pressures and influences to which the Commission is subject in the exercise of its policy initiation functions, the most important are those which emanate from the Council of Ministers.

When the Council indicates that it wishes to see certain sorts of proposals laid before it, the Commission is obliged to respond. However, important though the Council has become as a policy initiating body, (see Chapter 4), the extent to which this has produced a decline in the initiating responsibilities and powers of the Commission ought not to be exaggerated. Two factors in particular have ensured the retention of a key initiating role. First, the Council often finds it difficult to be bold and imaginative: it tends to be better at responding than at originating and proposing. Second, the Commission has been quite adept in responding to changes in the Community's policy needs and methods of functioning. This is perhaps best seen in the way in which the Commission's position on some issues has unquestionably been strengthened by gaining the support of national leaders at European Councils. Two examples, covering issues of great importance, illustrate this. First the Commission's 1985 White Paper *Completing the Internal Market*, (often referred to as the Cockfield White Paper after the Commissioner who pioneered it), which spelt out a rationale, a programme, and a timetable for completing the internal market by 1992, was approved at the June 1985 Milan summit. Six months later, at the Luxembourg summit, it was agreed that the institutional reforms that were necessary if the 1992 objective was to be achieved, would constitute a part of the Single European Act. Second, the Communication from the Commission to the Council entitled *The Single Act: A New Frontier for Europe*, which was launched amid considerable publicity early in 1987 – and which came generally to be referred to as 'the Delors package' – was central to the 1987–8 reform negotiations that culminated in major budgetary, agricultural and structural fund changes that were agreed at the February 1988 Brussels summit.

Executive Functions

The Commission exercises wide executive responsibilities. That is to say, it is closely involved in the management, supervision and implementation of Community policies. Just how involved varies considerably across the policy spectrum but, as a general rule, it can be said that the Commission's executive functions tend to be more concerned with monitoring and co-ordinating developments, laying down the ground rules, carrying out investigations and giving rulings on significant matters (such as proposed company mergers, state aids, and applications for derogations from Community law), than they are with detailed 'ground level' policy implementation.

Three aspects of the Commission's executive functions are worth special emphasis:

Rule-making Powers. It is not possible for the Treaties or for Council legislation to cover every possible area and eventuality in which a rule may be required. In circumstances and under conditions that are defined by the Treaties and/or Council legislation the Commission is, therefore, delegated rule-making powers. In this the Commission is in a similar position to national executives: because of the frequent need for quick decisions in that grey area where policy overlaps with administration, and because too of the need to relieve the normal legislative process of over-involvement with highly detailed and specialised matters, it is desirable to have truncated and special rule-making arrangements for 'administrative' and 'technical' law.

The Commission normally issues between 4000 and 5000 legislative instruments per year. These are in the form of directives, regulations, and decisions. (The Commission also issues a large number of other instruments – in particular recommendations and opinions – but these do not usually have legislative force.) Most of this Commission legislation is confined to the filling in of details, or the taking of decisions, that follow automatically from Council legislation. So, the greatest proportion of Commission legislation is made up of regulations dealing with price adjustments and market support measures under the Common Agricultural Policy. Exhibit 6.1 (p. 146) provides an example of such legislation. (See Chapter 6 for an examination of the differing nature of Community legislative instruments.)

But although most of the Commission's rule-making powers are confined to the routine and the straightforward, not quite all are. In at least three areas opportunities exist to make, not just 'administrative' law, but what verges on 'policy' law. First, under the ECSC Treaty, the Commission is granted extensive rule-making powers, subject, in many instances, only to 'consultations' with the Consultative Committee of the ECSC and with the Council of Ministers. Article 60, for example, gives the Commission powers to define what constitutes 'unfair competitive practices' and 'discrimination practices', and under Article 61 it may set maximum prices. If a state of 'manifest crisis' is declared, as it was in October 1980 because of the

Community's chronic over-production of steel, the Commission's powers are increased further: it may then set minimum prices (Article 61) and also, with the 'assent' of the Council of Ministers, establish a system of production quotas (Article 58). Second, the management of the Common External Tariff gives the Commission considerable manoeuvrability. It is, for example, empowered to introduce preventive measures for a limited period in order to protect the Community market from dumping by third countries. Third, in furtherance of the Community's competition policy, the Commission, supported by decisions of the Court of Justice, has taken advantage of the rather generally phrased Article 85 of the EEC Treaty to clarify and develop the position on restrictive practices through the issuing of regulations and decisions.

Management of community finances. On the revenue side of the budget Community income is subject to tight constraints determined by the Council. (See Chapter 11 for an explanation of budgetary revenue.) In overseeing the collection of this income the Commission has two main duties:

● To see that the correct rates are applied within certain categories of revenue.

● To ensure that the proper payments are made to the Community by the national authorities which act as the Community's collecting agents.

On the expenditure side, the administrative arrangements depend very much on the circumstances and the types of expenditure involved, but always the Commission must operate within the approved budget and on the basis of the guidelines laid down in Community law. The way in which the Community's three major funds operate indicates the variety of possible arrangements:

● General management decisions relating to the CAP – such as whether, and on what conditions, to dispose of surpluses – are taken by the Commission, usually via an appropriate management committee. The detailed application of policies occurs at national levels.

● Applications to the European Social Fund (ESF) must be channelled via national Ministries of Labour/Employment. Normally they are approved at this initial stage for forwarding to the

Commission so long as they are judged to be eligible within the Fund's guidelines and they satisfy nationally determined criteria. On reception by the Commission they are examined by senior officials from the viewpoints of eligibility and merit, and recommendations are then drawn up for consideration by the Committee of the European Social Fund. This is an advisory committee composed of governmental, trade union, and employer representatives, all of whom are appointed by the Council – which means that each state makes its own appointments. A major problem with the Committee is that it meets only occasionally and is, therefore, not in a position to give the many applications that are placed before it proper attention. What, therefore, occurs is that, after a certain amount of 'jockeying' between national delegations, the Commission's recommendations are approved without too much difficulty. Commission spokesmen claim that these recommendations are based purely on their assessment of which are the best applications, but to most outside observers it looks as though political considerations result in at least some attempt to spread the resources between the states.

● Applications to the European Regional Development Fund (ERDF) also have to receive initial national government approval: via appropriate agencies such as Ministries of Industry or Economic Development. Unlike the ESF, the ERDF works on the basis of national quota bands, which means that national ministries, by limiting the number of applications that are forwarded to Brussels, are strongly placed to decide which projects eventually receive funding. This is not to say that the Commission's role in the operation is unimportant. Commission officials in DGXVI (Regional Policy) look at applications, and a Regional Fund Committee – which is a management committee made up of officials from the member states – makes the final decision. But the choices before the Committee have usually been greatly cutailed by prior national sifting and Commission ordering.

Moving beyond the different parts of the Commission's financial management functions to look at the overall financial picture, it is clear that the Commission's ability to manage Community finances effectively is greatly weakened by its reliance on the Council. For the Council controls the upper limits of the revenue base, and framework spending decisions are taken by different Councils. In the past this meant that if it became obvious during the course of a financial year that expenditure was exceeding income the Commission could not step in at an early stage and take appropriate action by, for example, increasing the Value Added Tax ceiling on revenue or reducing agricultural price guarantees. All that it could, and regularly did do, was make out a case to the Council as to what should be done. It may be, however, that decisions taken at the February 1988 European Council meeting, which included a significant expansion of the Community's revenue base and provision for the imposition of financial penalties on farmers if production targets are exceeded, will, in the future, improve the Commission's general financial management capability (see Chapters 11 and 12).

As is clear from the previous few paragraphs, a number of different procedures apply with regard to how the Commission exercises its rule making and financial management functions. Aware that the arrangements were becoming ever more confusing and complex, and aware, too, that the projected completion of the internal market by 1992 would entail a host of implementing decisions, the Single European Act incorporated provisions for a clarification of the procedures. On the basis of the Act, and of a Council regulation approved in June 1987, the Commission's implementing and management powers in respect of Council decisions have now been streamlined. Three procedures are to apply:

1. The Commission will exercise its powers independently.
2. The Commission will exercise its powers through:
   (a) advisory committees (this procedure to be generally adopted in the case of internal market instruments).
   (b) management committees (this to be extended beyond agriculture, to which it is currently largely confined).
   (c) regulatory committees (the Commission failed to persuade the Council to give it more power under this procedure).
3. The Commission will exercise its powers by a special emergency procedure in the case of safeguard measures. (This is to apply principally under the Common Commercial Policy.)

Management and regulatory committees are thus confirmed as having important executive roles. Some discussion of them is, therefore, appropriate at this point.

Both types of committee are chaired and serviced by the Commission – with the chairman normally being a director or a head of division. The committee members are national representatives, with, in an average size committee, two or three middle-ranking officials from appropriate ministries attending on behalf of each state.

There is no hard and fast distinction of either principle or policy responsibility between management and regulatory committees. Most of the management committees are concerned with agriculture – and most of them, numbering over twenty, have specific sectoral responsibilites for the CAP's product regimes – but there are a few non-agricultural management committees too, of which the most important is the ERDF Committee. The regulatory committees tend to be concerned with harmonisation and vary greatly in their sectoral interests. Some, such as the Standing Committee on Foodstuffs and the Committee on General Customs Rules, have fairly broad briefs. Others, notably the numerous Committees for the Adaptation to Technical (and Scientific) Progress of Directives, are highly specialised: they include committees on Dangerous Substances and Preparations, Quality of Water Intended for Human Consumption, and Fertilisers. All of these committees, management and regulatory, meet as appropriate, which means weekly in the case of agricultural products requiring frequent market adjustments such as cereals and milk, and in other cases means hardly at all.

Both types of committees do similar things, with variations occurring not so much between management and regulatory committees as such, but rather between individual committees according to their terms of reference, the nature of the subject matter with which they are concerned, and how they are regarded by the Commission. Agenda items for committee meetings could include analysing the significance of data of various kinds, looking at how existing legislation is working, discussing a legislative proposal that is at an early draft stage, considering how existing legislation may be modified to take account of technical developments (the particular responsibility of the Technical Progress Committees), and assessing market situations (a prime task for the agricultural committees).

Where the distinction between management and regulatory committees can be important is when committees have to issue opinions on Commission legislation. For the Commission is in a much stronger position when acting through the former than it is through the latter. In both types of committees votes are distributed among the states on a weighted basis, with the national weights being the same as those which exist in the Council of Ministers (see Chapter 4 for details). Under the management procedure, if the committee issues a favourable opinion by a qualified majority (fifty-four votes out of seventy-six since 1 January 1986), or fails to deliver an opinion by not voting or by not being able to muster a positive or a negative qualified majority, the Commission may adopt the measure which becomes immediately applicable. If the committee delivers an unfavourable opinion by a qualified majority the Commission may still adopt the measure but it must inform the Council of Ministers which, acting within a specified period of time (usually one month) and by a qualified majority, may override the Commission's decision. Under the regulatory procedure committees operate in the same way as management committees in the case of favourable opinions, but where an unfavourable opinion or no opinion is delivered, the Commission submits the proposal to the Council and if it does not make a decision within a specified time (usually three months) the Commission can adopt the proposal.

The different powers given to the Commission under the two types of committee can result, when a new committee is being established, in a Council–Commission tug-of-war regarding which procedure is to apply.

Those who criticise the Community on the grounds that it is undermining national sovereignties sometimes cite regulatory and management committees as part of their case. They point to the rarity of adverse opinions, the low number of no opinions, the frequency with which measures go through without unanimous support, and the ability of the Commission – especially under the management procedure – to ignore or circumvent unfavourable votes. There is, however, another side to this; a side that suggests that the power of the Commission to control the committees and impose its will on the states ought not to be exaggerated. Three points in particular ought to be noted. First, although some of the committees do exercise important powers, they tend, for the most part, to work within fairly narrowly defined limits. Anything very controversial is almost invariably referred to a Council meeting. Second, many negative votes by states are cast tactically rather than as part of a real attempt to stop the proposal. That is to say, a national delegation might well recognise that a measure is going to be approved but will vote against it or will abstain to satisfy a political interest at home. Finally, as with all aspects of its activity, it is just not in the Commission's long-term interests to abuse its powers by forcing unwelcome or unpopular measures through a committee. It wants and needs co-operation, and if a proposal meets serious opposition in a committee a good chairman will, unless special circumstances prevail, suggest revisions rather than press a vote which may have divisive consequences.

Supervision of 'front line' policy implementation. Not many people in the Commission are engaged in 'front line' policy implementation. This is because most of this type of administration, which tends to be very labour intensive, has been delegated to appropriate agencies within the member states. Examples of such national agencies are: customs and excise authorities (which deal with most matters in relation to movements across the Community's external and internal borders); veterinary inspection teams (which check quality standards on foodstuffs); and agricultural intervention boards (which are responsible for controlling the volume of agricultural produce on domestic markets and which deal directly with farmers and traders about payments and charges).

To ensure policies are applied in a reasonably uniform manner throughout the twelve states the Commission attempts to supervise, or at least hold a watching brief on, the national agencies and the way they perform their Community duties. It is a task that carries with it many difficulties. Four of these are especially important.

First, the Commission is not, in general, well enough resourced for the job. It is, therefore, heavily dependent on the good faith and willing co-operation of the states. Even in those policy spheres where it is in almost constant communication with national officials the Commission cannot know everything that is going on. And with respect to those areas where contacts and flows of communication between Brussels and national agencies are irregular and not well ordered, it is almost impossible for Commission officials to have any very accurate idea as to what is happening 'at the front'.

The second difficulty is that even where they are willing to co-operate fully, national agencies are not always capable of implementing policies as the Commission would ideally wish. One reason for this is that some Community policies are, by their very nature, extremely difficult to administer. For example, the CAP requires that virtually all cross-border movement of produce must be checked – a task that even greatly enlarged national customs authorities could not possibly fully implement. Similarly, the Common Fisheries Policy is extremely difficult to police, with the provisions on fishing zones, total allowable catches, and conservation measures requiring surveillance measures such as obligatory and properly entered logbooks, port inspections, and aerial patrols. Another reason is that national officials are often poorly trained and/or are overburdened by the complexities of Community rules. The maze of rules may be illustrated by two examples: the import levy on biscuits varies according to their cereal, milk, fat and sugar content, while the export refund varies also according to their egg content; at the beginning of 1988 there were forty-three separate regulations in force on the export of beef and these were subject to eighty-two permanent and 145 temporary amendments.

The third difficulty is that agencies in the member states do not always wish to see Community law applied. Competition policy, for example, is rich in such examples, but there is often little the Commission can do given the range of policy instruments available to governments which wish to assist domestic industries, and given too the secretiveness with which these can often be arranged.

The fourth, and final, difficulty is that Community law can be genuinely open to different interpretations. Sometimes indeed it is deliberately flexible so as to allow for adjustments to national circumstances.

The Guardian of the Legal Framework

In association with the Court of Justice, the Commission is charged with ensuring that the Treaties and Community legislation are respected. This role links closely with the Commission's supervisory and implementing responsibilities. Indeed, the lack of a full Community-wide policy implementing framework means that a legal watchdog role acts, to some extent, as a substitute for that detailed day-to-day application of policies that at national levels involves, as a matter of routine, such activities as inspecting premises, checking employee lists, and auditing returns. It is a role that is extremely difficult to exercise: transgressors of Community law do not normally wish to advertise their illegal actions, and they are often protected by, or themselves may even be, national governments.

The Commission may become aware of possible illegalities in one of a number of ways. In the case of non-incorporation or incorrect incorporation of a directive into national law that is obvious enough, since directives normally specify a time by which the Commission must be supplied with full details of national incorporation measures.

A second way is through self-notification. For example, under Article 93 of the EEC Treaty, state aids must be referred to the Commission for its inspection. Another example arises under Article 85 of the EEC Treaty, because although it does not oblige parties to notify the Commission of possible restrictive business practices, they frequently do, either because they wish for clarification as to whether or not a practice is in legal violation, or because they wish to seek an exemption. (If notifications are not made within specified time limits exemptions are not permissible.) A third way is from the many representations that are made to the Commission by individuals, organisations, firms or member states who believe their interests are being damaged by the alleged illegal actions of another party. For example, Germany has complained about the amount of subsidisation given by many national governments to their steel industries. A fourth way is through the Commission's own efforts. Such efforts may take one of several forms: investigations by one of the small monitoring/investigatory/fraud teams that the Commission has in a few policy areas; careful analysis of the information that is supplied by outside agencies; or simply a Commission official reading a newspaper report that suggests a government or a firm is doing, or is not doing, something that looks suspicious under Community law.

Awareness of a possible infringement does not mean that the Commission will necessarily pursue it. Limited resources are one reason for this. In the field of competition policy, for example, there are always hundreds of cases awaiting examination and DGIV (Competition) is not especially anxious to increase this workload. The best tactic is often to press one case, issue a token fine, make a lot of fuss about it, and hope this acts as a warning to others. Political considerations may also act as a restraint. Neutral and independent though the Commission is supposed to be, it is not unaware of the ramifications of its actions, and it would not normally wish, without good reason, to pursue a case that might generate anti-Community feeling, that might jeopardise other policies, or that might antagonise a government by unearthing something that is politically embarrassing.

The most frequent causes of infringement proceedings against member states are for non-incorporation or incorrect incorporation of directives designed to approximate laws, non-application or incorrect application of rules on the free movement of agricultural produce and industrial goods, and infringements on customs duties and quotas.

Before any formal action is taken against a state it is informed by the Commission that it is in possible breach of its legal obligations. If, after the Commission has carried out an investigation, the breach is confirmed and continued, a procedure comes into force, under Article 169 of the EEC Treaty, whereby the Commission

> shall deliver a reasoned opinion on the matter after giving the state concerned the opportunity to submit its declarations. If the state concerned does not comply with the opinion within the period laid down by the Commission, the latter may bring the matter before the Court of Justice.

Since most infringements have implications for the functioning of the market, the Commission usually seeks to ensure that these procedures operate according to a tight timetable: normally about two months for the state to present its observations and a similar period for it to comply with the reasoned opinion.

Most cases, it must be emphasised, are settled at an early stage. So, in an average year, the Commission might issue around 500 letters of formal notice, deliver 150 reasoned opinions, and make fifty references to the Court of Justice. France and Italy, and more recently Greece and Spain, consistently figure high in these lists. One reason for so many early settlements is that most infringements occur not as a result of wilful avoidance of Community law but rather from genuine differences over interpretation or from national administrative and legislative procedures which have occasioned delay. Although there are differences between member states in their enthusiasm for aspects of Community law they do not usually wish to engage in open confrontation with Community institutions.

If states do not wish to submit to a Community law it is, therefore, more customary for them to drag their heels rather than be openly obstructive. Obstruction does, however, occur. For instance, in February 1982 the Court of Justice supported the Commission and ruled against Belgium for failing to implement six directives, four on waste disposal and two on water pollution. By 1987 the six directives had still been incorporated only in part. Additionally, new environmental directives, approved since 1982 – including directives on water and air pollution and on the major accident hazards of certain industrial activities – had not been incorporated as required. Further to all this, some directives which had been incorporated into Belgian law were not being implemented in practice.

The Commission has no power to impose penalties on member states which it holds to be in breach of Community law. Respect for its decisions is dependent on the goodwill and political judgement of the state concerned, backed up by the ability of the Commission to make a referral to the Court of Justice. However, in certain circumstances the Commission can fine individuals, firms and organisations, subject to their right to appeal to the Court of Justice. Article 85 of the EEC Treaty, which prohibits restrictive practices of various kinds, Article 86 which prohibits abuse of a dominant trading position, and a number of regulations and Court judgements provide the principal bases for this stronger Commission position *vis-à-vis* undertakings. Regulation 17/62, which gives effect to the principles set out in Articles 85 and 86, is especially important in this regard because it specifies the Commission's investigative and punitive powers. Under 17/62 the Commission can call for information, require that parties submit to an investigation, send in its own officials to examine the books, and issue fines. Of course, as with any law, implementation may be resisted. Such an instance occurred in February 1987 when officials from DGIV's investigative division attempted to enter the premises of the German chemical firm Hoechst in order to investigate reports of a cartel for polyethylene and PVC. Hoechst obtained a local court order enabling them to keep the officials out and subsequently initiated proceedings in the Court of Justice against the Commission for exceeding its authority. The Commission, in its turn, opened proceedings against the German government for failing to ensure that the officials could carry out their inspection.

If at all possible the Commission avoids taking formal action against firms. This is partly because of the ill-feeling that can be generated by open confrontations, and partly because formal action necessitates the use of cumbersome and protracted bureaucratic procedures within the Commission itself. Offending parties are, therefore, encouraged to fall into line or to reach an agreement with the Commission during the extensive informal processes that always precede formal action. If this fails, however, fines can result. Thus, in April 1986 a price-fixing cartel of petrochemical companies led by Montedison, ICI, Shell, and Hoechst, was fined a total of 55 million Ecu (£35m). It was deemed to be in breach of Community competition rules by fixing quotas for polypropylene (a plastic) which kept the price well above its real market level. Less punitively, in December 1986, the Commission issued a token fine of 50,000 Ecu

(£36,000) on three major acid manufacturers – Unilever, Henkel, and Oleofina – for exchanging confidential information between 1979 and 1982 about their sales of certain products. This was the first occasion the Commission had imposed fines for a pure exchange of information agreement. In explaining its action the Commission stated: 'This exchange of information, normally regarded as business secrets, provided each of them with a means to monitor the activities of its major competitors and to adjust its own behaviour accordingly.'

As with most of its other activities, the Commission's ability to exercise its legal guardianship role is blunted by a number of constraints and restrictions. Four are especially important. The first is the limited resources problem which means that choices have to be made about which cases are worth pursuing. The second is that relevant information can be difficult to obtain – either because it is deliberately hidden from prying Commission officials, or because, as is the case with many aspects of market conditions, reliable figures are just not available. The third is political considerations. And the fourth is practical difficulties. Points three and four are illustrated by the rather timid approach that the Commission has traditionally taken with regard to ensuring that multinational corporations are not in breach of Article 86 provisions on abuse of a dominant trading position. The fact is, that the taking of such action generates political opposition from those member states in which the multinational in question is based, risks being self-defeating by causing the company to transfer its activities elsewhere, and is very difficult to follow through because of the practical and legal difficulties of dealing with organisations which are located in several places, many of which are often outside Europe.

External Representative and Negotiator

Of the different aspects of the Community's external relations there are four in which the Commission plays a prominent role.

First, acting under the authority of Articles 228–231 of the EEC Treaty, the Commission represents the Community and participates in the work of a number of important international organisations. Four of these are specifically mentioned in the Treaty: the United Nations and its specialised agencies, the General Agreement on Tariffs and Trade (GATT), the Council of Europe, and the

Organisation of European Economic Co-operation (now OECD). A specific example of how the Commission links up with other organisations may be seen in its relations with the International Energy Agency (IEA). The IEA was established in 1974 as an autonomous agency within the OECD. It has twenty-one participating members: all the OECD countries except France, Finland and Ireland. Almost inevitably, it overlaps at many points in its work and its programmes with the Community – both, for example, pursue a minimum stock requirement policy – and hence a liaising framework, and if possible a co-ordinating one, is highly desirable. This is attempted principally by Commission participation in the Standing Groups which act as the IEA's main policy formulators and which bring together on a regular basis senior energy specialists from the IEA member states. In a less structured manner, mutual awareness between the two organisations as to what each is doing is also assisted by the fact that many of those who represent their countries on the IEA's Standing Groups and on the Agency's principal decision-making body, the Governing Board, are the very same people who appear in the Council of Ministers, and Council working groups, in Brussels.

Second, the Commission has responsibilities for acting as a key point of contact between the Community and non-member states. Over 130 countries have diplomatic missions accredited to the Community and the Commission is expected to keep them informed about Community affairs, either through the circulation of documents or by making its officials available for information briefings and lobbying. The Community, for its part, maintains an extensive network of diplomatic missions abroad, numbering over eighty delegations and offices, and these are staffed by Commission employees.

Third, the Commission is entrusted with important responsibilities in regard to applications for Community membership. On receipt of an application the Council normally asks the Commission to carry out a detailed investigation of the implications and to submit an opinion (an opinion that the Council need not, of course, accept – as it did not in 1976 when it rejected the Commission's proposal that Greece be offered a pre-accession period of unlimited duration and instead authorised negotiations for full membership). If and when negotiations begin, the Commission, operating within Council approved guidelines, acts as the Community's main negotiator except on show-piece ministerial occasions or when particularly sensitive or difficult matters call for an interministerial resolution of differences. The whole process – from the lodging of an application to accession – can take years. Portugal, for example, applied in March 1977; the Commission forwarded a favourable opinion to the Council in May 1978; negotiations opened in October 1978 and were not concluded until March 1985; and Portugal eventually joined in January 1986 – eight years and ten months after applying.

Fourth, the Commission is centrally involved in determining and conducting the Community's external trade relations. It represents the Community, both in formal negotiations, such as those conducted under the auspices of GATT, and in the more informal and exploratory exchanges such as are common between, for example, the Community and the USA over world agricultural trade, or between the Community and Japan over access to each other's markets.

The constitutional base for the Commission's external trade role is found in Article 113 of the EEC Treaty:

> The Commission shall submit proposals to the Council for implementing the common commercial policy. Where agreements [on trading matters] with third countries need to be negotiated, the Commission shall make recommendations to the Council, which shall authorise the Commission to open necessary negotiations. The Commission shall conduct these negotiations in consultation with a special committee appointed by the Council to assist the Commission in this task and within the framework of such directives as the Council may issue to it.

So, on the basis of a brief determined by the Council, with the outcome of negotiations subject to Council approval, and with national officials in the Article 113 Committee carefully monitoring its actions, the Commission acts as the Community's external trade negotiator. How much room for manoeuvre it has in undertaking this task varies according to circumstances. Usually, differences of both principle and special interest between the member states result in the negotiating brief being fairly tightly drawn – reflecting, often, a compromise between those countries which tend towards protectionism and those which favour free trade. While Commission officials acknowledge privately that the Council mandate is usually less of a dead weight than is often supposed, there is no doubt that the Commission's flexibility in negotiations is often constrained by the necessity of not disturbing compromises that have been agreed only with difficulty in the Council. (Although it should also be said that it is not unknown for the Commission to use Council reins to the Community's advantage: during negotiations it can be helpful to say, in response to an unwanted proposal 'the Council would never agree to that'.) In particularly difficult negotiations adjournments are sometimes sought to allow the Commission to return to the Council in order to seek approval for an amended brief which might break a deadlock. The use of a tandem arrangement, in which the Commission and the Council jointly represent the Community, has occasionally been used to increase flexibility.

Mediator and Conciliator

Much of Community decision-making, especially in the Council of Ministers, is based on searches for general agreements between competing interests. The Commission is very much involved in trying to bring these about and a great deal of its time is taken up looking for common ground which can create compromises that are somewhat more than the lowest common denominator. As a consequence, the Commission is often obliged to be guarded and cautious with its proposals. Radical initiatives, involving perhaps what it really believes needs to be done, are almost certain to meet with fierce opposition. More moderate proposals on the other hand, perhaps taking the form of adjustments and extensions to existing policy, and presented preferably in a technocratic rather than an ideological manner, are more likely to be acceptable. In other words, the Commission is subject to an enforced incrementalism.

The Commission is not the only Community body that consciously seeks to oil the wheels of decision-making. As is shown in the next chapter, the Council itself has taken steps to improve its own machinery. But the Commission is particularly well placed to act as mediator and conciliator. One reason for this is that it is normally seen as being non-partisan: its proposals may therefore, be viewed less suspiciously than any which come from, say, the chairman of a Council working group. Another reason is that in many instances the Commission is simply in the best position to judge what proposals are likely to command support, both inside and outside of the Council. This is because of the continuous and extensive discussions which the Commission has with interested parties from the earliest considerations of a policy proposal through to its enactment. Unlike the other institutions, the Commission is represented at virtually every stage and in virtually every forum of the Community's decision-making system.

Although there are naturally limitations on what can be achieved, the effectiveness with which the Commission exercises this mediating role can be considerably influenced by the competence of its officials. While, for example, one Commission official may play a crucial role in driving a proposal through a Council working group, another may be so incompetent as not only to prejudice the Commission's own position but threaten the progress of the whole proposal. Many questions must be handled with care and political sensitivity: when should a proposal be brought forward and in what form? At what point will an adjustment in the Commission's position open the way to progress in the Council? Is there anything to be gained from informal discussions with 'awkward delegations'? These, and questions such as these, call for highly developed political skills.

The Conscience of the Community

In performing each of the above tasks the Commission is supposed to stand above and beyond sectional and national interests. While others might look to the particular, it should look to the general; while others might look to the benefits to be gained from the next deal it should keep at least one eye on the horizon. As many have described it, it should be the 'conscience' of the Community.

Christopher Tugendhat, a former Commissioner, has described this role. Among other things, he states, the Commission exists 'to represent the general interest in the welter of national ones and to point the way ahead, but also drawing the attention of member states to new and more daring possibilities' (Tugendhat, 1986). Theoretically this may be so. But, in practice, it is very difficult to operationalise. One reason for this is that it is highly questionable whether such a thing as the 'general interest' exists: there are few initiatives which do not threaten the interests of at least some – were this not the case there would not be so many disagreements in the Council. Another reason is that many in the Commission doubt whether it is worth pursuing 'daring possibilities' if it is clear that they will be rejected and may even generate anti-Commission feelings.

In practice, therefore, the Commission tends not to be so detached, so far-seeing, or so enthusiastic in pressing the '*esprit communautaire*', as some would like. This is not to say that it does not attempt to map out the future or attempt to press for developments that it believes will be generally beneficial. But it operates in the real Community world, and that customarily involves looking to the short rather than to the long term, and to what is possible rather than what is desirable.

Concluding Remarks

It is frequently stated that there has been a decline in the powers of the Commission since the mid-1960s. Commentators have particularly stressed a diminution in the Commission's initiating role and a corresponding weakening in its ability to offer real vision and leadership to the Community. It has become, it is claimed, too reactive in exercising its responsibilities: reactive to the pressures of the many interests to which it is subject; reactive to the immediacy of events; and above all, reactive to the increasing 'instructions' which are given to it by the Council.

Unquestionably, there is something in this view. The explanation for why it has happened is to be sought in a combination of factors. The rather rigid vertical lines within the Commission's own organisational structure make it difficult for a broad vision to emerge. The tensions which are seemingly present between the politically creative elements of the Commission's responsibilities and the bureaucratic roles of administering and implementing have perhaps never been properly resolved, or even tackled. Beyond such internal considerations, factors as various as the international economic recession, the accession of states who are anxious to protect their independence, enlargement, and the placing on the Community agenda of more politically sensitive matters, have resulted in the states being very reluctant to give too much autonomy to the Commission.

But the extent to which there has been a decline should not be exaggerated. In some respects, indeed, there has been an increase in influence as the Commission has adapted itself to the ever-changing nature of, and demands upon, the Community. As has been shown, the Commission exercises, either by itself or in association with other bodies, a number of crucially important functions. It may not be quite the motor force that some of the founding fathers had hoped for, but in many ways it is still central and vital to the whole Community system.

4

The Council of Ministers

The Council of Ministers is the principal meeting place of the national governments, and it is the EC's main decision-making institution.

When the Community was founded in the 1950s many expected that in time, as joint policies were seen to work and as the states came to trust one another more, the role of the Council would gradually decline, especially in relation to the Commission. This has not happened. On the contrary, by jealously guarding the responsibilities that are accorded to it in the Treaties, by exercising influence in areas that are properly the responsibility of the Commission, and by adapting and extending its internal mechanisms to enable it more easily to cope with the EC's every increasing policy commitments, the Council has greatly enhanced its position in the Community. This has naturally produced some frustration in the Commission, and in the European Parliament. It has also ensured that national governments are centrally placed to influence most aspects of Community business.

There was also a general expectation when the Community was founded that governments would gradually come to be less concerned about national sovereignty considerations and that this would be reflected in an increasing use of majority voting in the Council. Again, this has not happened, or at least not as much as was anticipated. Even where the Treaties permit majority votes the Council has normally preferred to proceed on the basis of general agreements. This has been linked with a recognition of the right of states to exercise a veto on matters which, they claim, affect their national interests. These unwritten understandings have naturally bolstered the intergovernmental, as opposed to supranational, side of the

Community's nature. They have also resulted in Council decision-making processes tending to be slow and protracted.

Responsibilities and Functions

The principal responsibility of the Council is to take decisions which become Community law. As was shown in the previous chapter, the Commission also has law-making powers but these are usually limited, tightly drawn, and based on enabling Council legislation. Virtually all important proposals for legislation have to receive Council approval in order to be adopted. Normally, the Council has to act on the basis of proposals which are made to it by the Commission, and after receiving advice from the EP and the Economic and Social Committee (ESC), but, crucially, it alone decides. The Council is, therefore, in effect, the Community's legislature. In 1987 it adopted 40 directives, 458 regulations and 125 decisions.

But, if the Council is the Community's legislature in the sense that it converts proposals into legal acts, its legislative capacity is significantly restricted by the requirement of the Treaties that it can usually act only on the basis of Commission proposals. This means that it does not have the constitutional power to initiate or draft proposals itself. In practice, ways have been found, if not to completely circumvent the Commission, at least to allow the Council a significant policy initiation role. Article 152 of the EEC Treaty has been especially useful: 'The Council may request the Commission to undertake any studies the Council considers desirable for the attainment of the common objectives, and to submit to it any appropriate proposals.' In the view of many observers, the increasing use that has been made of Article 152, and the very specific instructions which have sometimes been issued to the Commission under its aegis, is against its intended spirit. Be that as it may, the political weight of the Council is such that the Commission is bound to pay close attention to what the ministers want.

In addition to Article 152, four other factors have also enhanced the Council's policy initiating role:

1. The increasing adoption by the Council of opinions, resolutions, agreements and recommendations. These are not legal texts but

they carry political weight and it is difficult for the Commission to ignore them. Sometimes they are explicitly designed to pressure the Commission to come up with proposals for legislation.

2. The movement of the Community into policy spheres which are not covered, or are not covered clearly, in the Treaties. This sometimes produces uncertainty regarding the exact responsibilities of Community bodies, and grey areas which the Council can exploit.

3. The increasingly developed Council machinery. There are now many places in the Council's network where ideas can be generated. The emergence of the Council Presidency as a key Community actor has played a particularly important role in enabling the Council to determine policy directions and priorities.

4. The increasing willingness of the states to found aspects of their co-operation not on Community law but on non-binding agreements and understandings. This is most obviously seen in European Political Co-operation and issues such as terrorism and drug control, but it does sometimes also happen in other, more conventional Community spheres where national differences make it very difficult for law to be agreed. Such non-legal arrangements do not have to be Commission initiated.

Not only has the Council encroached on the Commission's policy initiating function but it has also joined it in exercising important responsibilities in the key activities of mediation and consensus building. Of course, as the forum in which the national representatives meet, the Council has always served the function of developing mutual understanding between the states. Moreover, a necessary pre-requisite for successful policy development has always been that Council participants display an ability to compromise in negotiations. But, as the Community has grown in size, as more difficult policy areas have come onto the agenda, and as political and economic change has broken down some of the pioneering spirit of the early days, so has positive and active mediation come to be ever more necessary: mediation primarily between the different national and ideological interests represented in the Council, but also between the Council and the Commission, the Council and the Parliament, and the Council and non-institutional interests. The Commission has taken on much of this task but, so too, has the Council.

Composition

The Ministers

Ministerial meetings are at the apex of the Council machinery. Under the Merger Treaty there is only one Council of Ministers but, in practice, there are many in the sense that the work of the Council is divided into policy areas. The General Council, which is composed of Foreign Ministers, has the widest brief: it deals with politically sensitive matters, general issues relating to policy initiation and co-ordination, and various aspects of external relations. More sectoral matters are dealt with in the so-called 'Technical Councils' which are made up of departmental ministers such as Ministers of Agriculture, Energy, and Environment.

Often, the national representatives who attend Council of Ministers meetings differ in terms of their status and/or policy responsibilities. This can inhibit efficient decision-making. The problem arises because the states themselves decide by whom they wish to be represented, and their decisions may vary in one of two ways.

The level of seniority. Normally, by prior arrangement, Council meetings are attended by ministers of a similar standing, but circumstances do arise when delegations are headed at different levels of seniority. This may be because a relevant minister has pressing domestic business or because it is judged that an agenda does not warrant his attendance. Occasionally, he may be 'unavoidably delayed' because he does not wish to attend an unwanted or a politically awkward meeting. Whatever the reason, a reduction in the status and political weight of a delegation may make it difficult for binding decisions to be agreed.

The sectoral responsibility. Usually it is obvious which government departments should be represented at Council of Ministers meetings, but not always. Doubts may arise because agenda items may straddle policy divisions, or because member states organise their central government departments in different ways. As a result, it is possible for ministers from rather different national ministries, with different responsibilities and interests, to be present. The difficulties which this creates are sometimes compounded, especially in broad policy areas, by the minister attending not feeling able to speak on behalf of other ministries with a direct interest and therefore insisting on a reference back to national capitals.

States are not, therefore, always comparably represented at Council of Ministers meetings. But whether a country's principal spokesman is a senior minister, a junior minister, or, as occasionally is the case, the Permanent Representative or even a senior diplomat, care is always taken to ensure that national interests are defended. The main way in which this is done is by the attendance, at all Council of Ministers meetings, not only of the national spokesmen, but of small national delegations. The task of the supporting teams – which are comprised of appropriate national officials and experts – is to ensure that the head of the delegation is properly briefed, fully understands the implications of what is being discussed, and does not make negotiating mistakes. Sometimes, when very confidential matters are being discussed, the size of delegations may, on a proposal from the President, be reduced to 'Ministers plus two', 'Ministers plus one', or, exceptionally, 'Ministers and Commission'.

Council of Ministers meetings are normally convened by their President, but it is possible for the Commission or a member state to take the initiative. The Presidency rotates between the states on a six-monthly basis: January until June, July until December. The main tasks of the Presidency are as follows:

1. Arranging (in close association with the Council Secretariat), and chairing, all Council meetings from ministerial level downwards (apart from a few committees and working groups which have a permanent chairman). These responsibilities give to the Presidency a considerable control over how often particular Councils and Council committees and working groups meet, over agendas and over what happens during the course of meetings.
2. Launching and building a consensus for initiatives. A successful Presidency is normally regarded as one that gets things done. This can usually only be achieved by extensive negotiating, persuading, manoeuvring, cajoling, mediating and bargaining with and between the member states.
3. Ensuring some continuity and consistency of policy development. An important way in which this is achieved is via the so-called 'troika' arrangements which provide for co-operation

between the preceding, the incumbent, and the succeeding Presidencies.
4. Representing the Council in dealings with outside bodies. This task is exercised most frequently with regard to other Community institutions (such as regular appearances before the European Parliament), and with non-member countries in connection with certain external Community policies.

Holding the Presidency has advantages and disadvantages. Probably the main advantage is that it creates policy opportunities, for during its term of office an incumbent state can do much to determine, and set the pace of, Community goals. Another advantage is the prestige and status that is associated with the office. On the disadvantage side, the Presidency entails a heavy administrative burden which some of the smaller states find it difficult to carry.

Altogether there are some eighty Council of Ministers meetings in an average year, with a certain bunching occurring in relation to key features of the Community timetable: the budgetary cycle, the annual agricultural price-fixing exercise, and the ending of a country's six month Presidency. So, for example, in the closing week of the Dutch Presidency, in June 1986, six different sets of national ministers were brought together in an attempt to make progress on items as diverse as co-ordinated action against South Africa (Foreign Ministers) to liberalising the European aviation industry (Transport Ministers). The regularity of meetings of individual Councils reflects their importance in the Council system and the extent to which there is Community interest and activity in their policy area. So, Foreign Ministers and Agriculture Ministers naturally meet most frequently: about once a month on average. Economic and Finance Ministers (Ecofin), Industry Ministers, Internal Market Ministers, and Budget Ministers follow next with around six meetings a year. The least frequent meetings, numbering no more than one or two a year, are in fringe areas such as Education and Cultural Affairs.

Unless there are particularly difficult matters to be resolved meetings do not normally last more than a couple of days. So as to allow for travelling time to and from Brussels or Luxembourg, where most of the meetings are held, it is common to start after lunch and finish the next morning.

Outside the formal Council framework some groups of ministers, particularly Foreign Ministers and Ecofin Ministers, have periodic weekend gatherings which are used as an opportunity to discuss matters on an informal basis without the pressure of having to make decisions.

The Committee of Permanent Representatives

Each of the states has a national delegation, or Permanent Representation as they are more usually known, in Brussels which acts as a kind of Embassy to the Community. These are headed by a Permanent Representative, who is normally a diplomat of very senior rank, and are staffed, in the case of the larger states, by thirty to forty diplomats, plus back-up support. Some of the diplomats are permanently based in Brussels, others are seconded from national ministries.

Of the many forums in which governments meet 'in Council' below ministerial level the most important is the Committee of Permanent Representatives (COREPER). Although no provision was made for such a body under the Treaty of Paris, ministers established a co-ordinating committee of senior officials as early as 1953, and under the Treaties of Rome the Council was permitted to create a similar committee under its Rule of Procedure. Under Article 4 of the Merger Treaty these committees were merged and were formally incorporated into the Community system: 'A committee consisting of the Permanent Representatives of the Member States shall be responsible for preparing the work of the Council and for carrying out the tasks assigned to it by the Council.'

There are, in fact, two COREPERs. Each normally meets once a week. COREPER 2 is the more important and is made up of the Permanent Representatives. Because of its seniority it is the more 'political' of the two COREPERs and works mainly for the Foreign Ministers and Ecofin. It also usually deals with issues for other Council meetings that are particularly sensitive or controversial. COREPER 1 consists of the Deputy Permanent Representatives. Among the policy areas it normally deals with are environment, social affairs, transport and the internal market. Agriculture, because of the complexity and volume of its business, is not normally dealt with by COREPER at all but separately by the Special Committee on Agriculture (SCA). On agricultural matters the SCA is of comparable significance and status to COREPER and is staffed by senior officials, either from the Permanent Representations or from national Ministries of Agriculture. Like the two COREPERs it meets weekly.

Committees and Working Groups

A complicated network of committees and working groups assists and prepares the work of the Council of Ministers, COREPER and the SCA.

The committees are of different types. They include:

● Council committees in the strict sense of the term are those committees which are serviced by Council administrators. There are only a handful of these, of which the Energy Committee and the Committee on Education are examples. Council committees are composed of national officials and their role is essentially to advise the Council and the Commission as appropriate and, in some instances, as directed. A particularly important and rather special Council committee is the Article 113 Committee which deals with commercial policy. Any significant action undertaken by the Community in international negotiations is preceded by Community co-ordination via this Committee. It meets once a week: the full members – who are very senior officials in national Ministries of Trade or the equivalent – meet monthly, and the deputies – who are middle-ranking officials from the Ministries, or sometimes from the Permanent Representations – meet three times a month. The Committee performs two main functions: it drafts the briefs on which the Commission negotiates on behalf of the Community with third countries (the Committee's draft being referred, via COREPER, to the Ministers for their approval); and it acts as a consultative committee to the Council and the Commission by, for example, indicating to the Commission what it should do when problems arise during the course of a set of trade negotiations.

● The Standing Committee on Employment is also a Council serviced committee but is unusual in that it is not composed of national officials but of sectional interests. Its relationship to the Council is also unusual in that it regularly meets before meetings of the Social Affairs and Employment Council (which normally means at least twice a year) and its meetings are attended by the Commissioner responsible and by Ministers from the Council. It does not vote or consciously seek to negotiate common positions, but it considers the Ministers' agenda and then, on the basis of what emerges, the President of the Council usually prepares a paper for presentation at the Council meeting.

● Various committees, which are not technically Council committees, report to, or feed into, the Council, as well as the Commission, in an advisory capacity. Their access to the Council usually stems from their founding mandates, the importance of their policy considerations, the eminence of their memberships, or some combination of all three. The most important of these committees is the Monetary Committee which was established under Article 105 of the EEC Treaty: 'In order to promote co-ordination of the policies of Member States in the monetary field to the full extent needed for the functioning of the common market, a Monetary Committee with advisory status is hereby set up.' The Committee's prestige and power is explained by four main factors. First, it is given a broad brief in very important policy areas. The main focus of its work covers the European Monetary System, (it is crucial when realignments of currencies in the EMS are being considered), capital movements, international monetary relations, and, more generally, the implications of the economic policies of the member states for the Community as a whole. (On most of these matters the Committee works closely with another very important committee, the Committee of Governors of Central Banks.) Second, the Committee enjoys unusually privileged access to both the Commission and the Council. Indeed, in relation to the latter, the Committee's chairman normally reports several times a year directly to the Ecofin Council on the Committee's work. Third, the Committee meets regularly – normally about ten times a year – and is supported in most aspects of its work by an Alternates Committee and a small number of working parties. Finally, the members of the Committee – of which there are two from each member state, plus two from the Commission – are mostly senior and influential figures from Finance Ministries and national banks: people, in other words, who can normally communicate directly with whomsoever they wish, and people who are customarily listened to.

The role of the working groups (or working parties) is more specific than that of most of the committees in that they are responsible for carrying out a detailed analysis of formally tabled Commission proposals for Council legislation. The number of groups in existence at any one time varies according to the overall nature of the Community's workload and the preferences of the Presidency in office, but in recent years there have always been more than one hundred. At the beginning of the Belgian Presidency in 1987 there were 117. Members of the groups, of whom there are usually three or four per member state, are almost invariably national officials and experts based either in the Permanent Representations or in appropriate national ministries. Occasionally governments appoint non-civil servants to a working group delegation when highly technical or complex issues are under consideration.

Working groups meet as and when they are required. For some groups this may mean monthly or bi-monthly meetings, for others very few meetings at all if nothing much comes up within their terms of reference. Up to seven or eight different groups can be in session in Brussels on some days. On completion of their analyses of the Commission proposals, groups report to COREPER or to the SCA.

The Council Secretariat

The main administrative support for the work of the Council is provided by the General Secretariat. This has a staff of less than 2000, of whom around 200 are at 'A' grade, that is, diplomatic level. The Secretariat's base is in the Charlemagne Building which is next door to the Commission in Brussels.

The Secretariat's main responsibility is to service the Council machinery – from ministerial to working group levels. This it does by activities such as preparing draft agendas, keeping records, providing legal advice, processing and circulating decisions and documentation, translating, and generally monitoring policy developments so as to provide an element of continuity and co-ordination in Council proceedings. This last task includes seeking to ensure a smooth transition between Presidencies by performing a liaising role with officials from the preceding, the occupying, and the incoming Presidential states.

In exercising many of its responsibilities, the Secretariat works closely with representatives from the member state of the President-in-office. This is essential, not only because key decisions about such matters as priorities, meetings, and agendas are primarily in the hands of the Presidency, but also because there is a natural tendency for Presidents to rely heavily on their own national officials as they seek to achieve a successful six-month period of office by getting measures through. It is largely for this reason that the staff of a state's Permanent Representation increases in size during a Presidential tenureship. Something approaching a dual servicing of the

Presidency is apparent in the way at Council meetings, at all levels, the President sits with officials from the Council's General Secretariat on his one side and national advisers on the other.

The Operation of the Council

The Hierarchical Structure

As indicated above, a hierarchy exists in the Council consisting of the General Council, the Technical Councils, COREPER and the SCA, and the committees and working groups. The European Council is also sometimes thought of as being part of this hierarchy but, in fact, it is not properly part of the Council system, even though it does have the political capability of issuing what amount to instructions to the ministers (see Chapter 7).

The Council's hierarchical structure is neither tight nor rigidly applied. The General Council's seniority over the Technical Councils is, for example, very ill-defined, while important committees and working groups can sometimes communicate directly with Technical Councils. None the less, the hierarchy does, for the most part, work. This is best illustrated by looking at the Council's procedures for dealing with a Commission proposal for Council legislation.

The first stage is initial examination of the Commission's text. This is normally undertaken by a working group, or if it is of very broad application, several working groups. Since most groups are permanent it is usually clear to which group the proposal should go. If necessary, a new group can be established.

Progress, as at all Council levels, depends largely on the factors outlined in Table 4.1. Unless special circumstances apply, and an issue is forced, the general rule is that the group takes as long as is necessary to reach an agreement. This results both in high casualty rates and in many proposals dragging on for months, even years. Certainly the chances of eventual enactment are poor for any proposal that is not taken up and championed by at least one member state, and preferably several.

Those proposals that do progress are examined article by article. If all goes well, a document is eventually produced indicating points of agreement and disagreement, and quite possibly having attached to it reservations that states have entered to indicate that they are not yet

TABLE 4.1

Principal factors determining the progress of a proposal through the Council

The urgency of the proposal.

The controversiality of the proposal and support/opposition among the states.

The extent to which the Commission has tailored its text to accommodate national objections/reservations voiced at the pre-proposal stage.

The complexity of the proposal's provisions.

The ability of the Commission to allay doubts by the way it gives clarifications and answers questions.

The judgements made by the Commission on whether, and when, it should accept modifications to its proposals.

The competence of the Presidency.

The agility and flexibility of the participants to devise (usually through the President and the Commission) and accept compromise formulae.

The willingness of the states to use majority voting.

---

in a position formally to commit themselves to the text or a part of it. (States may enter reservations at any stage of the Council process. These can vary from an indication that a particular clause of a draft text is not yet in an acceptable form, to general withholdings of approval until the text has been cleared by appropriate national authorities.)

The second stage is the reference of the working group's document to COREPER, or, in the case of agriculture, to the SCA. In being placed between the groups and the Council of Ministers COREPER acts as a sort of filtering agency for ministerial meetings. It attempts to clear as much of the ground as possible so as to ensure that only the most difficult and sensitive of matters will detain the ministers in discussion. So, where the conditions for the adoption of a measure have been met in a working group, COREPER is likely to confirm the group's opinion and advance it to the ministers for formal enactment. Where, however, agreement has not been possible in a working group COREPER can do one of three things: try to resolve the issue itself (which its greater political status might permit); refer it back to the working group, perhaps with accompanying indications of where an agreement might be found; or pass it upwards to the ministers.

Whatever progress proposals have made at working group and

COREPER levels, formal adoption is only possible in Council of Ministers meetings. Such meetings thus constitute *the third stage* of the Council's legislative procedure. Items on Council of Ministers agendas are grouped under two headings. Matters which have been agreed at COREPER level, and on which it is thought Council approval will be given without discussion, are listed as 'A points'. These do not necessarily fall within the policy competence of the Council that is meeting but may have been placed on the agenda because the appropriate Technical Council is not due to meet for some while. Ministers retain the right to raise objections on A points, and if any do the proposal may have to be withdrawn and referred back to COREPER. Normally, however, 'A points' are quickly approved without debate. Such is the thoroughness of the Council system that ministers can assume they have been thoroughly checked in both Brussels and national capitals to ensure they are politically acceptable, legally sound, and not subject to outstanding scrutiny reservations. Ministers then proceed to consider the 'B points', which may include items left over from previous meetings, matters which it has not been possible to resolve at COREPER or working group levels, or proposals which COREPER judges to be politically sensitive and must be decided by the politicians. All 'B points' will have been extensively discussed by national officials at lower Council levels, and on most of them a formula for an agreement will have been prepared for the ministers to consider.

The position of the General Council rather suggests that there would, in certain circumstances – such as when a policy matter cuts across sectoral divisions – be a fourth Council legislative stage involving the Foreign Ministers. In practice, recourse to such a stage is by no means customary, even though it is frequently required. A principal reason for this is that the theoretical seniority enjoyed by the General Council over other Councils has no legal basis. Rather it stems only from a rather ill-formulated understanding that the General Council has special responsibility for dealing with disputes which cannot be resolved in the Technical Councils, for tackling politically sensitive matters, and for acting as a general co-ordinating body at ministerial level. Another factor limiting the role of the General Council is that often the Foreign Ministers are not able, or willing, to act any more decisively in breaking a deadlock than is a divided Technical Council. Members of the General Council may, indeed, have no greater seniority in rank, and may even be junior, to their national colleagues in say, the Budget or the Agriculture Councils. In any case Technical Councils are often not willing to refer their disputes 'upwards': Ministers, such as those of Agriculture, Trade, and Environment, have as much authority to make Community law as do Foreign Ministers and they normally prefer to take their own decisions – unless something which is likely to be very unpopular can be passed on elsewhere.

The General Council is thus of only limited effectiveness in resolving issues that have created blockages in the Technical Councils and in counteracting the fragmentation and sectoralism to which the Council of Ministers is unquestionably prone. The same is true of 'jumbo' Councils, which bring together, but only on a very occasional basis, different groups of ministers. This absence of clear Council leadership and of an authoritative co-ordinating mechanism has had the consequence of virtually forcing the European Council to assume responsibilities in relation to the Council of Ministers, even though it is not formally part of the Council hierarchy. Increasingly at their meetings the Heads of Government have gone beyond issuing general guidelines to the Council of Ministers, which was intended to be the normal limit of European Council–Council of Ministers relationships when the former was established in 1974. Summits have often been obliged to try and resolve thorny issues that have been referred to them by the Council of Ministers, and have also had to seek to ensure – principally via policy package agreements of the sort that were agreed at Fontainebleau in 1984, Luxembourg in 1985, and Brussels in 1988 – that there is some overall policy direction and coherence in the work of the Council of Ministers. The European Council can only go so far, however, in performing such problem solving, leadership, and co-ordinating roles: partly because it is timetabled to meet only twice a year, but also because many national leaders prefer to avoid getting too involved in detailed policy discussions.

Decision-making Procedures

The Treaties provide for three basic ways in which the Council can take a decision: unanimously; by a qualified majority vote; or by a simple majority vote. Unanimity is normally required where a new policy is to be initiated or an existing policy framework is to be modified or further developed. It is also required when the Council wishes to amend a Commission proposal against the Commission's wishes. Abstentions do not constitute an impediment to the adoption of Council decisions that require unanimity. Qualified majority voting or, much less often, simple majority voting, usually applies where proposals are designed to implement, clarify, or are otherwise within, established policy. Under the qualified majority voting arrangements France, Germany, Italy and the UK have 10 votes each; Spain has 8; Belgium, Greece, the Netherlands, and Portugal have 5; Denmark and Ireland have 3; and Luxembourg has 2. Of this total of 76 votes, 54 votes normally constitute a qualified majority. This means that the five larger states cannot outvote the smaller seven, and also that two large states cannot by themselves constitute a blocking minority.

In practice, proposals are not usually pushed to a vote in the Council when disagreements between the states exist, even when majority voting is perfectly constitutional under the Treaties. To appreciate why this is so it is necessary to go back to the institutional crisis of 1965.

In brief, events unfolded in the following way. The Commission, in an attempt to move progress in areas which had almost ground to a halt, put forward a package deal which had important policy and institutional implications. The most important aspects of its proposals were the completion of the Common Agricultural Policy, changing the basis of Community income from national contributions to own resources, and the granting of greater powers of control to the European Parliament over the use of those resources. The French government objected to the supranational implications of these proposals. It also used the occasion to register its opposition to what it saw as the increasing political role of the Commission and to the imminent prospect of the Community moving into a stage of its development in which there was to be more majority voting in the Council. When no agreement could be reached on these matters in the Council, France withdrew its representatives from the Community's decision-making institutions in July 1965, though it continued to apply Community law. This so-called 'policy of the empty chair' continued for six months and was ended only after the French government, under strong domestic pressure, agreed to attend a special Council meeting in Luxembourg in January 1966. The outcome of that meeting is usually referred to as the *Accords de Luxembourg* or the Luxembourg Compromise. In fact, there was little agreement or genuine compromise but rather a registering of differences. This is apparent from the official communiqué:

1. When issues very important to one or more member countries are at stake, the members of the Council will try, within a reasonable time, to reach solutions which can be adopted by all members of the Council while respecting their mutual interests, and those of the Community . . .
2. The French delegation considers that, when very important issues are at stake, discussion must be continued until unanimous agreement is reached.
3. The six delegations note that there is a divergence of view on what should be done in the event of a failure to reach complete agreement.
4. They consider that this divergence does not prevent the Community's work being resumed in accordance with normal procedure.

Although it has no constitutional status, the Luxembourg Compromise has profoundly affected decision-making in the Council at all levels. It has done so because point (2) of the communiqué has been interpreted as meaning that any state has the right to exercise a veto on questions which affect its vital national interests – and the states themselves determine when such interests are at stake. On only one occasion has the Compromise been openly breached. This was in May 1982 when the British government attempted to veto the annual agricultural prices settlement by proclaiming a vital national interest. The other states did not believe that such an interest was at stake (and with some reason given that the UK had already approved the constituent parts of the package). The view was taken (correctly) that the British were trying to use agricultural prices to force a more favourable outcome in concurrent negotiations over UK budgetary contributions. Agricultural ministers regarded this attempted linkage as quite invalid. They also thought it was over-demanding, since the dispute was played out to the background of the Falklands crisis in which the UK government was being supported by its Community partners even though some were unenthusiastic. Prompted by the Commission, the Belgian Presidency proceeded to a vote on the regulations for increasing agricultural prices and they were approved by seven (of the then ten) states. Denmark and Greece abstained, not because of any sympathy for Britain but because of reservations about the possible supranational implications of the majority vote. Subsequent events seem to have confirmed statements made by the majority seven at the time that no precedent was being set.

The Luxembourg Compromise did not, it should be emphasised, replace a system of majority voting by one of unanimous voting. On the contrary, before 1966 majority voting was rare and, indeed, it was its proposed phasing-in that the French were most concerned about. From 1966, the norm was not of unanimous voting but of no voting at all. Decisions came to be made by letting issues run until an agreement finally emerged. As a result, the veto has been formally invoked only occasionally, and then usually only for very short periods. Germany, for example, has only formally used a veto once: in 1985 it vetoed a modest cereals price cut which had been agreed by its nine partners. (With the interesting consequence that the Commission, acting under Articles 5 and 155 of the EEC Treaty, stated that the Council was not fulfilling its obligations and introduced Commission regulations on grain prices. No state challenged this course of action and the prices came into effect.)

The Compromise was, therefore, important, but its significance should not be overstated. The reluctance to use majority votes in the Council is not just a consequence of an unofficial agreement made over twenty years ago. There are strong positive reasons for acting only on the basis of unanimity. In many ways the functioning and development of the Community is likely to be enhanced if policy-making processes are consensual rather than conflictual. Thus, national authorities (which may be governments or parliaments) are unlikely to undertake with much enthusiasm the necessary task of translating Council directives into national law if the directives are perceived as domestically damaging, or if they are being unwillingly imposed following a vote in the Council. Nor is it likely that national bureaucracies will adopt helpful attitudes towards the implementation of unwanted legislation. More generally, the use of majority votes on important and sensitive matters could well create grievances that could have disruptive implications right across the policy spectrum.

For good reason, as well as perhaps some bad, decision-making in the Council thus usually proceeds on the understanding that difficult and controversial issues are not imposed. Where it is clear that a state or states have serious difficulties with a proposal they are normally allowed time. They may well be put on the defensive, asked to fully explain their position, pressed even to give way or at least to compromise, but the possibility of resolving an impasse by a vote tends to be avoided if possible. Usually, the item is held over for a further meeting, with the hope that in the meantime informal meetings or perhaps COREPER will find the basis of a solution. All states, and not just the foremost advocates of the retention of the veto (initially France, more latterly Denmark, Greece, the UK, and, to a more limited extent, Ireland) accept that this is the only way Council business can be done without risking major divisions.

But though there are good reasons for preferring unanimity, if the principle were to be applied too universally and too rigidly it could be as damaging as Council divisions, since the pace would be determined by the slowest and many much needed decisions would never be made at all. Such has often seemed to be the reality of the Community. However, majority voting has never been completely excluded. On internal staffing matters, and, more importantly, during the annual budgetary procedure where decisions cannot be indefinitely delayed and postponed, majority voting has long been common practice. (Though even on the budget the principle has been challenged from time to time. Christopher Tugendhat – Budget Commissioner from 1977 to 1984 – relates the tale of how the French, on threatening to invoke the Compromise when they were in a minority of one on a budgetary matter, were suddenly supported by some of the smaller states. A Belgian minister provided the explanation: 'To prevent the French from using the veto and so to preserve the practice of majority voting in this field at least.'). In recent years majority voting has also begun to be used in other policy areas. Though largely restricted to 'technical' issues it has begun to play a not insignificant part in helping to clear the Council's log jam of policy proposals. During 1986 over one hundred decisions were taken by majority vote, most of them in the three main areas provided for by the Treaty: budget, agriculture, and external trade.

Not only a vote, but the 'threat' of a vote has come to be an important way of breaking a deadlock. A state opposed to a proposal that otherwise commands general support often prefers to try and extract concessions in negotiations than run the risk of a vote being pressed and finding itself outvoted. Of course, in such circumstances, the veto can always be brought into play (though the term 'veto' is itself never officially used) but, in practice, countries rarely formally invoke the Luxembourg Compromise, and no country could do so regularly without ostracising itself in the Community, severely damaging its relations with its partners, and raising major questions about the whole Community decision-making method. Unless an important point of principle or a damaging political consequence is at stake a country in a minority thus often chooses not to create too much of a fuss, especially when, as is the case, for example, in agreeing external trade negotiating briefs for the Commission, qualified majority rules apply and a decision cannot be forever delayed.

There are reasons for believing that, in future, decisions will increasingly be taken by majority votes and be shaped by the threat of such votes. The first reason is that attitudes are slowly changing. There is an increasing recognition, even among the more rigid defenders of national rights and interests, that decision-making by unanimity is a recipe not only for procrastination and delay, but often for no decision-making at all. The situation whereby consensus is the rule even on issues where countries would not object too strongly to being voted down is increasingly being seen as unsatisfactory. Second, the Single European Act extends the number of policy areas in which majority voting is constitutionally permissible. Crucially, this involves those matters that are covered by the priority programme of completing the internal market by 1992: harmonisation of technical norms, opening up public procurement, removing restrictions in banking, insurance, capital controls, etc. Moreover, during the discussions which preceded the SEA, the assumption was that the new voting provisions would be used. Third, in July 1987, the General Council, in accordance with an agreement it had reached in December 1986, formally amended the Council's Rules of Procedure. Among the changes was a relaxation in the circumstances by which votes may be initiated: whereas previously only the President could call for a vote, under the new Rules any national representative and the Commission also have this right, and a vote must be held if a majority agree.

Nonetheless, important though these recent developments are, consensual decision-making remains, and can be expected to remain, the Council norm. Certainly, on important and sensitive issues many proposals will continue to lie on the table until agreement is found. This may involve delay, but the duty of the national representatives at all Council levels is not only to reach decisions but is also to defend national interests (see Chapter 13 for further discussion of this point). As long as governments are concerned not to cede too much of their national sovereignties to the Community, it can be anticipated that the unanimity principle will be retained for most major decisions in most policy areas.

The formal processes by which Council meetings are conducted and decisions are taken are broadly similar at Council of Ministers, COREPER, and working party levels. At one end of the table sit the representatives of the country occupying the Presidency; at the other end sit the Commission representatives; and ranged along the sides are the representatives of the other eleven member states. As indicated earlier, the Presidency plays the key role in fixing the agenda, both in terms of content and the order in which the items are taken. While it is difficult to exclude items which are clearly of central interest or which need resolution (and in COREPER and the Council of Ministers anyone can insist a matter is discussed provided the required notice is given), the broad shape is determined by the priorities of the Presidency. So, a President may come into office with the view that of forty proposed directives in his policy area he is going to try and get eight particular ones through. This will then be reflected in the organisation of Council business, so that by the end of his six-month term he may have succeeded with four, while another three may be at an advanced stage.

At ministerial level, Council meetings can often appear to be chaotic affairs. Officials come and go in relation to items on the agenda; ministers are constantly being briefed by officials as new points are raised; there are huddles of delegations during breaks; requests for adjournments and postponements are made to enable further information to be sought and more consideration to be given; and telephone calls may be made to national capitals for clarifications or even, occasionally, for authorisation to adopt revised negotiating positions. Not surprisingly, delegations which are headed by ministers with domestic political weight, which are well versed in the Community's ways, which have mastered the intricacies of the issues under consideration, and which can think quickly on their feet, are particularly well placed to exercise influence. (These points, apart from the first, also apply to COREPER and working parties.)

A characteristic of all Council meetings, and of Commission meetings where the member states are represented, is the *tour de table* procedure. By this, the President invites each delegation to give a summary of its thinking on the matter under consideration. This ensures that discussion is not totally dominated by a few, and, more importantly, establishes the position of each member state. It can thus help to clarify the possible grounds of an agreement and provide useful guidance to the President as to whether a compromise is possible or whether indeed he can attempt to move to a decision.

This last point highlights how important the President can be not only at the agenda setting stage but also during meetings themselves. An astute and sensitive chairman is often able to judge when a delegation that is making difficulties is not terribly serious: when, perhaps, it is being awkward for domestic political reasons and will not ultimately stand in the way of a decision being made. A poor chairman, on the other hand, may allow a proposal to drag on, or may rush it to the point that a state which, given time, would have agreed to a compromise may feel obliged to dig in its heels.

An extremely important feature of the whole Council network is the role of informal processes and relationships. Three examples demonstrate this. First, many understandings and agreements are reached at the lunches that normally precede ministerial meetings. These lunches are attended only by ministers and the minimum number of translators. (Most ministers can converse directly with one another – usually in French or English – although the entry of Greece, Spain, and Portugal has reduced this capacity).

Second, where difficulties arise in ministerial negotiations a good chairman can make advantageous use of scheduled and requested breaks in proceedings to explore possibilities for a settlement. This may involve holding off-the-record discussions with a delegation that is holding up an agreement, or it may take the form of a tour of all delegations – perhaps in the company of the relevant Commissioner and a couple of officials – to ascertain 'real' views and fall-back positions.

Third, many of the national officials based in Brussels come to know their counterparts in other Permanent Representations extremely well: better, sometimes, than their colleagues in their own national capitals or Permanent Representations. This enables them to make judgements about when a country is posturing and when it is serious, and when and how a deal may be possible. A sort of code language may even be used between officials to signal positions on proposals. So, for example, a veto would never be used in a working group or in COREPER for that would be to prejudge the 'political' discussion in the Council of Ministers. But if a representative was to state 'this is very important for my minister', or 'my minister is very strongly pressurised on this', other participants would recognise that signals were being given to them that further deliberations were necessary at their level if more serious difficulties were to be avoided when the ministers gathered.

Concluding Comments

The structure and functioning of the Council is generally recognised as being unsatisfactory in a number of important respects. In particular: power is too dispersed; there is insufficient cohesion between, or sometimes even within, the sectoral Councils; and decision-making processes are too cumbersome and too slow.

It seems unlikely that anything very radical will be done to tackle these problems in the foreseeable future, even though the number of policy issues and policy problems coming before the Council continues to increase. The obvious solutions can all be ruled out on the grounds of impracticability or political unacceptability. For example, the Council will not permit any significant reduction of its powers in relation to those of the Commission. Any movement to make majority voting the norm will be fiercely resisted. And the idea, which has sometimes been floated, of creating a 'super' Council with authority to impose an overall policy pattern on subsidiary Technical Councils does not convince many: it may be useful for knocking a few heads together, but as the experience of the European Council shows (see Chapter 7), the dream of authoritative national leaders rationally formulating policy frameworks in the 'Community interest' does not accord with political realities.

However, if major changes are unlikely, smaller, more gradual, shifts are possible and are indeed happening. The increasing use of majority voting, and the extension by the SEA of the spheres in which it is constitutionally permitted, is the most obvious case in point. Another development has been an increasing co-operation between succeeding Presidencies: ambitious rolling policy programmes have even been agreed. Developments of this sort may not produce the dynamic and streamlined institutional structure that many would like to see, but they are far from being insignificant or unimportant. As in so many spheres of Community life necessity may not be producing the transformation that is perhaps objectively or ideally desirable, but it is resulting in much needed adjustments.

5

The European Parliament

Powers and Influence

Since it was first constituted, as the Assembly of the European Coal
and Steel Community, the European Parliament – the title it adopted
for itself in 1962 – has generally been regarded as a somewhat
ineffective institution. It is a reputation which, today at least, is not
entirely justified. For while it is true that the EP's constitutional
powers are not comparable with those of national legislatures,
developments over the years have come to give it, in practice, some
influence in the Community system. As with national parliaments
this influence is exercised in three main ways: through the legislative
process, through the budgetary process, and through control and
supervision of the executive.

Parliament and Community Legislation

The EP has a number of opportunities to influence Community
legislation.

First, it sometimes participates in policy discussions with the
Commission at the pre-proposal legislative stage. The Commission
may, for example, float a policy idea before an EP committee or
committee members themselves may suggest policy initiatives to the
Commission.

Second, the EP can formally adopt its own ideas for suggested
legislation and then attempt to persuade the Commission to take
them up. The most usual way of doing this is via own initiative
reports, which are reports that the Parliament itself initiates. Around
100 own initiative reports are approved by the EP each year.

Third, the annual budgetary cycle provides some opportunities for exercising legislative influence. On the basis of an agreement it signed with the EP in 1982, the Council now sets expenditure limits within the budgetary process rather than attaching them to proposed legislation. The significance of this is that Parliament shares budgetary decision-making powers with the Council, whereas it only needs to be consulted on legislative proposals. Additionally, it has come to be accepted that if the EP puts appropriations into the budget for items for which there is no legal base, the Commission and the Council will seek to provide that base by drafting new legislation.

Fourth, and most importantly, the EP must be consulted on, though its approval is not necessary for, most significant Council legislation. If the Council acts prematurely, and does not wait for Parliament to declare an Opinion, the 'law' will be ruled invalid by the Court of Justice. Any uncertainty on this point was removed by the isoglucose case ruling in 1980 when the Court annulled a Council regulation on the grounds that it had been issued before Parliament's Opinion was known. The isoglucose case ruling does not give the EP an indefinite veto over Council legislation, for it is obliged by Treaty to issue Opinions, but it does give it a very useful delaying power.

Since July 1987, and the entry into force of the Single European Act, the precise nature of the EP's consultative powers has varied according to the Treaty articles under which the proposed Council legislation falls. For most articles, the traditional system of one reading, or consultation, remains. That is to say, Parliament is asked for an Opinion on Commission proposals for Council legislation on only one occasion. Once that Opinion is given the Council may take a decision. What use the EP is able to make of this single referral depends, in part at least, on its own subject competence and its tactical skills. The standard way of proceeding is to take advantage of Article 149 of the EEC Treaty which states: 'As long as the Council has not acted, the Commission may alter its original proposals, in particular where the Assembly has been consulted on that proposal.' If the Commission can be persuaded to alter a proposal so as to incorporate the EP's views, the prospects of those views becoming part of the text that is finally approved by the Council are greatly enhanced. With this in mind, the EP attempts to convince and to pressurise the Commission. Frequently, pressurising takes the form of amending proposals but withholding the final delivery of Opinions until after the Commission has stated, as it is obliged to do, whether or not it accepts the amendments. If the Commission's position on amendments is judged to be unsatisfactory, Parliament may choose to delay the progress of a proposal, perhaps by referring it to the appropriate Parliamentary committee for further consideration.

For ten EEC Treaty articles, the SEA extended the EP's consultative rights by creating a new co-operation procedure. In essence, what this does is to add extra legislative stages: whereas, where there is only a single referral, the Council can take final decisions after the EP has issued Opinions, under the co-operation procedure the Council is confined to adopting 'common positions' which must then be referred back to the EP for a second reading. At second readings the EP continues to lack full legislative powers – final decisions on legislative texts are still taken by the Council when, at its second readings, it considers EP responses to common positions – but the procedure does encourage the Commission, and even more importantly the Council, to take the EP's views seriously and to engage in inter-institutional bargaining. The most important Treaty article covered by the co-operation procedure is Article 100A, which was incorporated into the EEC Treaty under the SEA, and which deals with harmonisation measures that have as their purpose the establishment and functioning of the internal market (see Chapter 10 for a fuller explanation of the co-operation procedure).

It is very difficult to estimate the precise effect of EP deliberations on the final form of legislative acts. One reason for this is that a great deal of EP persuading and lobbying is impossible to monitor because it is carried out via informal contacts with Commission and Council representatives. Another reason is that the Commission and the Council often go halfway in agreeing to the sense of EP amendments, but object to the way in which they are phrased or to specific parts of them. In general, however, it is clear that the Commission is more sympathetic than is the Council: whereas the Commission, on average, accepts between about 70–80 per cent of EP amendments at the first or the single reading stage, with much of the remaining 20–30 per cent being rejected for technical rather than political reasons, the Council's acceptance rate is considerably lower, especially where there is only a single reading.

Around 150 resolutions embodying Opinions are normally passed by the EP each year. In 1987, the figure was 165, including 13 on first reading under the co-operation procedure. The number and proportion of Opinions on first reading will increase rapidly in the future as the momentum to complete the internal market gathers pace.

Having established that the EP does have a genuine legislative role, the weaknesses to which it is subject will now be outlined.

The first weakness is that the EP has only limited control over what happens to proposals once Opinions have been given. The Commission may, quite possibly as a result of discussions in the Council, amend proposals in such a way that they become significantly different from the texts considered and approved by the EP. The Council, if it acts unanimously, can overturn EP amendments accepted by the Commission. And the Council may choose not to act at all on proposals it does not like – at any one time there are usually in the region of 400–500 proposals on which Parliament has given an Opinion that still await a Council decision. (Proposals subject to the co-operation procedure are not exempt from such Council inaction, since the restricted timetable that is attached to the procedure only enters into force once the Council has adopted its common position.)

That all said, the EP's ability to follow up on its Opinions has unquestionably improved in recent years. New procedures charge relevant EP committee officers to monitor the progress of proposals on which Opinions have been given. The Commission and Council now report back to the EP and its committees on the course of proposals (although the Council is often accused by MEPs of providing insufficient information). There is some evidence that at conciliation meetings – which are meetings where delegations from the Council and the EP try to resolve differences on important Community decisions – the position of the Council tends not to be so fixed as formerly it was. And, finally, where, under the co-operation procedure, there is statutory provision for a second reading, Parliament can follow-up on the Council during the course of the legislative process itself, and in so doing can attempt to exert further pressure by rejecting or amending the common position.

The second weakness is that although the EP usually attempts to deliver Opinions as soon as possible, so as to ensure they are available to the Council at an early stage of its deliberations, occasions do occur when the Council has, in practice (though it cannot do so formally) all but agreed on its decision by the time the EP pronounces. This is especially likely if the initial referral to Parliament has been delayed, if there is some urgency about the matter, or if a Council President is anxious to push the proposal for reasons of his own.

The third weakness is that the EP is not consulted on all Council legislation. The greatest weakness in this regard is its lack of any right to be consulted on the range of external trade agreements which the Council concludes with third countries on behalf of the twelve under Article 113 (EEC). The Council and the Comission (which conducts the actual trade negotiations) may choose to discuss trade matters with the EP on an informal basis, but there is little evidence of Parliament bringing much influence to bear. In only two sets of circumstances does the EP have formal responsibilities on external trade matters: the SEA established that Parliament's assent, by a majority of current members, must be given before the Council can either accept applications for Community membership, or can, under Article 238 of the EEC Treaty, conclude special agreements with third countries. The first of these circumstances is obviously only for very occasional use. The second, however, has a more recurring application. Indeed, in the first six months of the SEA coming into force it was used on twenty occasions. Moreover, and somewhat controversially, on four occasions within the first twelve months the EP withheld its assent from additional financial protocols to the Community's agreement with Israel. The main reason for this was that Israel had allegedly done nothing about earlier Community complaints concerning the treatment of West Bank Palestinian farmers.

The fourth and final weakness is that the EP does not have to be consulted on Commission legislation which, numerically, makes up most Community legislation. There are different views on the significance of this. Pointing to the political and expenditure implications of some Commission legislation, critics argue that this is another example of executive power and of legislative and democratic weakness. Others, however, emphasise that Commission legislation is usually highly technical and of a kind that needs quick decisions; as such, it is similar to the decrees, ordinances and other minor legislative acts that national administrations issue and which are commonly accepted as an inevitable aspect of decision-making in the modern world.

Parliament and the Community Budget

Thanks mainly to the 1970 *Treaty amending Certain Budgetary Provisions of the Treaties* and the 1975 *Treaty amending Certain Financial Provisions of the Treaties* the EP enjoys considerable powers in relation to the Community's budget. These include:

1. The right to propose 'modifications' to compulsory expenditure. This expenditure is mainly concerned with agricultural price support measures and comprises about two-thirds of the total budget. Modifications that entail increases in total expenditure require qualified majority support in the Council to be accepted. Where increases are not involved, owing perhaps to a proposed increase being offset by a proposed decrease, a qualified majority vote in the Council is required for rejection – a negative majority as it is called.

2. The right to propose 'amendments' to non-compulsory expenditure. This expenditure includes most things apart from agricultural price support. Limitations are placed on the increases Parliament can propose (see Chapter 11 for details), and the Council can modify EP amendments at its second reading, but Parliament can reinsert, and can insist on, some of its amendments at its second reading of the budget.

3. Under Article 203(8) of the EEC Treaty as revised in 1975, Parliament 'acting by a majority of its members and two-thirds of the votes cast may, if there are important reasons, reject the draft budget and ask for a new draft to be submitted to it'. In other words the EP may reject the whole budget if it does not like the Council's final draft.

Following the introduction of direct elections for MEPs in 1979, extensive use was made of the powers just listed in the 1980s. Virtually every aspect of the rules, including the power of rejection, were tested to see how far they could be taken. Major confrontations with the Council, far from being avoided, seemed at times almost to be sought as the EP attempted to assert itself. Yet for all its efforts the Parliament could hardly be said to have re-shaped the budget in any fundamental way. Despite its periodic calls for a restructuring of Community expenditure – with, in particular, agriculture being brought under proper control and more funds being directed towards tackling unemployment and social needs – the allocations to the various chapters of the budget remained virtually undisturbed. There were developments which the EP welcomed – an increase in the overall size of the budget and, in some years, a proportionate improvement for non-compulsory expenditure – but both of these were extremely modest in scale given the range of problems most MEPs wished to see the Community tackle. Moreover, such 'gains' as there were owed as much to movements in world prices and the preferences of national governments in the Council as they did to Parliamentary pressure.

The reason for this relative ineffectiveness was that although the EP enjoyed joint decision-making powers with the Council on the budget, the powers of the two bodies were not equally balanced. Parliament was still very much restricted in what it could do: restricted by the Treaty which gave it very little room for manoeuvre in the major budgetary sector, compulsory expenditure; restricted by the Council's attitude which tended to be one of wishing to limit Parliament's influence as much as possible; and restricted by its own inability – because of conflicting loyalties and pressures – to be wholly consistent and resolved in its approach.

For the most part, these restrictions still apply. However, developments occurred in 1988 which are likely to have the long-term effect of bringing about at least some increase in the EP's influence on the Community budget. Following decisions taken by the European Council in February 1988 on budgetary matters, the EP, together with the Commission and the Council of Ministers, put its name, in June 1988, to *The Interinstitutional Agreement on Budgetary Discipline and Improvement of the Budgetary Procedure* (see Document 11.1). This commits all three institutions to a financial perspective for the years 1988 to 1992. Key features of the perspective are provisions for a significant increase in non-compulsory expenditure and a significant decrease in compulsory expenditure, and the setting of clear ceilings for both types of expenditure. The main benefits of the *Interinstitutional Agreement*, in power terms, for the EP are twofold. First, its influence over compulsory expenditure, which in the past has been very limited, is potentially increased. It is so because Parliament's approval is required for any upward movement of the ceiling. Second, the very act of the Council agreeing to sign a financial perspective with the EP, gives to the latter an extra element of leverage in budgetary discussions. (The EP's role in relation to budgetary decision-making is discussed further in Chapter 11.)

Control and Supervision of the Executive

Virtually all parliaments have difficulties in attempting to exercise controlling and supervisory powers over executives. On the one hand, they are usually hampered by the executives themselves, which do not welcome the prospect of being investigated and which therefore seek to protect themselves behind whatever constitutional, institutional and party political defences are available. On the other hand, parliamentarians themselves tend not to have the requisite information, the specialist knowledge, or the necessary resources that are required effectively to monitor, and if necessary to challenge, executive activity.

The EP shares these problems but additionally has two particular ones of its own. First, a key aspect of control and supervision of executives is with regard to policy implementation: is policy being implemented efficiently and for the purposes intended by relevant law? The Commission is the most obvious body to be called to account on these questions. But in many policy spheres the Commission's executive role is very limited and consists essentially of attempting to co-ordinate the work of outside agencies operating at different administrative levels. Such agencies, of which national governments are the most important, are often reluctant to open the books or to adopt co-operative attitudes towards EP investigators. Certainly there is little question of government ministers allowing themselves to be grilled by Parliament on the competency and honesty of their national bureaucracies.

The second problem specific to the EP is that on broad controlling and supervisory issues – such as whether the Community executive is acting responsibly in the execution of its duties, and whether it is fulfilling its Treaty obligations – problems arise from the blurring of roles between the Commission and the Council. In theory, the former proposes and implements while the latter decides but, as has been shown in Chapters 3 and 4, this distinction is not rigidly adhered to in practice. Insofar as the Council has assumed an increasing importance in what are theoretically Commission functions, the EP's supervisory powers have been weakened. This is because Parliament is not so constitutionally strong in relation to the Council as it is to the Commission, nor does it have the access to the former that it does to the latter.

The EP's ability to control and supervise the Commission and the Council will now be considered separately.

In relation to the Commission, the EP can use the following five powers and channels. First, by carrying a motion of censure by a two-thirds majority of the votes cast, including a majority of all MEPs, it can dismiss the College of Commissioners. In practice, it has never done so, because the power of dismissal is really too blunt a controlling instrument for most purposes: in all normal circumstances the EP has no wish to dismiss the Commission. Rather it just wishes to find out what the Commission is up to, what its plans are, and how effectively it is managing Community policies. In any event, even if the Commission were to be dismissed the EP would have no formal say in the appointment of the new Commissioners. An aggrieved Council could re-select the very same people.

Second, under Article 143 of the EEC Treaty the Parliament 'shall discuss in open session the annual general report submitted to it by the Commission'. This debate used to be one of the highlights of the Parliamentary year, but there is not much evidence of it ever having produced any concrete results. In recent years it has come to be superseded in importance by the debate on the Annual Programme of the Commission.

Third, under Article 205 of the EEC Treaty (which was added by the 1975 Treaty) 'The Commission shall submit annually to the Council and to the Assembly the accounts of the preceding financial year relating to the implementation of the budget. The Commission shall also forward to them a financial statement of the assets and liabilities of the Community'. On the basis of an examination of the accounts and the financial statement, and having examined also the annual report of the Court of Auditors, Parliament 'acting on a recommendation from the Council which shall act by a qualified majority, shall give a discharge to the Commission in respect of the implementation of the budget' (Article 206b EEC). Under its discharge powers the EP can require other institutions to take appropriate steps so as to ensure action on the comments appearing in the decision giving discharge.

Fourth, Parliament's standing committees have remits that are broad enough to allow them to attempt to exercise supervisory functions if they choose to do so. However, the Commission is not anxious to encourage investigations of itself, and the committees are not sufficiently well resourced to be able to probe very far. The Committee on Budgetary Control, which is specifically charged with monitoring policy implementation, is in a typically weak position: with only four grade-A officers employed to assist it, it cannot hope to do anything other than cover a small fraction of the Commission's work.

Finally, questions can be asked of the Commission. These may take the form of written questions, oral questions with or without debate, and questions asked in plenary sessions during Commission question time. In 1987, 2591 written questions and 714 oral questions were asked of the Commission. By and large, detailed and informative replies are given, but they can take rather a long time to be supplied – on average sixty days.

If the EP is not able to call the Commission fully to account it is even more restricted in its ability to exercise control over the Council. There are three main reasons for this.

The first arises from the very nature of the Council as the meeting place of the member states. To make it, or any of its members, directly responsible to the EP would be to introduce a measure of supranationalism into the Community that has been, and is, unacceptable to most governments. The view has been taken that insofar as Council members are to be responsible it should be principally to their national parliaments. In other words, the Council as a collective body is not to be responsible to anyone, while individual members are not to be responsible to another Community institution. (It might be added that if ministers do find themselves being pressed too hard in their national legislatures they can usually hide behind the closed doors of Council meetings and 'immovable' Community partners.)

Second, some important Council developments and activities have occurred outside the formal Community framework, with consequent difficulties for the EP in asserting a supervisory role for itself. European Political Co-operation and economic liaison/consultation between governments are examples of this. (Although on European Political Co-operation in particular, the case should not be overstated – ministerial appearances before EP plenaries and committees having gradually become institutionalised. Moreover the EP's influence in EPC may now increase following the provision in the SEA that member states 'shall ensure that the European Parliament is closely associated with European Political Co-operation. To that end the Presidency . . . shall ensure that the views of the European Parliament are duly taken into consideration'.)

Third, the very nature of the Council – with its ever-changing composition, its specialist Councils, and its rotating Presidency – makes continuity of relations between it and the EP difficult to establish. The amount of access the EP gets to ministers depends, in part, on the attitude of the country holding the Presidency. There are, however, certain set points of contact which, if they do not enable the EP to exercise an overall control on the Council, at least provide it with opportunities to challenge the Council on its general conduct of affairs. Thus Presidents of the Council attend EP committees from time to time, as occasionally do specialised ministers. MEPs can seek to use these occasions to open up discussions into wide-ranging question and answer sessions on the Council's priorities and performance. Presidents of the Council and specialised ministers also attend, and participate in, EP plenary debates. They tend to do so only on issues which are of particular importance to the Council, but again these are occasions that can result in useful EP–Council exchanges. And, as with the Commission, the EP can ask questions of the Council and the Council of Foreign Ministers (the two are distinct because of their different constitutional positions). The procedures used for asking questions are similar to those used for questions to the Commission. In 1987, 201 written questions and 221 oral questions were tabled to the Council and 150 written questions and 174 oral questions to the Council of Foreign Ministers.

Elections

Until 1979 MEPs were nominated by national parliaments from among their members. Various consequences followed from this: parties not represented in their national legislature could not be represented in the EP; virtually all MEPs were pro-integrationists, since sceptics and opponents in national parliaments were generally unwilling to allow their name to be considered for nomination; and MEPs were limited in the time they could give to their European responsibilities.

However, Article 138 of the EEC Treaty included the following provision: 'The Assembly shall draw up proposals for elections by direct universal suffrage in accordance with a uniform procedure in all Member States.' The Assembly approved such proposals as early as 1960, but found itself frustrated by another Article 138 requirement which stated: 'The Council shall, acting unanimously, lay down the appropriate provisions, which it shall recommend to Member States for adoption in accordance with their respective constitutional requirements.' That the first set of direct elections were not held until 1979 is witness to the feeling in some governmental quarters – initially mainly in France, later in Denmark and the UK – that direct elections were rather unwelcome: because they had supranational overtones and because they might be followed by pressures for institutional reform in the EP's favour. Even after the principle of direct elections was eventually won and it was agreed they would be held on a fixed five-year basis, no uniform electoral system could be agreed. Consequently, the first two sets of direct elections to be held – in 1979 and 1984 – have been contested on the basis of different national electoral arrangements (see Table 5.1). The strong opposition by UK governments to any form of proportional representation (outside Northern Ireland) seems likely to ensure that no uniform system will be introduced in the foreseeable future.

The widespread use not just of proportional representation but of proportional representation on the basis of single constituencies means that the EP can claim to be highly representative in its membership with respect to the ratio between votes cast and seats gained. In another respect, however, it is rather unrepresentative: populations per MEP vary enormously. This is because a conscious attempt has been made to ensure that the smaller countries are not swamped in the EP. So, for example, in Germany there is one MEP per 750,000 inhabitants; in Greece 1:412,000; in Ireland 1:233,000; and in Luxembourg 1:66,000.

A subject that has been much discussed in the context of EP elections is voter turn-out (see Table 5.2). Many have argued that a high turn-out would both enhance the EP's legitimacy and democratic base and also, partly in consequence, would place it in a strong position to press for increased powers. In the event, turn-out in the first two direct elections, held in 1979 and 1984, was relatively low. In 1979, only 62 per cent of those eligible to vote did so. In every country the turn-out was lower than it had been in the previous general election. The poll in 1984 was even worse: on average down two per cent to 60 per cent.

Various factors have been put forward to explain the low turn-outs. It has, for example, been argued that EP elections do not offer any prospect of a change of government, of switches in policy, or of the

TABLE 5.1

National arrangements for elections to the European Parliament[1]

	Number of MEPs	Entitlement to vote	Eligibility for election	Electoral system	Number of constituencies
Belgium	24	18	21	PR with PV[2]	3
Denmark	16	18	18	PR with PV	1
FRG	81	18	18	PR without PV[3]	10+1 (Berlin)
Greece	24	18	21	PR without PV	1
Spain	60	18	18	PR without PV	1
France	81	18	23	PR without PV	1
Ireland	15	18	21	PR with STV[4]	4
Italy	81	18	25	PR with PV	5
Luxembourg	6	18	21	PR with vote splitting	1
Netherlands	25	18	25	PR with PV	1
Portugal	24	18	18	PR without PV	1
United Kingdom	81	18	21	Majority vote system (Northern Ireland – PR with STV)	78+1 (Northern Ireland: 3 seats)
	518				

Notes:

[1]With the exception of Portugal and Spain, which did not hold their first direct election until 1987, the information in the columns refers to the 1984 elections. In most important respects all states used the same system in 1979 (1981 in Greece's case) as in 1984. Changes between the two elections were largely restricted to technical matters such as voter eligibility, the filling of vacant seats between elections, and rules for dual mandates.

[2]Proportional representation with preferential vote.

[3]Proportional representation without preferential vote.

[4]Proportional representation with single transferrable vote.

Source: Directorate General for Research, European Parliament (adapted).

making or unmaking of political reputations. In consequence they do not provide much of a base for the generation of popular interest or political excitement. It has also been contended that the election çampaigns have had little overall coherence or co-ordination. They have essentially been national contests, but of a secondary sort. In 1984, for example, there was little sense of the 1979–84 Centre-Right EP majority defending its record, or of the Left seeking to gain control. Nor did 'European' issues have much of an impact. Finally, observers have noted that many of the forces which do much to focus attention and generate interest in national electoral campaigns have approached the European elections in, at best, a half-hearted manner:

TABLE 5.2

Elections to the European Parliament: voter turn-out

	June 9/12 1979	June 14/17 1984
Belgium[1]	91.4	92.2
Denmark	47.8	52.2
France	60.7	56.7
Germany	65.7	56.8
Greece[1]	78.6[2]	77.2
Ireland	63.6	47.6
Italy	85.5	83.9
Luxembourg[1]	88.9	87.0
Netherlands	58.1	50.6
Portugal	—	71.6[3]
Spain	—	68.9[4]
United Kingdom	32.6	32.4
Total	62.0[5]	60.0[5]

Notes:
[1]Voting compulsory.
[2]Elections of 18 October 1981.
[3]Elections of 19 July 1987.
[4]Elections of 10 June 1987.
Both [3] and [4] turn-outs were inflated by national elections being held on the same day.
[5]Total averages refer only to the elections held in June 1979 and June 1984 respectively.

media interest has been limited; national political parties have been generally reluctant to commit resources to their Euro-campaigns; party activists have tended to be disinterested; and a conscious attempt has been made by some governments to play down the importance of the elections because they are invariably interpreted as being, in part at least, 'mid-term' national elections, or unofficial referenda on their performance in office.

Political Parties and the European Parliament

Party political activity is seen at three main levels in relation to the EP: the transnational, the political groups in the EP, and the national.

The Transnational Federations

Very loosely organised transnational federations, grouped around general principles, exist for co-ordinating, propagandist, and electioneering purposes. The three main federations were created in similar circumstances in the mid-1970s: out of existing, but extremely weakly based, liaising and information exchanging bodies, and as a specific response to the continuing development of the EC and the anticipated future use of direct elections for the EP. These three federations are: the European People's Party – Federation of Christian Democratic Parties of the European Community (EPP); the Federation of Liberal and Democratic Parties of the European Community (LDP); and the Confederation of the Socialist Parties of the European Community (CSP).

Some supporters of European integration have hoped that the federations might develop into organisations providing leadership, vision and co-ordination at European level, and perhaps might even serve as agents of unification to their heterogeneous memberships. They have failed to do so. Their principal weakness is that, unlike national parties or the EP political groups, they are not involved in day-to-day political activity in an institutional setting. They have, therefore, no very clear focus and cannot develop attachments and loyalties. From this, other weaknesses flow: low status; limited resources – they are heavily dependent on the EP political groups for administrative and financial support; and loose organisational structures based on periodic Congresses and bureaux meetings.

The federations have not, therefore, been able to do very much, even though there certainly are tasks for Community-based transnational parties to perform, such as long-term policy planning, the harmonisation of national party differences, and educating the electorate about Europe. Such influence as they have exercised has been largely confined to the EP elections, when manifestos have been produced and a few joint activities have been arranged. Even the manifestos, however, and the use made of them reinforces the general picture of weakness. To take the 1984 elections, the manifestos were developed in a similar way in all three federations – via working groups in which the EP political groups had an important influence, and adopted by Congresses. But because of the need to reconcile differences – which were usually along national lines – references to many key issues, such as the CAP, energy, and security, were often fudged. Where constituent parties were unhappy with parts of the manifestos – as, for example, the British Labour Party and the Danish Social Democrats were with references in the CSP manifesto to the need to increase the EP's influence – they either dissociated themselves from that part of the document or ignored it. In any event, with the transnational parties having no powers to impose themselves on their constituent members, and with the elections being contested in practice along national lines, it was completely up to the national parties to decide what use they wished to make of the 'Euro-manifestos'. Belgium, traditionally one of the most pro-European countries, encapsulated the varied response: the Christian Democratic parties did not draw up their own programmes but used the EPP's; both of the Socialist parties prepared their own detailed programmes before that of the CSP was even agreed; and the Liberal parties drew on the LDP manifesto but prepared their own as well.

Beyond the three main federations, other groupings of an even looser nature have surfaced from time to time. So, several such groups appeared at the time of the 1984 elections, tempted into existence, in part at least, by reimbursement payments which were made available to electoral alliances. They included the Green alliance which supported candidates in seven of the ten member states, a regional alliance made up of parties from Denmark, France, Greece and the Netherlands, and an alliance of the Communist parties of France, Italy, Belgium and Luxembourg. All were divided and were hard pressed to put together even minimalist common statements.

The Political Groups in the European Parliament

Political groups have existed in the EP since the earliest days of the Common Assembly. Under the current Rule of Procedure (4th edition, 1987) a minimum of twenty-three MEPs is required for a group to be formed if all the members come from a single state. If they come from two member states eighteen is sufficient, and if they come from three or more states the minimum is twelve.

Groups have been formed and developed for a number of reasons. The principal basis and unifying element of most of the groups is ideological identification. Despite the many differences which exist between them, MEPs from similar political families and traditions are naturally drawn to one another. All the more so when co-operation serves to maximise their influence, as it does in the EP in all sorts of ways – from electing the President to voting on amendments.

Organisational benefits provide another inducement to political group formation. For example, funds for administrative and research

TABLE 5.3

Political groups in the European Parliament*

Groups	Belgium	Denmark	Germany	Spain	France	Greece	Ireland	Italy	Luxembourg	Netherlands	Portugal	UK	Total
Socialist Group	8	3	33	28	20	10	—	12	2	9	7	33	165
European People's Party	6	1	41	1	10	8	6	27	3	8	4	—	115
European Democratic Group	—	4	—	17	—	—	—	—	—	—	—	45	66
Communist and Allies Group	—	2	—	3	10	4	—	26	—	—	3	—	48
Liberal and Democratic Reformist Group	5	2	—	2	12	—	1	6	—	5	10	—	44
European Democratic Alliance	—	—	—	—	19	1	8	—	—	—	—	1	29
Rainbow Group	4	4	7	1	—	1	—	2	—	2	—	1	20
Group of the European Right	—	—	—	—	9	1	—	5	—	—	—	1	16
Independent	1	—	—	8	—	—	—	3	—	1	—	1	15
Totals	24	16	81	60	81	24	15	81	6	25	24	81	518

*Situation in early 1988.

purposes are distributed to groups on the basis of a fixed amount per group (the non-attached being regarded as a group for these purposes) plus an additional sum per member. No-one is, therefore, unsupported, but clearly the larger the group the more easily it can afford a good back-up service.

There are also advantages in the conduct of Parliamentary business that stem from group status, since the EP arranges much of what it does around the groups. Although non-attached members are not formally excluded from anything by this – indeed they are guaranteed many rights under the Rules of Procedure – they can, in practice, be disadvantaged: in the distribution of committee chairmanships for example, or in the preparation of the agendas of plenary sessions.

Although a Centre-Right majority has always existed in the EP on most important votes, it has never been a wholly coherent or consistent political force. This is because of the large number of political groups in Parliament, which in turn is a reflection of the range of political opinion that exists across the Community, both as regards ideological and national affinities. In the 1984 elections candidates from no less than around sixty different national parties were elected, including eleven from Italy alone, nine from Belgium, and eight from Denmark. In mid-1988 the political groups were as follows.

The Socialists. The Socialists are the largest single group in the EP. Reflecting the breadth of European socialism the members of this group have found co-operation increasingly difficult since the early 1970s. In part, this has been a consequence of increased ideological diversity within the group, with opinions ranging from 'far left' state interventionists to 'moderate' social democrats. In part, it has been caused by national party groups being reluctant to concede national interests to wider European interests. And in part, too, it has stemmed from differences within the group on the very bases and direction of European integration. In spite of all this however, the Socialists, in plenary sessions, vote *en bloc* on most important issues.

The European People's Party. This is basically the Christian Democratic group and it is dominated by the German CDU/CSU and the Italian DC. The two parties are not as close as might be expected. The Germans are essentially a conventional conservative party; the

Italians are much more liberal, as is seen in the frequency with which they vote with the Socialists.

The European Democratic Group. Until the entry of Spain to the Community the dominance of British Conservatives made this group by far the most nationally homogeneous group. It was far from politically united, however, with a wide division existing between what might very broadly be described as a pro-Thatcher wing and a more outwardly 'European' wing. The entry of rather right-wing Spanish MEPs to the group in 1986 seemed to increase internal disharmony, and it was soon no secret that some of 'the Europeans' were canvassing the idea of the group linking up with one of the other Centre or Centre-Right groups.

The Communists and Allies. There is a considerable gulf between the two main constituent parties of this group: the parliamentary, democratic, some would say social democratic, Italian PCI, and the more orthodox, Moscow-oriented, French PCF. Since the brief blossoming of Eurocommunism in the mid-1970s the two have travelled in different directions and in the EP have little to do with one another. The national decline of the PCF has greatly altered the shape and balance of the group.

The Liberal and Democratic Reformist Group. In some respects this is the most divided group of all, and the most difficult to pinpoint in terms of its ideas. It contains certain Leftist influences, but it is basically a combination of the Centre and the Right. The 1984 elections played an important part in pushing it further to the Right, when the German FDP, an important Centrist influence (despite having only four MEPs), failed to surmount the German five per cent threshold barrier.

European Democratic Alliance. Beyond a common commitment to the CAP there are few natural points of agreement and identity between the two main components of this group: the French Gaullists and Irish Fianna Fail. However, neither has been large enough to constitute a group in its own right and both, for different reasons, have been reluctant to link up with one of the more established Centre-Right groups. The EDA has, therefore, served as little more than a useful marriage of convenience for them.

The Rainbow Group. As its name suggests, and as its composition certainly indicates – it is made up of Environmentalists, Ecologists, Anti-EEC Movement Danes, and Regionalists – this group is extremely heterogeneous. Insofar as it has any coherence it is in its attempts to protect minority interests.

The Group of the European Right. Although there was a sprinkling of Extreme Right MEPs prior to the 1984 election they were too small in number to constitute a group. This changed in 1984 with the election of members from the newly emerged and highly nationalistic, French *Front National*.

The political groups all contain, therefore, significant internal divisions, usually of both an ideological and a national character. Inevitably this has a weakening effect. So, for example, it is difficult, whatever their ideological principles might suggest to them, for French MEPs to vote for a cut in agricultural prices or for Portuguese MEPs not to support increases in the Regional Fund.

Two other factors also make for looseness and a limited ability on the part of the groups to control and direct their members. The first of these factors arises from the political powers of the EP and the institutional setting in which it is placed. With no government to sustain or attack, no government-sponsored legislation to pass or reject, MEPs do not have the same semi-automatic 'for' or 'against' reaction that is so typical of much national parliamentary behaviour. The second factor is structural. Unlike parties in national legislatures, the political groups are not part of a wider organisational framework from which emanate expectations of co-operative and united behaviour and generally recognised notions of responsibility and accountability. Rather they are, at best, quasi-federal bodies functioning in a multicultural environment. This is seen in a number of ways: the constituent member parties are likely to hold their own separate meetings and to have their own leaderships; in seeking to encourage group unity no sanctions can be invoked against, and few rewards can be withheld from, those who do not fall into line; and, in looking to their political futures, it is not only their political group or its leadership that MEPs must cultivate but also their national parties at home.

However, despite the many weaknesses of the groups, it is

important to emphasise that they are still of central importance in determining how the EP works. Some of the tasks they fulfil and the privileges they enjoy are specifically allocated to them under the Rules of Procedure or by decisions of Parliament. These include guaranteed representation on key EP bodies and committees and speaking rights in plenary sessions. Other functions have not been formally laid down, but have developed more out of political necessity, advantage, and convenience. This is most obviously seen in the way the groups are the prime determiners of tactics and voting patterns in the EP. The week prior to plenary sessions is set aside for political group meetings. At these meetings efforts are made to agree a common group position on matters of current importance. Should a deal be attempted with another political group on the election of the President? What is the group's attitude to a Commission proposal for a Council directive? What tactics can the group employ to present an unwelcome own initiative report being approved by a committee? In dealing with such questions internal group differences may have to be tackled. Sometimes they cannot be resolved. But, of the many influences bearing down on MEPs, political group membership is normally the single most important factor correlating with how they vote.

The National Parties

National political parties are involved in EP related activities in three main ways.

First, most candidates in the European elections are chosen by the national parties. This means that MEPs inevitably reflect national party concerns and are normally obliged, if they wish to be reselected, to continue to display an awareness of these concerns.

Second, European election campaigns are essentially national elections conducted by national parties. Use may be made of the transnational manifestos, but voters are directed by the parties primarily to national issues and the results are assessed primarily in terms of their domestic implications. That the European dimension is limited is no more clearly seen than in the lack of any consistent Left-Right movement in voting patterns across the member states in European elections.

Finally, in the EP itself, national party groups exist within the political groups. This is an obvious potential source of political group disharmony and in some cases has created great strains. Problems do not arise so much from the national groups having to act on specific domestic instructions. This may occur, but, for the most part, organisational links between the national groups and national party leaderships are weak and the former have a reasonably free hand within general party guidelines. The problem is simply that each national party group inevitably tends to have its own priorities and loyalties.

Composition

In addition to party political attachments there are other aspects of the composition of the EP which are also of interest and importance. Three are particularly worthy of comment.

The Dual Mandate

After the 1979 election some 30 per cent of MEPs were also members of their national legislature. This figure was inflated however, because many MEPs had contested the election primarily for domestic political reasons and had no firm commitment to completing their terms of office. By the end of the Parliament the number of dual mandates had been more than halved. What, therefore, seems to be a big drop after the 1984 election, to around 12 per cent of MEPs holding a dual mandate, in fact reflects a trend that was already well under way; a trend that was assisted in 1984 by some parties actively trying to discourage dual mandates and by Belgium forbidding it altogether under national law.

Among the consequences of this decline in the dual mandate has been a weakening of links between the EP and national parliaments. Most parties have procedures of some kind for maintaining contact between the two levels but they tend to be weak, and frequently the EP group is seen as something of a poor relation. A more positive outcome has been that MEPs with one mandate rather than two have more time and energy for their EP duties. This has been reflected in more days spent in plenaries and committees, more Parliamentary questions, and more reports.

Continuity

The degree of change and turnover in personnel affects the way most organisations work. The EP is no exception to this: the more effective MEPs tend to be those who have developed policy interests and expertise in European affairs over time, and who have come to know their way around the Community system.

Lack of continuity in membership was a problem during the 1979–84 Parliament, with nearly one-quarter of MEPs being replaced. However, as noted above, that was always likely to be an inflated figure, with many prominent politicians standing in 1979 who had no intention of making a political career in the EP. The 1984 intake gave promise of a much greater stability in the future: fewer dual mandates and over half of those elected being former MEPs.

Competence and Experience

It is sometimes suggested that MEPs are not of the same calibre and do not carry the same political weight as their counterparts in national legislatures. Because the EP is weak, the argument runs, it attracts mostly weak members, or members who regard it merely as a stepping stone to national transfer or advancement.

There is something in this view. Major national figures have tended either not to contest EP elections or not to have completed their terms of office. (The provision in the 1976 Act making national governmental office incompatible with EP membership has not helped in this regard.) Additionally, a few MEPs have transferred from the EP to national legislatures. But the situation should not be exaggerated. Competition to be an MEP is normally fierce, requiring all the customary political skills. Most MEPs do have considerable public experience, either in national or regional politics, or in an executive capacity with a major sectional interest. There is little evidence of a widespread desire on the part of MEPs to transfer to national politics. And, perhaps most importantly of all, it should not be assumed that those who choose to stand for, and work in, the EP are necessarily settling for second best: many are firmly committed to their responsibilities and have developed a competence and an experience which is different from, but which is not necessarily inferior to, that of national parliamentarians.

Organisation and Operation

The Multi-site Problem

The work of the EP is carried out on three sites in three different countries. Plenaries are held in Strasbourg at the Palais de L'Europe. Committees usually meet in Brussels, where the Parliament has office and meeting room facilities close to the Council and the Commission. Most of the Parliament's, 3200 staff (450 of whom are employed in the Secretariats of the political groups) are based in Luxembourg.

This situation is clearly unsatisfactory, and it is a source of grievance and annoyance among most MEPs. A reasonably conscientious MEP may well have to change his working location half a dozen times in an average month. His work diary is likely to look something like this: one week attending the monthly plenary at Strasbourg; from two to five days in committee(s), probably in Brussels but sometimes elsewhere; two to four days in political group meetings and group working parties, probably in Brussels; whatever time remains in his constituency (if he has one), visiting somewhere as part of an EP delegation, in Luxembourg consulting with officials on a report, or at home.

If the EP had one base, and especially if that was Brussels, it is likely that Parliament's efficiency, influence and visibility would all be increased. However, the Council has the power of decision on the matter, and hard lobbying from the Luxembourg and French governments has ensured that arguments for 'sense to prevail' and a single site to be agreed have not been acted upon.

Arranging Parliamentary Business

Compared with most national parliaments the EP enjoys a considerable independence in the arrangement of its affairs. That is not to say it can do whatever it likes. The Treaties oblige it to do some things, such as deliver Opinions on Commission proposals for Council legislation, and prevent it from doing others, such as censuring the Council. But, on many agenda, timetable and other organisational matters it remains, to a considerable degree, its own master.

A major reason for this independence is, once again, the special institutional setting in which the EP operates. The Community executive does not have to be as concerned to control what the EP does as do national governments with their legislatures. This is because although EP pronouncements and activities can be unwelcome to the Council and the Commission they do not normally have politically damaging or unmanageable consequences.

A second, and closely related, reason is the lack of any clear and consistent identification, of either a positive or negative kind, between the EP and the Community executive. In national parliaments business is shaped to a considerable degree by political attachments. But the Commission is made up of officials who are nominally non-partisan, while the Council is multiparty, multi-ideological, and multinational in its membership. As for the 'persuasive devices' that national executives have at their disposal to further encourage loyalty, neither the Commission nor the Council has patronage to dispense.

A third reason is that the EP is entitled to adopt its own Rules of Procedure. This it has done, amending and streamlining them in recent years in such ways as to make it both more efficient and more influential.

The EP thus largely makes its own decisions about its operation and functioning. In practice, the responsibility for this falls mainly to the President, the Bureau, and the Enlarged Bureau.

The President is elected to office for a two and a half year term. According to Rule 18 of the Rules of Procedure the President 'shall direct all the activities of Parliament and of its bodies under the conditions laid down in these Rules'. In practice, this means that the President has many functions, such as presiding over debates in the chamber, referring matters to committees as appropriate, and representing the EP in dealings with other Community institutions and outside bodies. An effective President must be an administrator and a politician, skilled in organising and also in liaising and bargaining.

The Bureau consists of the President and Parliament's fourteen Vice-Presidents. Like the President, the Vice-Presidents are elected for a two and a half year period of office, though by tradition the posts are distributed among the member states. Various organisational matters are dealt with by the Bureau such as making recommendations on the composition of committees and deciding on the composition and structure of the Parliament's Secretariat. To assist it in the performance of its duties, and in particular to take responsibility for financial and administrative matters concerning members, five quaestors, who are also elected, sit in the Bureau in an advisory capacity.

For certain key purposes the members of the Bureau are joined by the chairmen of the political groups or their representatives and two non-voting delegates from the non-attached groups. This constitutes the Enlarged Bureau. Its functions include: deciding on the seating arrangements in the Chamber – a potentially sensitive and highly symbolic issue when groups do not wish to be seated too far to the left or to the right of the hemicycle; drawing up the draft agenda of plenary sessions; and ruling on the permissibility and order of questions addressed to the Council and the Commission.

The Committees of Parliament

Much of the EP's work is carried out by committees. These are of two types. The first, and by far the most important, are standing or permanent committees. There are eighteen of these (see Table 5.4). The second are *ad hoc* committees which are established to investigate special topics.

TABLE 5.4

Standing Committees of the European Parliament

1. Political Affairs Committee
2. Committee on Agriculture Fisheries and Food
3. Committee on Budgets
4. Committee on Economic and Monetary Affairs and Industrial Policy
5. Committee on Energy, Research and Technology
6. Committee on External Economic Relations
7. Committee on Legal Affairs and Citizens' Rights
8. Committee on Social Affairs and Employment
9. Committee on Regional Policy and Regional Planning
10. Committee on Transport
11. Committee on the Environment, Public Health and Consumer Protection
12. Committee on Youth, Culture, Education, Information and Sport
13. Committee on Development and Co-operation
14. Committee on Budgetary Control
15. Committee on Institutional Affairs
16. Committee on the Rules of Procedure, the Verification of Credentials and Immunities
17. Committee on Women's Rights
18. Committee on Petitions

Assignment of MEPs to the permanent committees occurs at the beginning and half way through each five-year term. Assignment to the *ad hoc* committees is as required. According to the Rules of Procedure, all committee members are elected to their positions on the basis of proposals made by the Bureau to Parliament which are 'designed to ensure fair representation of Member States and of political views'. What this means, in practice, is that the political groups negotiate the share-out of committee memberships on a basis proportionate to their size. Most MEPs become a member of one standing committee – though a few are on as many as three – and a substitute member of another.

The permanent committees perform various duties, such as explore ideas with the Commission, foster own initiative reports, and, occasionally, discuss developments with the Council. Their most important task, however, is to examine legislative proposals on which an EP Opinion is required. In respect of proposals which only have a single reading, or at first reading stage under the co-operation procedure, the standard way of proceeding (other than where a proposal is completely straightforward and uncontroversial, which may result in it being dealt with by special procedures allowing for rapid approval) is as follows.

(1) Each proposal is referred to an appropriate committee. Should a proposal overlap the competency and interest of several committees up to three may be asked for their views but one is named as the committee responsible and only it reports to the plenary session.

(2) The responsibility for drawing up the committee's report is entrusted to a *rapporteur*. Though formally chosen by their fellow committee members, *rapporteurs* are, in practice, like committee chairman and many others in the EP who hold nominally elected positions, appointed as a result of negotiations between the political groups: negotiations that, in this case, are carried out by group 'co-ordinators' from the different committees. In drawing up his report a *rapporteur* can call on assistance from various places: primarily from Parliament's Secretariat, but also from his personal research assistant (the EP provides funds for each MEP to have at least one such assistant), from the Secretariat of his political group, from research institutes, and even from the Commission. Some *rapporteurs* hardly use these facilities and do most of the work themselves; others do little more than present what has been done on their behalf.

(3) A first draft is produced for consideration by the committee

according to an agreed timeable. Following changes that were introduced as part of the 1987 EP Rules of Procedure, drafts are normally presented in four main parts: Amendments to the Commission Proposal (if there are any); a Draft Legislative Resolution; an Explanatory Statement; and Annexes (if there are any), including Opinions of other committees. How much discussion the draft provokes, and how many committee meetings are required before a text is adopted that can be recommended to the plenary, depends on the complexity and controversiality of the subject matter. Factors likely to shape the reactions of committee members include national and ideological perspectives, lobbying by outside interests, and views expressed by the Commission (see Exhibit 5.1 for extracts from a committee report).

(4) The *rapporteur* acts as the committee's principal spokesman when the report is considered in the plenary. In this capacity he may have to explain the committee's view on amendments put forward by non-committee members, or he may be called upon to use his judgement in making recommendations to Parliament on what it should do when the Commission goes some, but not all, of the way in accepting committee-approved amendments. Occasionally – when, for example, the Commission offers a mixed package – committee meetings may be hurriedly convened during plenary sessions.

Where the co-operation procedure applies, the role and activity of committees at the second reading stage is similar to that at the first reading. That is to say, they examine a proposal – which is now in the form of the Council's common position – and make recommendations to the plenary. The responsibility for drawing up reports is conferred automatically on the committees involved in the first reading and the *rapporteur* remains the same. The reports normally have two main sections: Recommendations for the Second Reading (which may provide for approval of, rejection of, or amendments to, the common position – amendments often having the intention of re-establishing the EP's position as defined at the first reading, or to produce a compromise with the Council); and Justifications or Explanatory Statements.

A number of factors help to determine how the EP committees work, and how much influence they exercise. The most important of these factors are:

● *The significance of the policy area within the Community system.* The

EXHIBIT 5.1

Extracts from a European Parliament Committee Report

9 December 1987   SERIES A   DOCUMENT A 2–251/87

[*]   REPORT

drawn up on behalf of the Committee on the Environment, Public Health and Consumer Protection

on the proposal from the Commission of the European Communities to the Council (COM(87) 120 final – Doc. C2–34/87) for a decision amending Decision 86/85/EEC establishing a Community information system for the control and reduction of pollution of the sea caused by oil and other harmful substances

The Committee on the Environment, Public Health and Consumer Protection hereby submits to the European Parliament the following draft legislative resolution together with explanatory statement:

A

DRAFT LEGISLATIVE RESOLUTION

embodying the opinion of the European Parliament on the proposal from the Commission of the European Communities to the Council for a decision amending Decision 86/85/EEC establishing a Community information system for the control and reduction of pollution caused by spillage of hydrocarbons and other harmful substances at sea

The European Parliament,

– having regard to the proposal from the Commission to the Council (COM(87) 120 final),
– having been consulted by the Council pursuant to Article 130s of the EEC Treaty (Doc. C 2–34/87),
– having regard to, and approving, the legal basis proposed,
– having regard to the report of the Committee on the Environment, Public Health and Consumer Protection (Doc. A 2–251/87),
– having regard to the result of the vote on the Commission's proposal,
1. Approves the Commission's proposal;
2. Calls on the Council to notify Parliament should it propose to depart from the text approved by Parliament;
3. Calls on the Council to consult Parliament again should it propose to make substantial modifications to the Commission's proposal;
4. Instructs its President to forward to the Council and Commission, as Parliament's opinion, the text of the Commission's proposal as voted by Parliament and the corresponding legislative resolution.

B

EXPLANATORY STATEMENT

Although prevention of pollution should be the key element in environmental policy there will always be incidents involving the threat of pollution of the environment. Consequently, a preventive policy will always require the back-up of measures to control the effects of accidents.

The first stage in establishing adequate resources is to inventorize the resources already available for the control of accidents. To some extent existing Community information systems already meet this requirement. The expansion of the Community information system proposed by the Commission is a useful step towards controlling pollution of inland waterways and pollution of the sea into which such waterways discharge . . .

We therefore recommend that the Commission should, without delay, devise a programme capable of supporting the development of resources for controlling environmental accidents at sea and on inland waterways involving harmful substances other than oil.

 *   = Consultation procedure requiring a single reading

Committee on Agriculture, for example, deals with matters which simply loom larger in the Community scale of things than the Committee on Youth, Culture, Education, Information and Sport.

● *The power of Parliament within the policy area.* The influence of the Committee on Budgets is enormously enhanced by the real budgetary decision-making powers that the Treaties give to Parliament. Similarly, the Committee on Budgetary Control would be much weaker if the EP did not have the statutory responsibility to grant, postpone, or refuse a discharge to the Commission in respect of the implementation of the Community's budget.

● *Committee expertise.* Many committee members just do not have the requisite specialised skills or knowledge to be able to explore relevant issues in depth or to question the Commission on the basis of a fully informed understanding of policy. For example, few members of the Committee on Energy, Research and Technology have an appropriate technical background. The Committee on Agriculture, on the other hand, includes a large number of farmers, while the Legal Affairs Committee is composed mainly of lawyers or legal experts.

● *Secretariat support.* In terms of numbers, all committees are thinly resourced in their administrative back-up. Each has, on average, only about five senior officials and these, because of the EP's recruitment policy, are usually generalists rather than specialists. However, among these small teams there do appear to be variations in competence and enthusiasm.

● *Committee chairmanship.* The role of committee chairmen can be vital in guiding the work of committees. They can help to push business through; they can assist *rapporteurs* in rallying support for reports that are to be debated in plenaries; they can help to create committee harmony and a constructive working atmosphere; and they can do much to ensure that a committee broadens its horizons beyond simply reacting to initiatives that others present to it.

● *Committee cohesiveness.* One of the reasons why, for example, the Committee on Development and Co-operation is rather more influential than a number of other committees is that it tends to display a high degree of cohesiveness. With members of the committee being united on the desirability of improving conditions in the developing countries, discussions tend to revolve around questions of feasibility rather than ideological desirability. The Agriculture Committee, on the other hand, attracts MEPs who are both supportive and critical of CAP and hence it tends often to be sharply internally divided.

Plenary Meetings

There are usually twelve plenary meetings, or part-sessions as they are properly known, per year: one each month, apart from August when there is none and an extra meeting in October or November to consider the budget. Part-sessions last from Monday afternoon to Friday midday.

The agenda for plenaries is drafted by the President and the Enlarged Bureau in consultation with the committees, the political groups, and the EP's Secretariat. Their recommendations have to be approved by the plenary itself. With time so tight, items which many MEPs consider to be important inevitably do not get onto the agenda, while those that do make it normally have to be taken at pace. Strict rules govern who can speak, when, and for how long: the effect of these is often to restrict speakers to committee and political group spokesmen.

Plenaries have three standard elements. First, the bread and butter business is the consideration of reports from committees. As indicated earlier these reports produce around 150 resolutions embodying Opinions and 100 resolutions embodying own initiatives per year. Second, time is set aside for debates on topical and urgent matters. These usually result in about 150–200 resolutions being adopted every year. Finally, there is a 1½-hour Commission Question Time and a 1½-hour Council Question Time. Who answers on behalf of the Commission and the Council depends on the policy content of the questions (which are known in advance), preferences expressed by the Parliament, and who is available.

In addition to these three standard activities, there are a number of other possible agenda items. For example, statements by the Commission and the Council, reports by the President of the European Council on heads of government meetings, and addresses by distinguished foreign guests.

The EP in plenary does not, it should be said, give the impression of being the most dynamic of places. Attendance in the chamber is poor, the translation problem limits spontaneity, and much immediacy is lost by the practice of taking most votes in clusters at allocated voting times rather than at the end of debates. (These times are often not even on the same day as the debate.) None the less, working procedures have been gradually improved over the years, most notably by the removal of much minor business from the floor of the chamber. Furthermore, the recent innovation of focusing part-sessions on one or two major themes and grouping together reports from particular committees has allowed for a greater coherence and has also encouraged those who are interested and involved in the theme subjects to make the effort of travelling to Strasbourg.

Concluding Remarks

The EP is still commonly regarded as not quite being a proper parliament. Its limited constitutional powers are seen to relegate it to the role of a rather special sort of advisory body. But, in important respects, the EP is, in practice, little different from many parliaments of the democratic world. Certainly, since the introduction of direct elections, it can make a reasonable claim to be exercising the traditional parliamentary role of representing the citizenry. And with regard to influence on affairs a number of factors have combined to give it a significance that is comparable with that of at least some national parliaments. Among these factors are Treaty revisions, enhanced status and increased vigour stemming from direct elections, Court judgements, and formal and informal understandings with other Community institutions.

The granting of full legislative, budgetary, and supervisory powers to the EP cannot be anticipated in the foreseeable future. But the increased role which the Parliament has assumed in the Community system over the years – an increase that is visible in the growth of lobbying in and around the Parliament building, and also in the greater willingness of senior Commission and Council representatives to meet with, and appear before, Parliamentary bodies – should be recognised.

6

Community Law and the Court of Justice

The Need for Community Law

An enforceable legal framework is the essential basis of decision-making and decision application in all democratic states. Although not itself a state this also applies to the EC. It does so because the Community is more than merely another international organisation in which countries co-operate with one another on a voluntary basis for reasons of mutual benefit. Rather it is an organisation in which states have voluntarily surrendered their right, across a broad range of important sectors, to be independent in the determination and application of public policy.

If there was no body of law setting out the powers and responsibilities of the institutions and the member states of the Community, and if there was no authority to give independent rulings on what that law is and how it should be interpreted, effective Community decision-making would not be possible. Of course, law is not the only factor shaping the Community's decision-making processes. As in any organisation, practice evolves in the light of experience of what is possible and what works best. The tendency not to press for a vote in the Council even when it is legally permissible is an obvious example of this. But the law does provide the basic setting in which decisions are made. It lays down that some things must be done, that some cannot, and that some may be. So, for example, it is by virtue of Community law that agricultural prices can no longer be fixed in national capitals but must be agreed at Community level, that the Commission is entitled to take certain types of decisions without reference to other institutions, and that the European Parliament is permitted to increase the annual budget within specified limits.

The existence of Community law is also crucial with regard to policy implementation. For if decisions took the form only of vague intergovernmental agreements, and if those agreements could be interpreted by member states in whatever way was most beneficial and convenient for them, common policies would not, in practice, exist and the whole rationale of the Community would be undermined. The likes of the *common* agricultural policy, the *common* competition policy, the *common* commercial policy, and the harmonisation of matters as diverse as maximum axle weights of lorries and minimum safety standards at work, can be fully effective only if they are based on *common laws* that are capable of *uniform* interpretation in all member states.

The Sources of Community Law

A Community legal order is thus an essential condition of the Community's existence. The sources of that order are to be found in a number of places: the Treaties, Community legislation, international law, the general principles of law, and judicial interpretation.

The Treaties

The three founding Treaties plus the Treaties and Acts supplementing and amending the founding Treaties constitute the so-called primary legislation of the Community. They may also be regarded as making up the Community's written constitution.

National constitutions normally do two main things: they establish an institutional structure for decision-making, and they set out – often in a bill of rights – freedoms of the individual and restrictions on the power of decision-makers over the citizenry. The Treaties of the Community exercise the first of these tasks, but only in a very restricted way the second. The establishment of the institutional structure is seen, most obviously, in the identification of the Commission, the Council, the Court and the Parliament as the major institutions of the Community, and by the laying down of rules governing relations between them and also between them and the member states. As for the establishment of individual rights the scope is largely restricted to certain economic freedoms – a reflection of the concerns of the Community itself and of the fact that the EC does not carry the comprehensive responsibilities of nation states.

The economic character of the Community is seen in the way the founding Treaties, the Treaties of Accession, and the Single European Act are much concerned with something that is normally not considered to be appropriate subject matter for constitutions: policy. This takes the form of enunciation of general principles on the one hand and the identification of policy sectors that are to be developed on the other. The general principles include those in the EEC Treaty that are designed to promote competition and the free movement of goods, persons, services, and capital, all behind a common external tariff and a common commercial policy. The policy sectors that are identified, with varying degrees of precision regarding how they are to be developed, include: coal and steel (ECSC); atomic energy (Euratom); agriculture, social, and transport (EEC); and regional, environmental, and research and technological development (SEA).

Community Legislation

Laws adopted by the Community institutions constitute secondary legislation. They are concerned with translating the general principles of the Treaties into specific rules and are adopted by the Council or the Commission according to the procedures described in other chapters. While there is no hard and fast distinction between Council and Commission legislation the former tends to be broader in scope and concerned with more important or more controversial matters. Commission legislation, which numerically is by far the most voluminous of the two, is largely administrative/technical in nature and subject to tight guidelines laid down in enabling Council legislation.

The Treaties distinguish different types of Community legislation (Article 14 ECSC, Article 189 EEC, Article 161 Euratom): regulations, directives, decisions, and recommendations and opinions.

Regulations (called general decisions under the ECSC). A regulation is:

1. Of 'general application', that is, it contains general and abstract

provisions which may be applied to particular persons and circumstances.

2. 'Binding in its entirety', that is, it bestows rights and obligations upon those to whom it is addressed, and member states must observe it in full and as written.

3. 'Directly applicable in all Member States', that is, without the need for national implementing measures, it takes immediate legal effect right across the Community on the date specified in the regulation. (Normally this is the same day as, or very shortly after, the regulation is published in the *Official Journal of the European Communities*. This, in turn, is usually only a day or two after the regulation has been adopted.)

Most regulations are adopted by the Commission and concern highly specific and technical adjustments to existing Community law. The majority relate to the CAP. Exhibit 6.1 is a typical regulation.

Directives (recommendations under the ECSC). 'A directive shall be binding, as to the result to be achieved, upon each Member State to which it is addressed, but shall leave to the national authorities the choice of form and method' (Article 189 EEC).

In theory, a directive is thus very different from a regulation: it is not binding in its entirety but only in 'the result to be achieved'; it is addressed to member states and does not claim general applicability; it is not necessarily addressed to all member states; and appropriate national measures need to be taken to give the directive effect. As a consequence directives tend to be rather more general in nature than regulations. They are not quite so much concerned with the detailed and uniform application of policy, as with the laying down of policy principles which member states must seek to achieve but which they can pursue by the appropriate means under their respective national constitutional and legal systems. (Such appropriate means can vary from administrative circulars to new laws approved by national legislatures.)

The distinction between regulations and directives should not, however, be exaggerated, because, in practice, a number of factors often result in a blurring. First, directives are almost invariably addressed to all states and are so because they are usually concerned with the harmonisation of laws and practices in fields of Community activity. Exhibit 6.2 is a typical harmonising directive. Second, many

EXHIBIT 6.1

COMMISSION REGULATION (EEC) No 2755/87

of 15 September 1987

fixing the aid for soya beans

THE COMMISSION OF THE EURO-PEAN COMMUNITIES,

Having regard to the Treaty establishing the European Economic Community,

Having regard to the Act of Accession of Spain and Portugal,

Having regard to Council Regulation (EEC) No 1491/85 of 23 May 1985 laying down special measures in respect of soya beans([1]), as amended by Regulation (EEC) No 1921/87([2]); and in particular Article 2(7) thereof,

Whereas the amount of the aid referred to in Article 2(1) of Regulation (EEC) No 1491/85 was fixed by Commission Regulation (EEC) No 2638/87([3]);

Whereas it follows from applying the rules and other provisions contained in Regulation (EEC) No 2638/87 to the information at present available to the Commission that the amount of the aid at present in force should be altered as set out in this Regulation,

HAS ADOPTED THIS REGULATION:

Article 1

1. The aid referred to in Article 2 of amended Regulation (EEC) No 1491/85 is hereby fixed in the Annex.

2. In cases of advance fixing of the aid the amount shall however be confirmed or altered with effect from 16 September 1987 to take account, where appropriate, of the effects of application of the system of maximum guaranteed quantities for soya seed.

Article 2

This Regulation shall enter into force on 16 September 1987.

This Regulation shall be binding in its entirety and directly applicable in all Member States.

Done at Brussels, 15 September 1987.

For the Commission
Frans ANDRIESSEN
Vice-President

_____

([1]) OJ No L 151, 10. 6. 1985, p. 15.
([2]) OJ No L 183, 3. 7. 1987, p. 19.
([3]) OJ No L 248, 1. 9. 1987, p. 50.

ANNEX

Aid for soya beans([1])

(ECU/100 kg)

	Seed harvested in		
	Spain	another Member Portugal	State
Seed processed in:			
— Spain	0,000	33,910	33,910
— Portugal	22,084	0,000	33.910
— another Member State	22,084	33,910	33,910

([1]) Subject to confirmation of the amount to be deducted in accordance with the system of guaranteed maximum quantities.

EXHIBIT 6.2

COUNCIL DIRECTIVE

of 16 February 1987
fixing guidelines for the assessment of additives in animal nutrition

(87/153/EEC)

THE COUNCIL OF THE EUROPEAN COMMUNITIES,

Having regard to the Treaty establishing the European Economic Community,

Having regard to Council Directive 70/524/EEC of 23 November 1970 concerning additives in feedingstuffs([1]), as last amended by Commission Directive 86/525/EEC([2]), and in particular Article 9 thereof,

Having regard to the proposal from the Commission,

Whereas Directive 70/524/EEC provides that the examination of additives must be performed on the basis of a dossier forwarded officially to the Member States and to the Commission;

Whereas such dossiers must make it possible to verify that additives comply, in respect of their proposed use, with the general principles laid down in the Directive for their inclusion in the Annexes thereto;

Whereas it has been found necessary to provide for the dossiers to be compiled in accordance with common guidelines defining the scientific data which make it possible to identify and characterize the products concerned and the studies necessary in order to evaluate, in particular, their efficacy and their safety for man, animals and the environment;

Whereas the guidelines are intended primarily as a general guide; whereas, depending on the nature of the additive or its conditions to use, the extent of the studies necessary in order to evaluate its properties or its effects may vary;

([1]) OJ No L 270, 14. 12. 1970, p. 1.
([2]) OJ No L 310, 5. 11. 1986, p. 19.

Whereas it is indispensable to apply the principles of good laboratory practice when developing additives intended for use in feedingstuffs to ensure that the results of laboratory tests are not disputed; whereas recourse to procedures involving the use of laboratory animals for experimental or other scientific purposes should be kept to a minimum;

Whereas the guidelines have been drawn up on the basis of present scientific and technical knowledge and they may be adapted if necessary to any developments in this sphere,

HAS ADOPTED THIS DIRECTIVE,

Article 1

Member States shall prescribe that the dossiers which must accompany every request for the inclusion of an additive or a new use of an additive in the Annexes to Directive 70/524/EEC are to be compiled in accordance with the guidelines set out in the Annex to this Directive.

Article 2

This Directive shall apply without prejudice to provisions on:

(a) good laboratory practice for the purposes of mutual acceptance of data for the evaluation of chemical products; and

(b) the protection of animals used for experimental or other scientific purposes.

Article 3

Member States shall bring into force the laws, regulations or administrative provisions necessary in order to comply with this Directive by 31 December 1987 at the latest. They shall forthwith inform the Commission thereof.

Article 4

This Directive is addressed to the Member States.

Done at Brussels, 16 February 1987.

For the Council
The President
L. TINDEMANS

directives are drafted so tightly that there is very little room for national authorities to incorporate adjustments. Third, directives contain a date by which the national procedures to give the directive effect must have been complied with. The Commission has to be notified of national implementing measures, and states which do not comply by the due date are liable to have proceedings initiated against them which can, ultimately, result in a case before the Court of Justice. Fourth, the Court has ruled that in some instances directives are directly applicable; for example, where national implementing legislation has been unduly delayed or where it has departed from the intent of the original directive.

Decisions (called individual decisions under the ECSC). 'A decision shall be binding in its entirety upon those to whom it is addressed' (Article 189 EEC). It may be addressed to any or to all member states, to undertakings, or to individuals. Many decisions are highly specific and are, in effect, adminstrative rather than legislative acts. Others are of a more general character and can be akin to regulations or even, occasionally, directives.

Decisions are adopted in a whole range of circumstances. For example: to institute a pilot action programme; to authorise grants from one of the Community's funds; to allow an exemption from an existing measure; or to counter dumping from a third country.

Recommendations and Opinions (Opinions only under the ECSC). Recommendations and Opinions have no binding force and so, strictly speaking, do not formally constitute part of Community law. However, the Court of Justice has on occasions referred to them, so their legal status is not always completely clear. The same applies to some of the other non-binding devices which the Community institutions use for such purposes as floating ideas, starting a legislative process, promoting co-ordination, and encouraging harmonisation. These include memoranda, communications, conventions, programmes, guidelines, agreements, declarations, resolutions, and decisions not made under Article 189.

In order to accommodate the mosaic of different national circumstances and interests which often exist on a particular issue, the Community's legislative framework has to be flexible, creative, and innovative. The variety of formal and quasi-formal legislative instruments that have just been outlined is the most obvious way in which it is so. A second way is in the variations between directives regarding the time periods permitted for member states to introduce the necessary measures to comply with the directive. So, for example, amending directives may have immediate effect; while innovative or controversial directives may not be required to take effect for three or four years or even longer. A third way is in the frequent attachment to legal acts, or in the granting of permission by the Commission after acts have come into force, of devices which allow for adaption to local conditions and needs: devices which take the form, for example, of exemptions, derogations, and safety clauses.

The complexity of Community legislation is closely linked with its considerable volume. In an average year as many as 13,000 instruments of all types may be adopted. Most of these are administrative measures of a routine, non-political, recurring kind such as price adjustments. With regard to the major, or clear, categories of legislation, around 4000 regulations are usually produced, about 500 decisions, and around 80 directives. Of these, the Council issues approximately 500 of the regulations, 170 of the decisions, and 70 of the directives.

International Law

International law is notoriously vague and weak, but the Court of Justice has had occasional recourse to it when developing principles embodied in Community law. Judgements have also established that insofar as the Community is increasingly developing an international personality of its own and taking over powers from the states the same rules of international law apply to it as apply to them: regarding treaty law, for example, and the privileges and immunities of international organisations.

The many international agreements to which the Community is a party are sometimes viewed as another dimension of international law. However, since they are implemented by legislative acts they are probably better viewed as constituting part of Community legislation.

The General Principles of Law

All three Treaties charge the Court of Justice with the task of ensuring 'that in the interpretation and application of this Treaty the law is observed' (Article 164 EEC, Article 136 Euratom, Article 31 ECSC). The implication of this, and of certain other Treaty articles, (notably 173 and 215 EEC) is that the Court need not regard written Community law as the only source of law to which it may refer.

In practice, this has meant that the Court, in making its judgements, has had regard to the general principles of law when they have been deemed to be relevant and to apply. Now, exactly what the general principles of law are, gives rise to controversy. Suffice to note here that they are usually regarded as ranging from such general principles as adherence to legality and prohibition of denial of justice to more technical principles such as rights acquired under an administrative act. In the Community context they have had their greatest impact in the broad, and as far as the Treaties are concerned, largely silent, area of fundamental human rights.

Judicial Interpretation

Although case law has traditionally not played a major role as a source of law in most of the member states of the Community (the United Kingdom and Ireland are the main exceptions), the rulings of the Court of Justice have played an important part in shaping and making Community law. This stems partly from the Court's duty of ensuring that Community law is interpreted and applied correctly. It stems also from the fact that much of Community statute law is far from clear or complete.

The lack of precision in much of the Community's statute law arises from a number of factors: the relative newness of the Community; the problems of the decision-making processes that so often lead to weak compromises and to avoidance of necessary secondary legislation; and the speed of change in some spheres of Community activity which makes it very difficult for the written law to keep abreast of developments. In many fields of apparent Community competence the Court thus has to issue judgements from a less than detailed statutory base. In the different types of cases that come before it – cases of first and only instance, cases of appeal, cases involving rulings on points of Community law that have been referred by national courts – the Court, therefore, inevitably and frequently goes well beyond merely giving a technical and grammatical interpretation of the written rules. It fills in the gaps in the law and, by so doing, it not only clarifies the law, but it creates new law. This is seen both in the way national courts are expected to – and generally do – respect its judgements, and in the way the Court has increasingly come to cite its own case law.

In short, the Court is, in effect, extending Community law and making judicial legislation.

The Content of Community Law

The content of Community law is described at some length in Chapter 9, in the context of the examination that is presented there of Community policies. Attention here will, therefore, be confined to briefly noting some points of general significance.

The first point is that Community law does not range as widely as national law. It is not, for instance, directly concerned with criminal law or family law. Nor does it have much to do with policy areas such as education or health. What Community law is primarily concerned with – and, in this, it reflects the aims and the provisions of the Treaties – is economic activity. More particularly, Community law is strongly focused in the direction of, to quote Article 2 of the EEC Treaty, 'establishing a common market and progressively approximating the economic policies of the Member states'. To these ends, much of Community law is to be found in the overlapping, and often highly technical, areas of commercial law, competition law, business law, and law relating to the free movement of goods, services, capital and labour within the Community market.

The second point is that no policy area contains a comprehensive code of Community law. Even in areas where there is a high degree of Community regulation, such as external commercial relations and the functioning of agricultural markets, national laws covering various matters still exist. Community law thus sits side-by-side with national law, constituting an important part of the overall legal framework of member states in some policy spheres, being of only marginal significance in others.

The third point is that the range of Community law has broadened out considerably over the years. Certainly, as noted above, Community law is primarily economic in character, but less dominantly so than it was. A good illustration of this is seen in the way Community environmental laws now exist dealing with matters as diverse as disposal of toxic wastes and protection of endangered bird species. This expansion of Community law into an increasing number of policy areas has occurred, and is still occurring, for several reasons. Prominent among these reasons are: sectional pressures; increasing recognition of the benefits which can accrue in many fields of activity from joint action; and growing feelings that the Community market can only function smoothly, efficiently, and equitably, if there are common rules covering matters such as health and safety at work, entitlements to social welfare benefits, and mutual recognition of educational and professional qualifications.

The Status of Community Law

In Case 6/64 *Costa v. ENEL* the Court of Justice stated:

> By creating a Community of unlimited duration, having its own institutions, its own personality, its own legal capacity of representation on the international plane and, more particularly, real powers stemming from limitation of sovereignty or a transfer of powers from the states to the Community, the Member States have limited their sovereign rights, albeit within limited fields, and have thus created a body of law which binds both their individuals and themselves'.

Community law thus constitutes an autonomous legal system imposing obligations and rights on both individuals and member states, and limiting the sovereignty of member states. There are three main pillars to this legal system: direct applicability, direct effect, and primacy.

Direct Applicability

Community law is directly applicable where there is no need for any national measures to be taken in order for the law to have binding force within member states. Of the different statutory sources of Community law only regulations are always directly applicable. However, it has been established, principally via Court of Justice judgements, that other legal acts may also be directly applicable when their structure and content so allow and certain conditions are satisfied.

Direct Effect

This term refers to the principle whereby certain provisions of Community law may confer rights or impose obligations on individuals which national courts are bound to recognise and enforce. Having initially established the principle in 1963 in the case of *Van Gend en Loos* (Case 26/62) the Court, in a series of judgements, has gradually strengthened and extended the scope of direct effect so that it now applies to most secondary legislation except where discretion is explicitly granted to the addressee. Many of the provisions of the Treaties have also been established as having direct effect, although the Court has ruled that it does not apply in some important spheres, for example, free movement of capital.

(Although the details of what is an extremely complicated legal debate cannot be rehearsed here, it should be noted that the distinction that has just been drawn between direct applicability and direct effect is not one that all lawyers accept. A consequence of this is that the terms have given rise to considerable confusion and much debate. Even official Community sources, including the Court itself, have not used the terms consistently or with precision.)

Primacy

Somewhat surprisingly, there is no explicit reference in the Treaty of Rome to the primacy or precedence of Community law over national law. Clearly the principle is vital if the Community is to function properly, since if member states had the power to annul Community law by adopting, or giving precedence to, national law then there could be no uniform or consistent Community legal order: states could apply national law when Community law was distasteful or inconvenient to them. The Court, therefore, from an early stage, took an active part in establishing the primacy of Community law. National courts, it has consistently asserted, must apply Community law in the event of any conflict, even if the domestic law is part of the national constitution. An example of Court statements on primacy may be taken from *Simmenthal* v. *Commission* (Case 92/78) where the Court concluded:

> Every national court must, in a case within its jurisdiction, apply Community law in its entirety and protect rights which the latter

confers on individuals and must accordingly set aside any provision of national law which may conflict with it, whether prior or subsequent to the Community rule.

In general, national courts have accepted this view of the Court and have given precedence to Community law. A few problems do still remain – notably in relation to fundamental rights guaranteed by national constitutions – but for the most part the authority and binding nature of Community law is fully established.

Powers and Responsibilities of the Court of Justice

The Court of Justice – which is based in Luxembourg and which must not be, though it often is, confused with the Strasbourg-based European Court of Human Rights – has two main functions. First, it is responsible for directly applying the law in certain types of cases. Second, it has a general responsibility for interpreting the provisions of Community law, and, in so doing, it must attempt to ensure that the application of the law, which on a day-to-day basis is primarily the responsibility of national courts, is consistent and uniform.

Inevitably, for the reasons that were explained earlier, these duties result in the Court making what is, in effect, judicial law. This is most clearly seen in three respects.

First, Community competence has been extended by Court judgements. There is no doubt, for example, that rulings of the Court have been a major factor in helping to create the internal market. In some cases, this has been as a result of practices being ruled to be illegal, in others it has been a consequence of judgements forcing the Commission and the Council to act.

Social security entitlements provide another example. This is an area where most governments have not wished to do anything more than co-ordinate certain aspects of their social security systems. The Court, however, has pushed them into a certain amount of harmonisation – with regard to the rights of migrant workers for example. It has also extended the provisions of regulations in a way the states did not envisage when they gave them their approval in the Council. Interestingly, in issuing judgements in social security cases, the Court has often used the EEC Treaty and not regulations as its legal base – because the Council can change regulations much more easily than it can the Treaty.

Second, Court judgements have saved the Community the need to make law in existing areas of competence. A particularly influential judgement in this respect was issued in February 1979 in the *Cassis de Dijon* case (Case 120/78) which concerned the free circulation of the French blackcurrant liqueur. The Court ruled that national food standards legislation cannot be invoked to prevent trade between member states unless it is related to 'public health, fiscal supervision and the defence of the consumer'. The principle of 'mutual recognition' was thus established, with the result that the need for legislation to harmonise standards so as to facilitate trade was much reduced. Of course, the *Cassis de Dijon* judgement does not rule out challenges to the principle of 'mutual recognition' or to its application. For example, in a case that was lodged before the Court in July 1984 and which attracted much attention, the German government attempted to protect its brewers by arguing that whereas their product was pure, most so-called foreign beers contained additives and needed to be excluded from the German market on health grounds. In March 1987 the Court upheld the 'mutual recognition' principle and ruled that a blanket ban on additives was quite disproportionate to the health risk involved; the German insistence on its own definition of beer amounted to a barrier to trade.

Third, the powers of the institutions have been clarified, and in important respects have been significantly affected, by the Court. Two judgements have been especially influential. In October 1980 in the isoglucose case (Case 138/79) the Court ruled that the Council could not adopt legislation until it had received Parliament's Opinion. In July 1986, in a case brought by the Council and supported by Germany, France and the United Kingdom against the Parliament (Case 34/86) the Court specified limitations on the EP's budgetary powers.

In fulfilling its responsibilities, the Court cannot itself initiate actions. It must wait for cases to be referred to it. This can happen in one of a number of ways:

Failure to Fulfil an Obligation

Under Articles 169 and 170 (all subsequent Treaty references in this Chapter are to the EEC Treaty except where otherwise stated) the Court rules on whether member states have failed to fulfil obligations under the Treaty. Actions may be brought either by the Commission or by other member states. In either case, the Commission must give the state(s) concerned an opportunity to submit observations and must then itself deliver a reasoned opinion. Only if this fails to produce proper compliance with Community law can the case be referred to the Court of Justice.

In practice, failures to fulfil obligations are usually settled well before they are brought before the Court. When an action is brought, the Commission is almost always the initiator, partly because the states are obliged to refer the matter to the Commission in the first instance and partly because states are extremely reluctant to engage in direct public confrontations with one another. (Though they do sometimes try to encourage the Commission to, in effect, act on their behalf.) Such cases in recent years have led to rulings against Italy that its duties on imported gin and sparkling wine were discriminatory, against the UK that it had taken insufficient national measures to give full effect to the 1976 directive on sexual discrimination, and against Belgium for failing to implement three directives which harmonise certain stock exchange rules.

Application for Annulment

Under Article 173, the Court may be called upon to review the legality of Council or Commission acts that have binding force by either a member state, the Council or the Commission. The Court itself has also ruled, most notably in its July 1986 judgement on the powers of the Parliament under the budgetary procedure, that 'an action for annulment may be brought against the acts of the European Parliament which are intended to have legal effects *vis-à-vis* third parties'. In the words of the Treaty, grounds for annulment are 'lack of competence, infringement of an essential procedural requirement, infringement of this Treaty, or of any rule of law relating to its application, or misuse of powers'.

Article 173 also allows any 'natural or legal person' (that is to say, private individuals or companies) to institute proceedings for annulment, although only on a restricted basis. Rulings under this provision have tended to serve as useful underpinnings to some Community policies, notably competition policy, commercial policy and the highly controlled and directed policies for steel that were pursued in the 1980s.

Unlimited Jurisdiction With Regard to Penalties

In certain limited spheres of activity, notably competition policy, the Commission is empowered to impose penalties to ensure compliance with Council regulations. Under Article 172, the Council regulations may grant unlimited jurisdiction to the Court regarding the penalties provided for in the regulations. In practice, this means that aggrieved parties may appeal against Commission decisions and the penalties it has imposed. As such, this is another form of action for annulment. The Court may annul or confirm the decision and increase or decrease the fine. In the great majority of judgements the Commission's decisions are upheld. There has been no example of a fine being increased.

Failure to Act

Should the Council or the Commission fail to act on a matter provided for by the Treaty, the member states, the institutions of the Community, and, in restricted conditions, 'natural or legal persons' may initiate an action before the Court under Article 175 to have the infringement established. Such actions are rare, but one that attracted much attention was initiated by the Parliament, with the support of the Commission, against the Council in 1983. The case concerned the alleged failure of the Council to take action to establish a Common Transport Policy, despite the provision for such a policy in the EEC Treaty. The judgement, which was delivered in May 1985, was not what the Parliament or the Commission had hoped for. The Court ruled that while there was a duty for legislation to be produced, it had no power to enforce it because the Treaty did not set out a detailed timetable or an inventory for completion; it was incumbent upon the national governments to decide how best to proceed.

Actions to Establish Liability

'In the case of non-contractual liability, the Community shall, in accordance with the general principles common to the laws of the Member States, make good any damage caused by its institutions or by its servants in the performance of their duties' (Article 215). Under Article 178, the Court has exclusive jurisdiction to decide whether the

Community is liable, and if so, whether it is bound to provide compensation.

This means that the Community may have actions brought against it on the grounds of it having committed an illegal act. The complex mechanisms of the Common Agricultural Policy have produced by far the most number of such cases, threatening indeed to overwhelm the Court in the early 1970s. As a consequence the Court became increasingly unwilling to accept non-contractual liability cases, at least on the basis of first instance, and made it clear that they should be brought before national courts.

In the 1970s the Court also ruled that the circumstances in which the Community could incur non-contractual liability and be liable for damages were strictly limited. Of particular importance in this context were judgements in 1978 on two joined cases concerning skimmed milk. (Cases 83 and 94/76 and 4, 15 and 40/77). Community legislation obliged the food industry to add skimmed milk to animal feed as part of an effort to reduce the surplus of powdered milk. A number of users challenged the legality of this, on the grounds that the Community's solution to dealing with the problem was discriminatory. In its first judgement, the Court ruled that the powdered milk regulations were, indeed, invalid because they did not spread the burden fairly across the agricultural sector. In its second judgement, however, it ruled that it was only exceptionally and in special circumstances, notably when a relevant body had manifestly and seriously exceeded its powers, that the Community should be liable to pay damages by virtue of a legislative measure of a political and economic character being found to be invalid.

References for Preliminary Rulings

The types of cases referred to above are known as direct actions. That is to say, the Court is called upon to give a judgement in a dispute between two or more parties who bring their case directly before the Court. References for preliminary rulings are quite different, in that they do not involve the Court determining cases itself, but rather require it to give interpretations on points of Community law to enable national courts to give judgement in cases which they are hearing.

References are made under Article 177 which states that national courts may, and in some circumstances must, ask the Court to give a

TABLE 6.1

Cases brought before the European Court of Justice since 1953
(situation at 31 December 1987)

	ECSC				EEC												
	Scrap compensation	Transport	Common petition	Other²	Free movement of goods and customs union	Right of establishment and freedom to supply services	Taxation	Competition	Social security and free movement of workers	Agriculture	Transport	Article 220 Conventions	Other³	Euratom	Privileges and immunities	Proceedings by staff of Community institutions	Total
Actions brought	167	35	66	252 (24)	603 (45)	107 (12)	210 (35)	377 (34)	382 (35)	1004 (81)	46 (5)	62 (4)	269 (40)	14 (3)	12	2289 (77)	5895 (395)⁴
Cases not resulting in a judgement	25	6	24	107 (16)	124 (19)	26 (3)	39 (1)	40 (9)	31 (4)	87 (10)	9 (3)	4 (1)	75 (24)	1 —	2 (1)	1340 (10)	1940 (101)
Cases decided	142	29	41	119 (14)	394 (19)	63 (11)	107 (9)	275 (13)	304 (30)	793 (66)	31 (6)	54 (3)	135 (33)	10 (7)	9 —	846 (106)	3352 (317)
Cases pending	—	—	1	26	85	18	64	62	47	124	6	4	59	3	1	103	603

Notes:
The figures in brackets represent the cases dealt with by the Court in 1987.

¹ Cases concerning more than one subject are classified under the most important heading.

² Levies, investment declarations, tax charges, miners' bonuses, production quotas.

³ Contentious proceedings, Staff Regulations, Community terminology, Lomé Convention, short-term economic policy, commercial policy, relations between Community law and national law and environment.

⁴ Of these 144 were references for preliminary rulings.

Source: General Report on the Activities of the European Communities, 1987.

preliminary ruling where questions arise concerning the interpretation of the Treaty or the validity and interpretation of acts of the
institutions of the Community. The Court cannot choose to make a
pronouncement on a case which happens to come to its attention and
parties to a dispute have no power to insist on a reference or to object
to one being made. It is the exclusive prerogative of the national judge
to apply for a preliminary ruling. Once a reference has been made, the
Court is obliged to respond but it can only do so on questions which
have been put to it and it may not pronounce on, or even directly
attempt to influence the outcome of, the principal action. Interpretations made by the Court during the course of preliminary rulings must
be accepted and applied by the national court that has made the
referral.

Preliminary rulings now constitute the largest category of cases
that come before the Court. With only occasional dips, references
have progressively increased: from one in 1961, to 32 in 1970, to 106 in
1979, to 144 in 1987. Preliminary rulings serve three principal
functions. First, they help to ensure that national courts make legally
'correct' judgements. Second, because they are generally accepted by
all national courts as setting a precedent, they promote the uniform
interpretation and application of Community law in the twelve
member states. Third, they provide a valuable source of access to the
Court for private individuals and undertakings who cannot directly
appeal to it, either because there is no legal provision or because of
inadequacy of funds.

Membership and Organisation of the Court

The Court consists of thirteen judges, each of whom is appointed for a
six-year term of office which may be, and frequently is, renewed. To
ensure continuity turnover is staggered in three yearly cycles.

According to the Treaties, judges are to be appointed 'by common
accord of the Governments of the Member States' from amongst
persons 'whose independence is beyond doubt and who possess the
qualifications required for appointment to the highest judicial offices
in their respective countries or who are juriconsults of recognised
competence'. In practice, there is something of a gap, in spirit at least,
between these Treaty provisions and reality. First, because each state
is permitted one nomination that is automatically accepted, leaving

only the thirteenth judge to be appointed by a common accord. Secondly, because in making their choices governments have tended not to worry too much about the judicial qualifications or experience of their nominations, but have looked rather for a good background in professional activities and public service. There is no evidence of 'political' appointments being made, in the way in which they are to the United States Supreme Court, but the fact is that soundness and safeness seem to be as important as judicial ability. At the time of his initial appointment the typical judge is a legally qualified 'man of affairs', who has been involved with government in his native country in some way, but who has, at best, served in a judicial capacity for only a limited period.

The judges elect one of their number to be President of the Court for a term of three years. His principal function is to see to the overall direction of the work of the Court by, for example, assigning cases to the Court's Chambers, appointing judge-rapporteurs to cases, and setting schedules for cases. He is also empowered, on application from a party, to order the suspension of Community measures and to order such interim measures as he deems to be appropriate.

Assisting the judges in the exercise of their tasks are six advocates-general. The duty of advocates-general is 'acting with complete impartiality and independence, to make, in open court, reasoned submissions on cases brought before the Court of Justice . . .' (Article 166 EEC). This means that an advocate-general, on being assigned to a case must make a thorough examination of all the issues involved in the case, take account of all relevant law, and then present his conclusions to the Court. The conclusions are likely to include observations on the key points in the case, an assessment of Community law touching on the case, and a proposed legal solution.

In principle, advocates-general are appointed on the same Treaty terms and according to the same Treaty criteria as the judges. In practice, since not all states can claim an advocate-general, appointments are more genuinely collective than is the case with judges – but only up to a point, since the larger states have usually been able to ensure that they are each allocated a post. As regards the calibre of the appointees, their judicial experience tends to be even more questionable than that of the judges; certainly few have ever served in a judicial capacity in their own states.

In addition to the judges and the advocates-general, each of whom is entitled to appoint two legal secretaries to assist them, the Court employs a staff of around 650. Most of these are engaged either in administrative duties – such as registering and transmitting case documents – or in providing language services.

The increasing number of cases coming before the Court – in the 1960s there were around 50 in an average year, by the late 1980s there were usually between 300 and 400 (295 in 1987) – has made it impossible for everything to be dealt with in plenary session. There has, therefore, been an increasing tendency for cases to be assigned to Chambers. However, cases brought by a member state or by one of the Community institutions, cases deemed to be especially important, and cases where a member state so requests, must be heard by the Court sitting in plenary session. (A quorum for the plenary Court is seven judges.) In general, a matter is referred to a Chamber of three judges if it is based upon relatively straightforward facts, raises no substantial points of principle, or where the circumstances are covered by existing case-law. Cases involving complex findings of fact, or novel or important points of law, which do not require to be heard by the full Court, are assigned to a Chamber of five judges.

Under the Single European Act the Court was given an additional means of enabling it to deal more expeditiously and more effectively with its constantly expanding workload: the Council was empowered to establish, at the request of the Court, a Court of First Instance. Such a request was quickly made, and in July 1988 establishment of a Court of First Instance was agreed following the resolution of a dispute between the member states on what should be the new Court's jurisdiction. When it starts work in the Autumn of 1989 (which is the anticipation at the time of writing), the Court will have jurisdiction in the areas of competition law, certain ECSC law, and cases involving disputes between the Community and its staff. It will not be able to hear actions brought by member states or by one Community institution against another, nor will it be able to deal with references for preliminary rulings. All decisions of the Court of First Instance will be subject to appeal to the Court of Justice on points of law. The new Court will consist of twelve members, with most of its work being done in Chambers of three or five judges. Unlike in the Court of Justice, members of the Court of First Instance will be subject to being called upon to perform the task of an advocate-general in certain cases. The conditions of appointment and terms of office of the members of the new Court are to be similar to those of the members of the Court of Justice.

The Procedure of the Court

Court procedure involves both written and oral stages. The former are more important, with cases being conducted largely away from the public eye via the communication of documents between interested parties and Court officials. Not much happens in open court.

Without going into all the details and possible variations, cases proceed broadly along the following lines:

● Relevant documentation and evidence is assembled. In preliminary ruling cases, the national court making the reference should have provided with its submission a summary of the case and of relevant facts, a statement of the legal problem, and the (abstract) question it wishes the Court to answer. Interested parties, the member states, the Commission, and the Council if appropriate, are then notified and given an opportunity to present their views. In direct action cases the procedure is necessarily rather different and the Court, under the direction of a duly appointed judge-rapporteur, may have to take a more active role in gathering the evidence. This can involve holding a preparatory enquiry at which oral and documentary evidence is presented.

● A public hearing is held at which the essentials of the case are outlined, at which the various parties are permitted to present their views orally, and at which the judges and advocates-general may question the parties' lawyers.

● Following the public hearing, the advocate-general appointed to the case examines it in detail. He and his staff look at all relevant Community law and then come to a decision that appears to them to be correct in legal terms. A few weeks after the public hearing the advocate-general presents his submission to an open session of the Court.

● Acting on the advocate-general's submission, and on the basis of a draft drawn up by the judge-rapporteur, the Court prepares its decision. Deliberations are in secret and decisions are made, where there is a disagreement, by majority vote. (Hence the need for an odd number of judges.) Judgements must be signed by all the judges who have taken part in the proceedings and no dissenting opinions may be published. (In their oath of office members swear to preserve the secrecy of the deliberation of the Court.)

Three problems associated with the Court's proceedings ought to be mentioned. First, there is a lengthy gap between cases being lodged at the Court and final decisions: on average, about twelve to fifteen months for preliminary rulings and nearly two years for direct actions. The intention is that the newly-established Court of First Instance will reduce these delays. It should also be noted that, in special cases, interim judgements are issued and accelerated procedures are used. Second, lawyers' fees usually mean that going before the Court can be an expensive business, even though there is no charge for the actual proceedings in the Court itself. This does not, of course, place any restriction on the ability of member states or Community institutions to use the Court, but it can be a problem for individuals and small firms. There is a small legal aid fund, but it cannot remotely finance all potential applicants. Third, the use of majority voting coupled with the lack of opportunity for dissenting opinions has encouraged a tendency, which perhaps is inevitable given the different legal backgrounds of the judges, for judgements sometimes to be less than concise; occasionally even to be fudged.

Community Law and the Court of Justice: Concluding Observations

The legal framework described in the previous pages constitutes the single most important feature distinguishing the Community from other international organisations. The member states do not just co-operate with one another on an intergovernmental basis but have developed common laws designed to promote uniformity. The claim to legal supremacy in the interpretation, application and adjudication of these laws constitutes a central element of the supranational character of the Community.

This has necessarily involved the states in surrendering some of their sovereignty. They are obliged to submit to a legal system over which they do not have control. As a corollary, their governments are also sometimes prevented from introducing national laws they themselves desire.

The Court of Justice has played an extremely important part in establishing the Community's legal order. Whether it is acting as an international court, a court of review, a court of appeal, or a court of referral, (roles which, in practice, greatly overlap), it is frequently as much a maker as an interpreter of law. Of course, judges everywhere help to shape the law, but this is especially so in the Community where the Court has had much more manoeuvrability available to it than is customary within states. It has used this potential to considerable effect: to help clarify relations between the institutions and between the institutions and the member states; to help determine and clarify policy content in many different spheres; and to help develop and foster the *esprit communautaire*.

7

The European Council

Origins

Although no provision was made in the founding Treaties for summit meetings of Heads of Government a few such gatherings did occur in the 1960s and early 1970s. In 1974, at the Paris summit, it was decided to institutionalise these meetings with the establishment of what soon became known as the European Council.

The main reason for the creation of the European Council was a growing feeling that the Community was failing to respond adequately or quickly enough to new and increasingly difficult challenges. Neither the Commission, whose position had been weakened by the intergovernmental emphasis on decision-making that was signalled by the Luxembourg Compromise, nor the Council of Ministers, which was handicapped both by sectoralism and by its practice of proceeding only on the basis of unanimous agreements, were providing the necessary leadership. A new focus of authority was seen as being required to try to make the Community more effective, both domestically and internationally. What was needed, argued France's President Giscard d'Estaing, who, with West Germany's Chancellor Schmidt, was instrumental in establishing the European Council, was a body which would bring the Heads of Government together on a relatively informal basis to exchange ideas, to give direction to policy development, and perhaps sometimes to break deadlocks and clear log-jams. It was not anticipated that the leaders would concern themselves with the details of policy. Rather, the intention was that they would operate at a very general level. In a similar manner to the Western Economic Summits, which were also established at this time, it was hoped the European Council would promote the co-ordination and clarification of interstate relations and would serve to further understanding at the highest political level.

The formal creation of the European Council was very simple: a few paragraphs were issued as part of the Paris communiqué. The two key paragraphs were these:

> Recognising the need for an overall approach to the internal problems involved in achieving European unity and the external problems facing Europe, the Heads of Government consider it essential to ensure progress and overall consistency in the activities of the Communities and in the work on political co-operation.
>
> The Heads of Government have therefore decided to meet, accompanied by the Ministers of Foreign Affairs, three times a year and, whenever necessary, in the Council of the Communities and in the context of political co-operation. The administrative secretariat will be provided for in an appropriate manner with due regard for existing practices and procedures.

Two points about this communiqué are particularly worth emphasising. First, it was vague and left a number of questions largely unanswered, especially as regards the precise role and functioning of the European Council. Subsequent summit declarations (notably London 1977 and Stuttgart 1983) have done something, but not a great deal, to clarify matters. As a result, the evolution and operation of the European Council has owed much more to the preferences of participants and practical necessities than it has to agreed rules and requirements.

Second, the communiqué had no constitutional or legal standing. It announced a political agreement between the national leaders but it did not formally or legally integrate the European Council into the Community framework. In a somewhat similar fashion to the Luxembourg Agreement and European Political Co-operation, the European Council was thus to be part of the 'unofficial' approach to integration rather than the 'official' Treaty-based approach. Even when, in the Single European Act, the European Council was eventually accorded legal recognition it was so only in two short paragraphs that were confined to clarifying membership, and reducing the minimum number of meetings per year from three to two. The paragraphs, moreover, were not incorporated into the Treaties.

Membership and Organisation

The relevant paragraphs of the Single European Act state:

> The European Council shall bring together the Heads of State or of Government of the Member States and the President of the Commission of the European Communities. They shall be assisted by the Ministers for Foreign Affairs and by a Member of the Commission.
>
> The European Council shall meet at least twice a year.

This means that there are twenty-six negotiating participants in plenary sessions of the European Council: two from each member state (usually the Head of Government and Foreign Minister – although the French President, who is Head of State, has always been present, and under the 1986–8 'co-habitation' arrangement was accompanied by his Prime Minister), plus two from the Commission. In addition to these twenty-six, only a very restricted number of other people are permitted to be present in the room: seven officials – three from the country holding the Presidency, three from the secretariat of the Council of Ministers, and the Secretary General of the Commission; interpreters; and national civil servants, but only on the basis of one adviser per country being allowed entrance at any one time (each delegation has a suite in the vicinity of the plenary meeting room and officials are summoned as required). The membership of the European Council is thus based on the Council of Ministers model in the sense that it is made up of national delegations, plus the Commission. Unlike in the Council of Ministers, however, the delegations are not physically accompanied by four or five national officials.

In addition to plenary sessions, three other sorts of meetings also occur at European Councils. First, the Heads of Government plus the President of the Commission hold at least one meeting of their own. The emphasis here is on informality – they, are indeed, often referred to as 'fireside chats' – and they are normally held after dinner on the first day. (European Council meetings are held over two days, usually from lunchtime on day one to around teatime on day two.) Second, the Foreign Ministers hold at least one separate session. European Political Co-operation usually ranks high on their agenda, but they may also be deputed to tackle a particularly difficult item on the plenary agenda or to undertake the preparation of a communiqué.

Third, numerous bilateral meetings are held over breakfast, during natural breaks, and late at night. Some of these meetings are related to European Council agenda items and have as their aim the resolution of differences or the co-ordination of tactics; others, such as the frequent Irish-UK Heads of Government meetings, are not directly related to Community matters at all.

Much of the responsibility for preparing European Council meetings rests with the President in Office – a post that is held concurrently with the Presidency of the Council of Ministers. The 'standard' procedure is for senior officials from the Presidency, working with the Secretariat of the Council of Ministers (the European Council does not have its own Secretariat) and in liaison with the Commission, to identify topics that can be, ought to be, or need to be discussed. These are then channelled through COREPER, or, in the case of EPC matters, through the Political Committee (which is made up of Political Directors from Foreign Offices). Finally, about ten days before the European Council meeting, Foreign Ministers meet to finalise the agenda and, usually, to engage in exploratory pre-summit negotiations.

Often, of course, circumstances intervene to produce departures from, or more commonly additions to, the 'standard' procedure. Among such circumstances are: instructions from a previous summit (the most obvious example of this being the decision taken at the 1985 Milan summit to establish an intergovernmental conference to report to the next summit on institutional reform); an urgent need for decisions to be taken on divisive, technical or detailed matters (which might necessitate countless preparatory meetings of officials and the convening of extra meetings of the Council of Foreign Ministers and of appropriate Technical Councils); and attempts to use the European Council to make significant policy breakthroughs or to launch major initiatives (which, in addition to numerous pre-meetings, might result in the President or a representative of the initiating party touring capitals in advance of the summit meeting in an attempt to clear at least some of the ground in advance – as President Mitterrand did prior to the 1984 Fontainebleau summit).

The basic format of a European Council meeting is as follows:

● Participants gather over lunch. (The two regular meetings

provided for in the SEA are held in the country of the President in Office and any extra meetings are held in Brussels.) Informal discussions begin immediately.

● On the basis of the (normally loose) agenda, that has been agreed in advance, a full plenary session is held in the afternoon.

● In the evening two dinners, one for Heads of Government and the President of the Commission, one for Foreign Ministers and the Vice-President of the Commission, provide an opportunity for further informal discussions.

● The dinners drift into informal sessions. The Heads have their 'fireside' chat, the Foreign Ministers often discuss EPC matters.

● During the night Presidency and Council Secretariat officials prepare a draft of conclusions on the first day's business and/or work on a form of words that can serve as a basis for further negotiations the next day.

● Another plenary session is held in the morning, and perhaps afternoon, of day two. This usually picks up from the previous day's discussions, but with the draft that has been worked on during the night now tabled. With the leaders now trying to move towards conclusions breaks in proceedings may be called for, most usually by the Presidency, so as to permit delegations to carefully study the implications of proposals or so as to allow for informal discussions.

● The summit normally ends some time in the afternoon with the publication of a concluding statement. The statement is customarily agreed to by all, although some states may attach reservations. Thus, for example, the preamble to the conclusions of the 1985 Luxembourg summit which, in effect, agreed the SEA, included the following: 'Denmark has stated that it was unable to take a position on these texts. A blanket reservation on the part of Denmark therefore remains. Italy has made its final acceptance conditional upon examination by the Italian Parliament. There are also a few reservations on specific points.' On only one occasion has a vote been taken in regard to the concluding statement: at Milan in 1985 when Denmark, Greece and the UK were outvoted on the establishment of the intergovernmental conference.

● Before leaving for home the delegations each hold a press conference, where different versions of what has happened are often given.

As with the preparation of summits, so with their operation, this basic format can vary according to circumstances. Such, for example, was the case at the specially called 1988 Brussels summit which, after failures in 1987 at Brussels and Copenhagen, was called to try to resolve a number of pressing interrelated issues – notably on controlling the CAP, increasing non-agriculture expenditure, and expanding the Community's resource base. One departure from the basic format arose from the depth of differences between the delegations (where, in broad terms, the Dutch and the UK were most isolated because of their strong line on the need for CAP controls) which had the effect of preventing the German Presidency from being able, on the morning of day two, to formally table a text which would serve as a basis for further discussions. This, in turn, led to a second departure: the summit broke up on the morning of day two into a series of smaller groups with which the President, Chancellor Kohl, and advisers held 'confessionals', i.e. informal discussions designed to identify 'ideal' and 'acceptable' solutions. One of the key 'confessionals' involved the President meeting the Dutch and UK Prime Ministers and the President of the Commission. When the plenary eventually recommenced a third departure ensued: the continuation of the summit until after midnight. At midnight, the President informed the participants that UK resistance to a compromise that the other eleven (including the Dutch) were prepared to accept left him with no option but to close the meeting. At this point, the Spanish Prime Minister called for a few minutes adjournment so as to allow for a final reconsideration by all parties, and when the leaders returned Mrs Thatcher announced that, subject to Foreign Ministers later agreeing to certain still unresolved matters on CAP controls, the UK would accept the package. (Her principal reasons for agreeing to the deal were, in all probability, a desire not to allow another summit breakdown to endanger the proposed completion of the internal market, and also advice from her officials that postponement of the issues until the next summit would not improve the UK's negotiating position or produce further concessions from the other states.) Eventually, at 2.00 a.m., the agreement was announced and press conferences were held.

Activities

The European Council has a relatively free hand with regard to what it may, and may not, do. This is, as noted above, partly because there are no constitutional or other legal provisions setting out its responsibilities, and it is partly because the political status of the participants is such as to put them generally beyond much challenge.

As a result, the activities undertaken by the European Council have tended to vary, according both to the preferences of the personalities involved and changing circumstances and requirements. So, in the second half of the 1970s when Giscard d'Estaing and Schmidt determined much of the direction and pace, considerable time was given over to general discussions of major economic and monetary problems. In the 1980s, by contrast, with some participants – notably Mrs Thatcher and the Commission – strongly pressing particular distributional questions, and with policy issues increasingly being referred 'upwards' from the Council of Ministers for resolution, the summits came to be much more taken up with quite detailed decision-making.

Borrowing (with an adaptation) the categories suggested by Bulmer and Wessels (1987) the main areas of European Council activity can be categorised under five broad headings:

The Economic and Social Situation Within the Community

Summits have frequently reviewed both the overall economic and social situations within the Community, and also particular questions relating to economic growth, trade patterns, inflation, monetary instability, and unemployment. However, differences between the states on what should be done, coupled with a widely shared determination to ensure that national hands remain firmly placed on key economic controls, has meant that these discussions have not usually been able to produce very much beyond general exhortations on topics such as controlling inflation, tackling unemployment, and encouraging investment. The two major exceptions to this are the European Monetary System, which was created over four summits (supplemented by numerous meetings outside the summits) in 1978–9, and the prioritisation of the programme to complete the internal market which was agreed at Milan in June 1985 and was confirmed later the same year at Luxembourg.

International Economic and Monetary Issues

Economic growth, inflation, trade and similar issues, are not, of course, purely internal Community matters. They have vitally important international dimensions, and the summits have often explicitly looked to these: usually either with a view to co-ordinating the Community's position in international negotiations (notably the Western Economic Summits), or with a view to putting pressure on other economic powers (especially the USA and Japan) to revise their economic, monetary, or trading policies.

International Political Issues

The European Council has issued many declarations on important aspects of international affairs: for example, on East–West relations, South Africa, Afghanistan, Poland, and the Middle East. There is not, it has to be said, much evidence of these having had any effect – except perhaps in respect of the Arab-Israeli conflict where the Community's leaders' attempts (which were signalled in their 1980 Venice Declaration) to steer a middle way between the two sides and to encourage a dialogue in which the Palestine Liberation Organisation is a participant, has at least made an important contribution to the dialogue as to how the dispute might eventually be resolved.

Specific Community Policy Issues

Despite the original intention that the European Council should operate at a fairly general level it has, in practice, often concerned itself with quite specific policy issues. There are three main reasons for this: some Heads of Government are not averse to being involved in sectoral policy deliberations; some issues are so sensitive and/or so intractable that it has required the authority of national leaders to deal with them; and the European Council is, because of its non-sectoral nature, often the best placed institution to put together the package deals that are frequently required to reach agreements on issues that cut across policy sectors, or which can only be resolved by linking up issues in one sector with issues in another. Sometimes, this involvement with specific policy issues has taken the form of playing a significant role in policy initiation. This was the case with the creation of the New Community Instrument at the Brussels 1977 summit, the establishment of the Integrated Mediterranean Programme at Dublin in 1984, and the laying down of a timetable for the completion of the internal market at Luxembourg in 1985. At other times, it has involved tackling issues that the Council of Ministers have been unable to resolve. For example, at summits in the early 1980s, CAP reform, UK rebates, and budgetary resources were constantly on European Council agendas until a package deal was eventually agreed at Fontainebleau in 1984. Within a couple of years of Fontainebleau all these issues had reappeared as problems and, along with demands for expanding the size of the social and regional funds, dominated two unsuccessful summits in 1987 and an ultimately successful special summit at Brussels in 1988.

Constitutional and Institutional Matters

These have come up in the European Council in three main forms. First, the summits have discussed, and have agreed the general arrangements for, the three Community enlargements. (The approval for the first enlargement was given at the 1969 Hague summit, i.e. before the European Council was formally established.) Second, the summits have considered, and have sometimes taken action on, a range of specific institutional matters. For example: direct elections to the EP; the location of the EP; the administrative support for European Political Co-operation; and the efficiency of the Commission. Third, the European Council has stimulated debate and has taken limited decisions within the context of what is commonly referred to as 'European Union' – by which is meant a more integrated Community with stronger, more federal, institutional structures. The stimulation of debate has primarily been through the issuing of declarations (notably the Solemn Declaration on European Union which was issued at the 1983 Stuttgart summit), and the commissioning of reports (such as the Report of the Three Wise Men commissioned at the 1978 Brussels summit and the Dooge Committee Report commissioned at the 1984 Fontainebleau summit). The follow-up to these declarations and reports is to be found mainly in the SEA, which was agreed to at the 1985 Luxembourg summit and which provided for some integrationist developments, including constitutional revisions. On the whole, however, the SEA package was rather modest, reflecting the unwillingness of most governments to commit themselves firmly to political integration: commissioning reports and agreeing to general declarations does not demand very much; ceding sovereignty – by agreeing to proposals for a stronger Commission, more majority voting in the Council of Ministers, and real legislative powers for the EP – does. (It might be added that the SEA appears as particularly timid and cautious when set alongside the EP's 1984 Draft Treaty on European Union, which included proposals for Council–EP joint decision-making: proposals which, despite EP hopes and intense lobbying, the European Council did not seriously consider.)

The European Council thus exercises a number of functions, the relative importance of which can vary from summit to summit. In general, the most important functions are: a forum, at the highest political level, for the exchange of views, the exploration of possibilities, and the building of mutual understanding and confidence; a policy initiator and dispenser of policy guidelines; a decision-maker – both on matters which it has come to be commonly accepted fall within its sphere of responsibility (notably constitutional and major institutional issues), and matters where it acts as a sort of court of appeal for problems unresolved by the Council of Ministers.

Other functions tend to be of secondary importance. In some cases this is not because of their intrinsic nature, but rather because, in practice, they do not add up to very much. So, foreign policy declarations rarely have much noticeable effect on their intended targets. Pronouncements on long-term Community goals are usually couched in language that is far too vague for practical application. And as for the potentially extremely important function of co-ordination of policy sectors, that can hardly be said to be seriously attempted at all – except, perhaps, and almost indirectly, via periodic package deals where some attempts have been made to link developments in different sectors. (The already quoted 1988 Brussels summit provides such an example: the different parts of the agreement – covering improved budgetary discipline measures, tighter CAP controls, expansion of the structural funds, and an increase in the Community's budgetary resources – were seen, by at least some of the participants, as being interdependent.)

One function, it must be emphasised, that the European Council does not exercise is that of legislator. It does have the potential to make Community law – by transforming itself into a special Council of Ministers – but it has never done so. Its decisions are thus political decisions. Where the intention is that its decisions should be given legal effect, the customary Community legislative procedures have to be respected. (There is no guarantee that an agreement in the

European Council will automatically produce ease of passage through these procedures. One reason for this is that the guidelines laid down by the European Council are sometimes insufficiently precise to clear all political obstacles. Another reason is that governments occasionally decide after a summit that their delegation gave too much away and that ground must be recovered by taking a tough line in the Council of Ministers.)

The European Council and the Community System

Institutionalised summitry in the form of the European Council has inevitably increased the influence of the states in the Community system. It has also added an extra intergovernmental element to the nature of the Community: by virtue of the fact that the leaders customarily act on the basis of unanimous agreements – either because they prefer to or, where subsequent Council legislation is required to give their decisions effect, because they may in effect be required to.

However, although the European Council has unquestionably become an important Community institution, its role is still by no means clear. Certainly, the original idea that it would provide overall strategic direction, but would not get involved with policy detail, has not been rigorously followed. What happens at individual summits is not part of any regularised or consistent pattern. So, some summits have been relatively low key affairs and have done little more than pronounce on some aspect or aspects of current international developments, indicate one or two policy initiatives in fringe policy areas, and cobble together a concluding statement exuding general goodwill. Other summits, by contrast – and this type has been common since the early 1980s – have been surrounded by atmospheres of crisis and by prophecies of catastrophe should they fail to produce firm decisions on key and pressing issues: frequently they have failed, but the catastrophes have never quite happened, and the next summit, or next but one, has usually been able to find an agreement via the customary Community method of compromise.

The creation and development of the European Council has inevitably had implications for the roles and functioning of the other principal Community institutions.

The Commission has seen some further undermining of its special position regarding policy initiation. 'Further' because, as shown in Chapters 3 and 4, the Council of Ministers has increasingly exercised policy initiating and mediating responsibilities. On the other hand, the Commission has, to some extent, been compensated by being permitted to enter into political discussions with national leaders at the summits, and also by being able – and sometimes being required – to submit reports and documents to the summits (see Chapter 3 for examples of very influential Commission submissions to summits).

The Council of Ministers has lost power to the European Council by virtue of the increasing tendency of most major issues to go through the summits in some form. However, the extent of the loss should not be exaggerated. First, because there is certainly no clear hierarchical relationship between the two bodies in the sense that the Council of Ministers feels obliged to refer all significant matters 'upwards'. Second, there is no consistent line of division between the two regarding who does what, other than the Council of Ministers alone being responsible for making legislation. Certainly, there is no question of the European Council taking 'first order' decisions and the Council of Ministers being confined to 'second order' decisions. And, third, since the European Council only meets for four, or perhaps six, days a year, it cannot normally hope to do anything more than sketch outlines in a restricted number of areas.

The EP has been largely by-passed by the European Council and so must be regarded as having experienced some net loss of power. It is true that, since 1981, the President of the European Council has given a verbal report on each summit meeting to the next EP part-session, and it is also the case that, more recently, the practice has begun to develop of the EP President being permitted to address summits on specific matters. However, there is no evidence of either of these procedures producing much in the way of influence. Far more important is the almost complete lack of influence of the EP on European Council agendas or deliberations, and the tendency of the Council of Ministers to take the view that legislation which stems from European Council decisions is non-negotiable.

Since the European Council operates largely on an extra-constitutional basis, and since its decisions are political rather than legal in character, its existence has had few implications for the Court of Justice. Or, rather, it has had few direct implications. It can, however, be argued that any increase in a non-constitutional approach to integration necessarily constitutes a corresponding decrease in the influence of the Court of Justice given its attachment to, indeed its restriction to, questions that have a legal base.

Concluding Comments

The record of the European Council is mixed. Unquestionably, there have been positive achievements. Understandings between national leaders have been furthered, certain medium-term goals have been identified and given an impetus (such as on the internal market and agricultural reform), and agreements have been worked out on important matters that were either unsuitable for, or could not be resolved by, the Council of Ministers. At the same time, however, there have been failures, or at least the non-fulfilment of hopes. So, summits have become rather routinised and bureaucratised, too often time has been devoted to policy detail rather than to mapping out the future, and the decisions that have been taken on institutional reforms have hardly been pioneering or wide-ranging.

But that there should be pluses or minuses in the record is not altogether surprising. The summits were, after all, established on a very loose and ill-defined basis and it was thus perhaps inevitable, given the status of the participants, that they would be drawn into attempting to do a host of different things. It was also perhaps inevitable, given the composition and mode of functioning of the summits, that they would experience some of the problems of intergovernmental conflict that are so characteristic of the Council of Ministers.

8

Other Institutions and Actors

The Economic and Social Committee

Origins

In the negotiations which led to the Rome Treaties it was decided to establish a consultative body comprised of representatives of socioeconomic interests.

There were four principal reasons for this decision. First, five of the six founding states – Germany was the exception – had such bodies in their own national systems. The main role of these bodies was to provide a forum in which sectional interests could express their views, and in so doing could supplement the popular will as expressed via parliaments. Second, the essentially economic nature of the Community meant that sectional interests would be directly affected by policy developments and would be key participants in, and determiners of, the development of integration. Third, it was not thought that the Assembly (as the EP was then called) would be an effective forum for the expression of sectional views. Fourth, the institutional framework of the Rome Treaties was based on the Treaty of Paris model, and that had provided for a similarly constituted socioeconomic advisory body in the ECSC Consultative Committee.

Accordingly, the EEC and Euratom Treaties provided for a common Economic and Social Committee. It was to have an advisory role and it was to be made up of representatives of various types of economic and social activity.

179

Membership

Since the 1986 Community enlargement the ESC has had 189 members. These are drawn from the member states as follows:

Belgium	12	Italy	24
Denmark	9	Luxembourg	6
France	24	Netherlands	12
Germany	24	Portugal	12
Greece	12	Spain	21
Ireland	9	United Kingdom	24

Members of the Committee are proposed by national governments and formally appointed by the Council of Ministers. The term of office lasts for four years, which may be renewed.

To ensure that a broad spectrum of interests and views are represented the membership is divided into three, more or less equally sized, groups. Each national complement of members is supposed to reflect this tripartite division. The three groups are:

Group I – employers. Just less than half of this group are drawn from industry. The rest are mostly from public enterprises, commercial organisations, banks, insurance, etc.

Group II – workers. The great majority in this group are members of national trade unions.

Group III – various interests. About half of this group are associated either with agriculture, small and medium-sized businesses, or the professions. The rest are mostly involved with public agencies and local authorities, consumer groups, environmental protection organisations, etc.

All members are appointed in a personal capacity and not as delegates of organisations. However, since most members are closely associated with, or are employees of, national interest organisations (organisations that are, in many cases, affiliated to Euro-organisations) it is inevitable that they do tend to act as representatives of, and spokesmen for, a cause.

The administrative and linguistic support for the Committee is provided by a Secretariat which employs a staff of around 480.

Organisation

The Committee elects a Chairman and a Bureau from among its members, each for a term of two years. The main responsibility of the Chairman is to act as the ESC's principal representative in relations with other Community institutions, member states, and non-EC organisations and states. The Bureau, which has 30 members – the President, two Vice-Presidents, and nine members from each group – assists with outside relations and is also responsible for the general organisation of the Committee's work.

The groups operate in a somewhat similar fashion to the political groups in the EP. That is to say, they meet on a regular basis – normally once a month on average – to review matters of common concern, to discuss their work, and (particularly in the more cohesive groups I and II) to attempt to agree voting positions on Opinions that are due to be submitted to plenary sessions. Group representatives in sections and study groups (see below) also sometimes meet together to co-ordinate their activities.

Most of the work of the ESC consists of giving Opinions on Community related matters. In a manner similar to the way in which the detailed work on Opinions in the EP is undertaken by committees, so in the ESC it is undertaken by sections, each of which draws its membership from the groups. There are nine sections:

Agriculture
Industry, Commerce, Crafts and Services
Economic, Financial and Monetary Questions
Social, Family, Educational and Cultural Affairs
Transport and Communications
External Relations
Energy, Nuclear Questions, and Research
Regional Development
Environment, Public Health and Consumer Affairs

The sections appoint *rapporteurs* to prepare draft Opinions on their behalf. How *rapporteurs* go about this depends on circumstances and preferences. They may well make use of a subcommittee or a study group; they may call for assistance from the ESC Secretariat – though resources for this purpose are thin; or – a common occurrence – they may seek, or be offered help from, Euro or national sectional interests.

In the sections an attempt is usually made to develop a common position on Opinions, though on controversial issues this is not always possible to achieve. In an average year there are usually around 70–80 section meetings and some 250 meetings of subcommittees and study groups. (In addition, there are 300–400 miscellaneous meetings and meetings sponsored by the three groups. Many of these are concerned in some way with the preparation of Opinions.)

Plenary meetings are held in Brussels, over a two-day period, usually nine or ten times a year. Agendas are dominated by consideration of reports from the sections. The standard procedure for dealing with reports is for each to be introduced by its *rapporteur*, for a debate to be held, and for a vote to be taken. On uncontroversial items the vote may be taken without discussion or debate.

Functions

The ESC engages in a number of activities:

1. It issues information reports on matters of contemporary interest and concern.
2. It liaises, via delegations, with a host of other international bodies and groupings.
3. It seeks to promote understanding between sectional interests by, for example, organising conferences, convening meetings, and being represented at congresses and symposia.
4. It seeks to take advantage of various contacts it has with other Community institutions to press its views. The most regularised of these contacts is with the Commission: Commissioners themselves quite frequently attend plenaries and meetings of sections. Occasionally ministers address plenaries.
5. Above all, as noted above, it issues Opinions on a range of Community matters. Opinions are issues in one of three sets of circumstances:

Mandatory referral. Under Article 198 (EEC) and Article 170 (Euratom): 'The Committee must be consulted by the Council or by the Commission where this Treaty so provides.' Compared with the EP there are not so many issues where the Treaties do so provide, but many important policy areas are none the less included. So, under the EEC Treaty the ESC must be consulted on matters pertaining to agriculture, freedom of movement for workers, the right of establishment, transport, approximation of laws, social policy, the European

Social Fund, and vocational training. Under the Euratom Treaty the Committee has to be consulted on such matters as research and training programmes, health and safety, and investment. Under the SEA these areas of mandatory consultation have been further extended to include internal market issues, economic and social cohesion, environment, and research and technology.

Optional consultation. The Committee may be consulted by the Council or the Commission 'in all cases in which they consider it appropriate' (Article 198 – EEC, and Article 170 – Euratom). Until the entry into force of the SEA some 80 per cent of ESC Opinions were based on optional consultation. With the widening of the scope of mandatory referral this figure will now fall.

Own initiatives. Following pressure over a long period, the 1972 summit of Community leaders granted the ESC the right to issue Opinions on its own initiative. It can thus pronounce on almost any Community matter it wishes other than those which fall under the European Coal and Steel Community. The reason for this exclusion is, as noted above, that the ESC has a separate Consultative Committee. With ninety-six members – who are divided into three equal groups of producers, workers, consumers and dealers – the Consultative Committee performs similar functions for the ECSC as does the ESC for the EEC and Euratom. The Consultative Committee meets about six times a year.

The ESC normally issues about 120 Opinions in an average year. Of these, some ten to fifteen are own initiatives. In 1987, Opinions on Council/Commission referrals included ones on the 1987/8 economic report (Opinions on the economic report are given each year), social developments in the Community, a proposal for a Council regulation on action by the Community relating to the environment, and a proposal for a Council directive amending an existing directive on the approximation of laws of the member states relating to the permissible sound power level of tower cranes. (Exhibit 8.1 is typical of an Opinion given on request.) Own initiative Opinions given in 1987 included ones on the consequences of the Chernobyl nuclear accident, the impact of US economic and political developments on GATT negotiations and international trade, and the economic situation of the Community in mid-1987. (Like the Opinions on the economic

EXHIBIT 8.1

An Opinion of the Economic and Social Committee

No C 328/8   Official Journal of the European Communities   22. 12. 86

Opinion on the proposal for a Council Directive on the approximation of the laws of the Member States relating to materials and articles intended to come into contact with foodstuffs([1])

(86/C/328/03)

On 29 April 1986 the Council decided to consult the Economic and Social Committee, under Article 198 of the Treaty establishing the European Economic Community, on the abovementioned proposal.

The preparatory work was referred to the Section for Protection of the Environment, Public Health and Consumer Affairs. This appointed Mr Poul Antonsen as rapporteur.

The Section adopted its opinion on 1 and 2 September 1986.

At its 239th plenary session (meeting of 17 September 1986) the Economic and Social Committee adopted the following opinion unanimously:

1.   General comments

1.1.   The Committee approves the Commission's proposal subject to the following comments.

1.2.   The Committee has reservations regarding the proposed 'Advisory Committee Procedure', but this subject is dealt with in its opinion on 'Completion of the Internal Market: Community Legislation on Foodstuffs'.

2.   Specific Comments

2.1.   *Article 2*

The Committee welcomes the emphasis put by the Commission on public health, and stresses the need to treat

2.4.   *Article 3*

The Committee feels it should be made clear that rules on composition can be applied, as well as rules on migration. Care should be taken to ensure that Article 3 is not administered in such a way as to constitute a trade barrier.

2.5.   *Article 5*

The Committee draws attention to the need for labelling to take acount of the requirements of the blind and weak-sighted.

2.6.   *Article 9*

The Committee feels that this article should specify a time limit, consistent public health as a matter of the utmost importance.

with those set in Article 10, for repeal of Directive 76/893/EEC.

2.2   *Article 2*

2.7.   *Annex I*

There seems to be a discrepancy between the English (bring about an unacceptable change in the composition of the foodstuffs or a deterioration in the organoleptic characteristics thereof) and German versions of the second indent. The discrepancy is also found in the present Directive 76/893/EEC.

The Committee proposes that the Commission add 'covering materials made of paraffin or microcrystalline wax' as these are not considered to be plastics for the purposes of Article I of Directive 82/711/EEC.

2.8.   *Annex II.2*

2.3   *Article 2*

The word 'unacceptable' is imprecise, its meaning should be specified.

The Committee finds that the expression 'suitable' is not clear and does not give any indication of what toxicological testing would be needed in a given case. (The Commission has, however, at the Section meeting referred to reports of the Scientific Committee for Food, Third series, 1977: Toxicological evaluation of a substance for materials and articles intended to come into contact with foodstuffs.)

(¹) OJ No C 124, 23.5.1986, p. 10.

Done at Brussels, 17 September 1986.

*The Chairman
of the Economic and Social Committee*
Gerd MUHR

report, own intiative Opinions on the economic situation are also given annually.)

A point of contrast worth noting between ESC and EP Opinions is that the ESC is not as concerned as the EP to reach a single position which excludes all minority views. It is quite possible for minority positions to be attached as annexes to EP Opinions which have received majority support in the plenary. So, for example, in April 1987 the plenary rejected the Opinion proposed by the Section on Agriculture on the 1987–8 agricultural price proposals; to the Opinion that was approved, an annexe was attached in the form of a 'Statement by the Farmers'.

Influence

There is not much evidence of the ESC exercising real influence on Community policy and decision-making. Those of its recommendations that are taken up usually cover relatively minor points, and, in any event, are sometimes as much a consequence of pressure that is exerted elsewhere as ESC pronouncements. There are a number of reasons why the Committee is in a relatively weak position to exercise power.

First, the Council and the Commission are not obliged to act upon its views. This also, of course, applies to the EP on most non-budget matters but at least in its case it *has* to be consulted on *most* important proposals, its Opinion *must* be delivered before proposals can be given legislative effect, and delaying powers are available to strengthen its bargaining position. The ESC is not so well placed: the range of issues on which consultation is mandatory is more restricted, the deliverance of its Opinion is often therefore not necessary for further progress, and even when its Opinion is required it can be made subject to a timetable that is so tight as not to allow sufficient time for a considered response – the Council and the Commission can, if they consider it necessary, set a time limit as short as ten days for the submission of an ESC Opinion.

The second weakness follows on from this last point: it is by no means uncommon for proposals to be referred to the ESC at a stage of advancement when agreements between the key decision-makers have already been made in principle and are difficult to unscramble.

Third, the ESC is not the only, and in many circumstances is not even the most important, channel available to interests wishing to exert pressure on Community decision-makers. Direct access to Council representatives and to Commission officials, and representation in advisory committees, is seen by many as being more useful than activity in the ESC – not least because these other channels often offer greater opportunities than does the ESC for influencing issues at the pre-proposal stage.

Finally, members of the ESC serve only in a part-time capacity and are, therefore, very restricted in what they can do. In addition, the fact that they serve – in theory at least – in a personal rather than a representational capacity means that there are rarely any very strong reasons why the Commission or the Council should listen to them if they do not wish to do so.

The ESC is sometimes described as the Community's 'alternative' or 'additional' assembly. As is evident from the above discussion, this description does not stand up – especially since the introduction of direct elections in 1979 which have had the effect of further enhancing the standing, capacity, and influence of the EP in relation to the ESC.

What the ESC basically does is two things. First, it provides a useful forum in which representatives of sectional interests can come together on a largely co-operative basis to exchange views and ideas. Second, it is a consultative organ that gives some limited – but in most cases only very limited – opportunities for interests to influence Community policy and decision-making.

The European Investment Bank

Functions

The European Investment Bank (EIB) was established under Articles 129 and 130 of the EEC Treaty. Its members are the member states of the Community. The Bank is located in Luxembourg.

According to Article 130 the task of the EIB is to contribute, on a non-profit making basis, via the granting of loans and the giving of guarantees, to the 'balanced and steady development of the Community'. What this means, in practice, is that the Bank's main job is to act as a source of investment finance for projects which further certain Community goals. In so doing, it is by far the largest provider of Community loan finance: in 1987 the Community loaned a total of 8.6 billion Ecu, of which 7 billion came from EIB sources, 9.7 million from ECSC sources, 4.5 million from New Community Instrument (NCI) sources, and 2.1 million from Euratom sources. Of the EIB sources, just over 90 per cent was for projects within the member states and the remainder was for projects outside.

In respect of the loans made within the Community, two main criteria have to be satisfied for the Bank to consider providing finance.

First, the project must comply with the economic policy objectives laid down in Article 130 of the EEC Treaty. These objectives are interpreted fairly broadly but at least one of the following normally has to be met:

1. The project must further the economic development of the Community's less prosperous regions. Over 50 per cent of loans in recent years have gone to the more underdeveloped areas – with Italy being the largest national beneficiary.
2. The project must involve modernisation and generally improve the competitiveness of Community industry. Under this heading, particular support has been given to the introduction and further development of advanced technology.
3. The project must be of common interest to several member states or to the Community as a whole. In this connection, the Community's energy objectives have been given a high priority – notably by financing projects designed to reduce dependency on oil imports through encouraging energy saving, developing indigenous resources, diversifying imports, etc.

Second, the project must be economically viable, and the loan must be guaranteed by adequate security. This is because although the EIB is not a profit-making body it is not a loss-making one either: apart from in certain specified and strictly limited circumstances, the Bank's loans are not subsidised from the Community budget but must be financed from the Bank's own capital. This capital comes from two sources: subscriptions by the member states, and borrowing – in the EIB's own name and on its own credit – on capital markets inside and outside the Community. Of these two sources, borrowing is by far the largest element and since the sums raised must be repaid from the Bank's own financial operations the Bank must take appropriate steps to protect itself.

A major attraction for potential EIB borrowers is that loans are offered at very competitive rates. They are so because the Bank enjoys a first class international credit-rating and is thus itself able to borrow at favourable rates. Other advantages of EIB loans are that they are generally made available at fixed interest rates, and repayments can often be deferred for the first two or three years.

Two other features of EIB loans are also worth noting. First, the Bank does not usually lend more than 50 per cent of the investment cost of a project. Borrowers need to find additional sources of loan finance, with the consequence that the Bank very frequently operates on a co-financing basis with national banks. Second, the Bank generally only deals directly with large loans – of more than about two million Ecu. This does not, however, mean that only large-scale investment is supported because, mainly via its global loan facility, the Bank opens lines of credit to intermediary institutions – such as regional development agencies and, more commonly, national financial institutions – which then lend the money on in smaller amounts. Global loans account for around 25 per cent of total EIB lending and are directed principally towards small and medium sized enterprises. An administrative problem with global loans is that the intermediary agencies which act on the EIB's behalf and which are delegated responsibility for appraising applications and negotiating with the potential borrowers tend to make their decisions according to traditional banking criteria and not with much of an eye to Community objectives.

In addition to the activities which have just been described, certain other EIB responsibilities should also be mentioned.

● Under the New Community Instrument the Commission is empowered to borrow money on the capital markets. It does so under conditions and for purposes that are specified in guidelines laid down by the Council of Ministers. Once the Commission has decided upon the eligibility of projects the Bank decides whether to grant loans and administers those which are approved.

● The Commission may also borrow funds on capital markets in connection with certain Euratom activities. The Commission decides on the granting of loans, and the Bank is responsible for financial appraisal and management.

● Many projects are eligible for both EIB loan finance and for Community grant aid. Where this is the case – and it applies mainly where grants from the European Regional Development Fund or from the Integrated Mediterranean Programmes are available – the Bank works closely with other interested parties, especially the Commission, to work out appropriate financial arrangements. So, for example, regarding finance for the regions: when it starts looking at a project the Bank notifies the Commission and member states so as to ensure that any loan it may grant conforms with Community and national policies; the Bank is represented on the Community's Regional Policy Committee (the advisory committee consisting of representatives of the member states) and the ERDF management committee; and there are regular contacts at officer level between DGXVI (Regional Policy) and the Bank.

Organisation

The Bank is not legally or formally linked in with 'mainstream' Community policy and decision-making processes. It liaises with other Community institutions and actors as appropriate, but it is not subject to the usual pattern of Commission initiatives, EP scrutiny, Council approval, and Court of Justice interpretation. The Bank's decision-making bodies are, thus, fairly autonomous. They consist of the following:

1. The *Board of Governors*, which decides on total funding and lays down general directives on the Bank's activities. It is also responsible for formally appointing members of the Board of Directors and the Management Committee. The Board of Governors is composed of one minister per member state – usually the Minister of Finance – and normally meets once a year. Certain major decisions of the Board have to be made unanimously, others can be made by a majority of members representing at least 45 per cent of subscribed capital.

2. The *Board of Directors*, which has a general responsibility for ensuring that the Bank is managed according to the provisions of the Treaty, the Bank's Statute, and directives issued by the Governors. More specifically the Board has sole responsibility for deciding on loans and guarantees, raising funds and fixing interest rates. There are twenty-two directors: twenty-one are nominated by the member states and are senior figures in national financial institutions or national Ministries of Finance/ Economics/Industry; one is nominated by the Commission. The Board of Directors normally meets every four to six weeks.

3. The *Management Committee*, which controls current operations, makes recommendations to the Board of Directors and is responsible for implementing decisions made by the Directors. The Committee is a full-time body consisting of the Bank's President and six Vice-Presidents. It meets every working day.

Supporting, and operating under, these decision-making bodies is the EIB's administration. This is divided into seven Directorates: General Administration; Operations in the Community 1; Operations in the Community 2; Operations outside the Community; Finance and Treasury; Research; Legal. There is also a Technical Advisory Service. In all, the EIB employs around 700 staff.

Concluding Comments

The EIB is a bank, not a grant-dispensing body. This means that it must observe certain basic banking principles. At the same time, however, it is a Community institution charged with furthering a number of policy objectives. These two responsibilities do not always sit easily together.

The scale of EIB borrowing and lending is small when compared with the total operations of commercial banks across the member states. The role of the Bank should not, however, be underestimated: after the World Bank it is the second largest institutional borrower on the international capital markets; and though the impact of its lending activities may be slight across the Community as a whole, it is by no means insignificant in targeted spheres and regions. What the Bank basically does is to act as a useful complement to the private sector by financing Community-oriented projects which commercial institutions do not wish to finance, do not wish to finance wholly, or do not wish to finance on terms that are sufficiently attractive to proposers.

The Court of Auditors

The 1975 *Treaty amending Certain Financial Provisions of the Treaties . . .*, which came into force in 1977, replaced the then two existing Community audit bodies – the Audit Board and the ECSC Auditor – with a single Court of Auditors. The Court is based in Luxembourg.

Membership and Organisation

There are twelve members of the Court: one from each member state. They are appointed by a unanimous vote of the Council of Ministers on the basis of nominations made by national governments and after there have been consultations with the EP. At the time of their appointment, members of the Court must belong or have belonged to an external audit body in their own country, or be persons who are appropriately qualified in some other capacity. Appointment is for a six-year period, which may be renewed. As with other 'non-political' Community bodies, a condition of appointment is that the members will act in the general interest of the Community and will be completely independent in the performance of their duties.

The members elect one of their number to be the President of the Court. His term of office is for three years and is renewable. The President sees to the general efficient running of the Court and also represents it in its external relations.

Members are assigned a specific sector of activity for which they hold a particular responsibility regarding the preparation and implementation of the decisions of the Court. Each sector falls under one of three audit groups which act primarily as co-ordinating agencies and filters for plenary sessions. All important decisions are taken in plenaries, by majority vote if need be.

As with several other Community institutions, the administration supporting the Court is rather small in size given the potential importance of the work to be done. At the beginning of 1988 there were 310 permanent posts and fifty-six temporary posts. Inevitably such modest staffing resources greatly restricts the number of things the Court can attempt to do.

Activities of the Court

The Court engages in two main types of activity.

First, it carries out annual audits to see whether revenue has been received and expenditure has been incurred in a lawful and regular manner, and also to examine whether the financial management of Community authorities has been sound. The auditing powers of the Court cover the general budget of the Community, plus certain financial operations that are not included in the budget such as borrowing and lending facilities of the ECSC and aid to developing countries that is financed by national contributions.

The auditing of the general budget, which is the Court's most important single task, and the related process of granting a discharge to the Commission on its implementation of the budget, proceed as follows:

● The Commission is required to draw up, for each financial year, accounts relating to the implementation of the budget, a financial statement of the assets and liabilities of the Community, and an analysis of the financial year. The main responsibility for collecting and presenting this information (the internal audit) lies with DGXX

(Financial Control). The documentation must be forwarded to the Council, the EP, and the Court of Auditors by no later than 1 June of the following financial year.

● The Court undertakes its audit (the external audit) partly on the basis of an examination of the Commission documentation and partly on the basis of its own independent investigations. The latter, which begin before the Commission documentation arrives, involves examining records supplied by, and requested from, Community institutions and member states (which in the latter case means liaising closely with national audit bodies and appropriate national agencies) and also, where necessary, carrying out on-the-spot investigations. The purpose of this Court audit is not to replicate what has already been covered by the internal audit, but rather to add an extra dimension to the Community's overall auditory control by examining the adequacy of internal procedures – particularly with regard to their ability to identify significant irregular and unlawful transactions and to properly evaluate the extent to which correct financial management (in terms of economy, efficiency and effectiveness) is being practiced. By 15 July, the Court transmits to all relevant institutions any comments which it proposes to include in its annual report to which it believes there should be, or there may wish to be, a reply. After the receipt of replies, which must be submitted by 31 October, the Court adopts the final version of its annual report. This has to be communicated to the Community's other institutions by 30 November.

● The EP, acting on a recommendation of the Council, is supposed to give discharge to the Commission in respect of the implementation of the budget by 30 April of the following year. To this end, the EP's Budgetary Control Committee examines all relevant documentation, particularly that produced by the Court of Auditors. Normally, discharge is given by the due date, but in 1987 dissatisfaction with several matters resulted in the discharge for the 1985 financial year being deferred and it was only after the Commission had taken remedying measures that discharge was eventually given in January 1988.

The second main activity of the Court is to submit observations and deliver opinions on a range of subjects. This it does in three sets of circumstances: special reports on specific aspects of the audit are prepared, either on the Court's own initiative or at the request of another institution; a Community institution may ask the Court to submit an Opinion on a matter, usually concerning financial aspects of draft legislation; and when the Council enacts a financial regulation it is obliged to seek an Opinion from the Court on the draft text. From its establishment in 1977 to the end of 1987 the Court adopted fifty-four special reports and delivered forty-nine Opinions.

The Effectiveness of Financial Controls

Unquestionably, controls over Community revenue and expenditure could be improved were the political will to exist. For example, procedures could be tightened so as to prevent member states from imposing the limitations they occasionally apply to the audit enquiries considered necessary by the Court of Auditors. The Court's own attempts to extend its influence beyond questions of financial rectitude into considerations of policy efficiency could be encouraged, and even formalised. And the particular problem of fraud – which is generally thought to account for at least 10 per cent of the Community budget, most of it in connection with agriculture payments – could be more effectively tackled if resources at both Community and member state levels were expanded and if proposals that have long been advocated by the Court for streamlining administrative practices were adopted.

But though the Community is often criticised for being financially profligate the case should not be overstated. For the most part the institutions themselves work to tight budgets and within limited resources, and their operations and programmes are subject to reasonably rigorous, if not as extensive as is perhaps ideally desirable, investigations via the internal and external audits.

Interests

Different Types

A vast range of non-governmental interests cluster around Community processes. These interests are of four main types.

Regional and local authorities. Many subgovernmental decision-making bodies in the member states seek to have a direct role in Community processes. How extensive a role depends partly on the amount of autonomy and manoeuvrability they enjoy at national level. The German *Lander* (states), for example, which enjoy a considerable measure of independence within Germany's quasi-federal system, have opened up several lines of – primarily informal – contact with the Commission, and some have established their own economic promotion offices in Brussels. This is not usual, however, and a more common practice is for regional and local authorities to work through occasional *ad hoc* delegations and/or via the locally-based Community liaison officers which many have appointed with the brief to attract funds from the various sources of Community finance.

Private and public companies and corporations. In addition to any involvement they may have via interest group organisations (see below) some economic undertakings seek to have direct dealings with Community authorities. Ford, for example, have taken worries about the competitiveness of the motor industry to the Commission, and electronics manufacturers such as Philips and Thomson have lobbied for higher and more uniform tariff levels on products from Japan.

National interest groups. Many circumstances result in nationally-based interest groups attempting to involve themselves in Community processes. For example, an association representing beer producers may wish to press for the removal of discriminating excise duties that have the effect of preventing its members competing in the market of another member state on an equal basis with domestic producers. Or an environmental interest group may want to see more effective implementation of existing Community legislation on disposal of sewage into the sea. In seeking to play a part in Community processes, most national interest groups are confined to working from their national offices or via a European interest group, but a few of the larger industrial and agricultural groups have, in addition to a domestic and a European group base, their own representatives and agents permanently based in Brussels.

European interest groups. There are somewhere in the region of 500 'Euro'-groups. Such groups have three main distinguishing characteristics: they are not based on individual national membership but on affiliation by national groups from at least several Community countries; they look to further the European – as opposed to national –

interests of a sector or a cause; and they enjoy some sort of contact with, and recognition by, the Commission.

Given their particular Community orientation it is worth looking at the Euro-groups in a little detail.

Their *policy interests* naturally reflect the policy priorities and policy concerns of the Community. This is most obviously seen in the variety of the agriculture lobby where over 150 Euro-groups are to be found. These range in nature from the broadly based umbrella group COPA, which seeks to represent most types of farmers on most issues, to highly specialised groups representing the likes of yeast producers and pasta manufacturers. Pressure groups usually go where power goes, and what has happened in agriculture, quite simply, is that as considerable policy responsibilities have been transferred from national capitals to the Community then so has a Euro-lobby developed to supplement – not replace – the domestic lobbies.

In addition to agriculture, other areas of activity prominently represented among the Euro-groups are industrial employer interests, commerce, service industries (banking, insurance, transport and the liberal professions are all well represented), trade unions, consumers, and evironmentalists.

The *membership* of Euro-groups also varies considerably. It does so in four main respects.

First, some groups – the so-called umbrella groups – have a broad membership base and seek to represent a whole sector or area of activity. Examples of such groups are COPA, UNICE (industrial employers), ETUC (trade unions), *Federation Bancaire* (commercial banks), EEB (environment), and BEUC (consumers). Most groups, however, are more narrowly focused and seek to speak on behalf of a specific industry, process, service or cause.

Second, since most Euro-groups are based on national affiliates, the number of people they can claim to represent naturally reflects the factors determining group membership at national levels. So, sectional interests are usually better placed than promotional interests. Similarly, among sectional interests, Euro-groups representing interests which are well mobilised at national levels, such as dairy farmers and textile manufacturers, naturally tend to be much more genuinely representative than groups acting on behalf of poorly mobilised sections of populations such as agricultural labourers or consumers.

Third, there are considerable variations in the number of national affiliates in Euro-groups. At one end of the spectrum, many Euro-groups draw their members from only a few states – which, in the case of activities which are carried on throughout the Community, can weaken the group's representational claims. At the other end of the spectrum, some groups are not EC specific and draw members from most European states: ETUC for example has thirty members from twenty countries, while UNICE has associate members from ten non-Community states. Membership of this latter sort, which goes beyond the geographical borders of the Community, has advantages and disadvantages: on the one hand, it can help to promote international co-operation and increase group resources; on the other hand, and this is a charge that has frequently been laid against ETUC, it can serve to dilute group concentration on, and therefore influence within, the Community.

Fourth, national and sectional differences between member organisations results in many groups having considerable difficulty in maintaining internal cohesion and presenting a common front. The umbrella groups naturally have the greatest problems: ETUC, for example, has traditionally had to reconcile differences between Socialist, Christian, and Communist unions, while COPA has had considerable difficulty in recent years in managing the differential agricultural sectoral implications of proposals for reform of the CAP.

In terms of *resources*, only a few large umbrella groups have well appointed offices with a full-time staff that is numbered in double figures. Among these are COPA (by far the best resourced, with a full-time staff of around forty-five), UNICE, ETUC, CEA (European Insurance Committee), and GCECEE (Savings Banks Group of the EEC). More commonly, groups rely heavily on the resources of national affiliates and themselves employ only one or two full-time officials – who often do not have their own separate offices but work either from home or from accommodation that is made available to them by an affiliate (usually the Belgian) or an appropriate umbrella group. Many groups do not even stretch to one permanent employee and work purely through affiliates or through part-time and temporary representatives and agents whose services are called upon as and when the need arises.

The *organisational structure* of most Euro-groups is extremely loose. The central group organs usually enjoy only a very limited independence from the national affiliates, while the affiliates themselves are autonomous in most respects and are not subject to central discipline. In addition, key decisions made at central level are usually taken only on the basis of unanimous votes (though some groups, including COPA, do have provisions for weighted majorities on some issues). These loose structures can weaken the effectiveness of Euro-groups, by making it difficult for them to put forward collective views which are anything more than rather vague lowest common denominators. At the same time, however, moves to create stronger structures risks groups not affiliating, or national affiliates concentrating almost exclusively on their national level activities.

Just how extensive and complex a group's organisational structure is depends largely on its size. The more specialised and poorly resourced groups usually operate on a fairly rudimentary basis, often merely via an annual meeting and an executive committee which meets as required. The large umbrella groups, by contrast, usually have an extensive structure, typically made up of a general meeting which meets at least once a year, an executive committee which meets once every 4–6 weeks, specialist policy committees whose frequency of meetings depends on the business in hand, a President, and a full-time Secretariat which is headed by a Secretary General. COPA has the most developed structure (see Figure 8.1).

Finally, with regard to their *functions*, Euro-groups normally attempt to do two main things. First, they seek to gather and exchange information – both in a two-way process with Community organs and with and between national affiliates. Second, they seek to have their interests and views incorporated into Community policy, by persuading and pressurising those who make and implement policy. Not all Euro-groups, of course, attempt or are able to exercise these functions in equal measure: for example, in those sectors where Community policy is little developed they often choose to give a higher priority to the first than to the second function.

Access to Decision-makers

The long, complex and multi-layered nature of Community processes provides many points of access for interests, and so many opportunities for them to keep themselves informed about developments and to press their cases with those who influence, make and implement decisions. The points of access can be grouped under three broad headings: national governments, the Commission, and the European Parliament and the Economic and Social Committee.

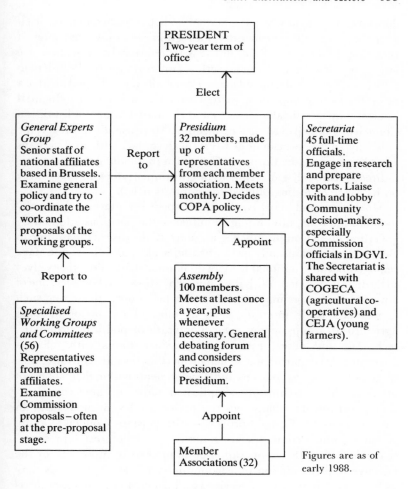

FIGURE 8.1
Organisational structure of COPA

National governments. A major problem for interests is that they cannot normally directly approach either the European Council or the Council of Ministers. This is partly because there are practical problems involved in lobbying what are, in effect, international negotiations, it is partly because the meetings are held behind closed doors, but it is mainly because neither body has wished to make itself available, as a collective identity, for regularised or intensive interest targeting. Only a few direct linkages therefore exist, and these are largely restricted to the most powerful of interests. So, the President in Office of a Technical Council may occasionally meet the president of a powerful Euro-group, or a written submission from an influential interest may be officially received and circulated prior to a European Council or Council of Ministers' meeting. More usually, however, the only way an interest can hope to establish contact with, and perhaps exert pressure on, the European Council or the Council of Ministers is indirectly: through a government or governments looking favourably on its cause or feeling obliged to act on its behalf.

Much time and effort is, therefore, spent by interests, especially national interests, attempting to influence the positions adopted by governments in Community negotiations. In the case of the European Council, this task usually has to be undertaken at at least one stage removed because national leaders do not normally allow themselves to be directly lobbied. With the Council of Ministers, however, one of a number of factors may result in doors being opened. Among such factors are: some interests, such as most of the major national agricultural groups, enjoy – for a mixture of political, economic, technical, and other reasons – an insider status with relevant governmental departments, which means that they are consulted as a matter of course on proposals and developments within their sphere of interest; when a technically complicated matter is under considera-tion, governments usually seek the advice of relevant interests at an early stage of the Council process – with perhaps Council working group members communicating directly with interest representa-tives; and when the co-operation of an interest is important for the effective implementation of a Community proposal, its views may well be actively sought, or received and listened to if an approach is made.

This last point touches on another reason, in addition to trying to influence Council decision-making, why interests may approach national governments: they may wish to influence the way Community decisions are implemented. If relevant ministries can be persuaded to, say, delay, or not to monitor too closely, the implementation of directives on disposal of pollutants, or safety standards in the workplace, some interests may well have much to gain financially.

The Commission. The Commission is the main target for most interests. It is so, primarily, because of its central importance in so many different respects: in policy initiation and formulation; in taking many final decisions; in following proposals through their legislative cycle; in managing the Community's spending programmes; and in policy implementation. An important contributory reason why the Commission attracts so much interest attention is simply that it is known to be approachable.

The Commission makes itself available to interests because several advantages accrue to it from so doing. First, interests often have access to specialised information and to knowledge of how things are 'at the front' which the Commission needs if it is to be able to exercise its own responsibilities efficiently. Second, the Commission's negotiating hand with the Council of Ministers is strengthened if it can demonstrate that its proposals are supported by influential interests. Third, and this is in some ways the other side of the coin to the previous point, if the Commission does not consult with and try to satisfy interests, and comes forward with proposals to which influential interests are strongly opposed, the proposals are likely to meet with strong resistance at Council of Ministers level. Fourth, with regard specifically to Euro-groups, where groups come forward with broadly united and coherent positions they can greatly assist the Commission by allowing it to deal with already aggregated views and by enabling it to avoid becoming entangled in national and ideological differences between sectional interests.

Until about the mid-1970s the Commission displayed a strong preference for talking to Euro-groups rather than national groups, and to governments rather than subgovernmental national authorities. In more recent years, however, this attitude has been relaxed and most interests of significance have been able to have their views at least considered by the Commission. The procedures by which the contacts and communications occur are many and are of both a formal and informal nature. They include: the extensive advisory committee system which exists for the precise purpose of allowing interests to make their views known to Community authorities, and in particular to the Commission (see Chapter 3); representatives of the Commission receive numerous delegations from interests; representatives of the Commission travel to member states to meet interests and to attend conferences and seminars where interests are represented; a few of the larger Euro-groups invite Commission representatives to attend some of their working parties and committee meetings; informal meetings and telephone conversations between Commission and interest representatives occur constantly; and, finally, interests present the Commission with a mass of written documentation in the form of information, briefing and policy documents of different sorts.

Naturally, the extent and nature of the communications between any one interest and the Commission vary considerably according to a number of factors. A small national interest in a specialised area may only require occasional contact at middle ranking official level with one particular Directorate General. By contrast, an active umbrella group may wish to be permanently plugged into the Commission at many different points. As an indication of how extensive the links can be, some of the access channels available to COPA are worth noting: about every four to six weeks the Presidium of COPA meets the Commissioner for Agriculture; the Secretary General of COPA and the Director General of DGVI (Agriculture) meet regularly and often speak to each other several times a week on the telephone; at all levels, the staff of COPA are in almost constant touch with staff in DGVI and, less frequently, are in close contact with staff in other DGs – notably DGXIX (Budgets); and COPA is strongly represented, both in its own right and via affiliates, on all the agricultural advisory committees and also on certain other leading advisory committees such as the Standing Committee on Employment and the Harmonisation of Legislation Committee.

The European Parliament and the Economic and Social Committee. The special advisory positions held by the EP and the ESC in the Community makes them natural, albeit generally second-ranking, targets for interests.

In the case of the ESC there are, of course, factors which put it in a special position *vis-à-vis* interests: its membership is largely made up of interest representatives and its very *raison d'être* is to act as the Community's principal forum for interest representation and expression. The ways and the extent to which the ESC exercises these representative and expressive roles were examined earlier in the chapter.

With regard to the EP, it has been very noticeable, not least in the swelling ranks of lobbyists who attend the Strasbourg plenaries, that as the role and influence of the Parliament in the Community system has grown, so has it increasingly attracted the attention of interests. Among the possibilities offered to interests by the EP are the following: a general circulation of literature among MEPs may have the effect of improving the image of an interest or changing the climate of opinion in the interest's area of concern; MEPs can be directly approached with a view to persuading them to vote in a particular way on a particular issue (which may well be possible given the lack of voting discipline in the EP), or with a view to persuading them to support the interest's view in a committee or a political group; interests have some opportunities for direct contacts with committees and political groups – committees, for example, occasionally travel to member states for the precise purpose of meeting interest representatives, while political groups sometimes allow themselves to be addressed when they judge it to be appropriate; attempts can be made to encourage an MEP to seek permission to draw up an own initiative report which, if it makes progress, may possibly have the effect of pressurising the Commission and/or the Council into action of a desired sort; officials and MEPs engaged in preparing reports for EP committees often approach appropriate interests for their views, or allow themselves to be approached; and attempts can be made to persuade individual MEPs to take matters up with governments and with the Commission

Many possible avenues are thus available to interests to enable them to promote their causes. Which are the most suitable, the most available, and the most effective, naturally vary according to circumstances. A regional authority, for example wishing to attract ERDF funds, would be well advised to establish contacts with DGXVI (Regional Policy), but it should also court good relations with national civil servants and ministers, since applications to the Regional Fund must be channelled via national governments. By contrast, an environmental group in a country where the government is not noted for its sympathy to 'green' issues might be most effective working as part of a Euro-group – from which widely-based public information and relations campaigns can be launched that attempt to persuade the EP to pass a resolution, that may be able to pressurise the Commission into ensuring that existing Community legislation is properly implemented and new measures are considered, and that may provide a route to the Council of Ministers via other national affiliates successfully leaning on their governments.

Influence

The factors which determine the influence exercised by interests in the Community are similar to those which apply at national levels. The more powerful and more effective interests tend to be those which have at least some of the following characteristics:

Control of key information and expertise. Effective policy-making and implementation requires a knowledge and understanding of matters which can often be provided to Community authorities only via interests. This obviously puts some interests in potentially very influential positions – as is seen, to some extent, in the way in which the influence interests exercise via official forums is often much greater in specialised advisory committees than it is in more general settings such as the ESC or the Standing Committee on Employment.

Adequate resources. The better resourced an interest is, the more likely is it to be able to make use of a variety of tactics and devices at a number of different potential access points. So, regarding proposed legislation, a well-resourced interest is normally in a position to lobby the Commission from the initiation stage, the EP at the consultation stage, and the Council of Ministers – usually through national governments – at the decision-making stage. Similarly, a regional or local authority hoping for Community funds is more likely to be successful if it employs people who know what is available, how to apply, and with whom it is worth having an informal word.

Economic weight. Important economic interests – whether in the form of major companies or representational organisations – usually have to be listened to, not least because their co-operation is often necessary in connection with policies designed, for instance, to encourage Community-wide investment, to expand employment in the less prosperous regions, to stimulate cross-border rationalisations, and to improve industrial efficiency. Examples of economic weight being an important factor in successful lobbying include: the chemical industry – via its Euro-group CEFIC – has managed to persuade the Commission to investigate numerous cases of alleged dumping, often by US industry; the Esprit programme to strengthen the European base in information technology stemmed from major companies in the sector warning the Commission that unless something was done quickly the US and Japan would totally dominate the market; and EUROFER – the larger steel manufacturer's association – has worked closely with the Commission and governments to limit the damage to its members of the Community's steel rationalisation programme.

Political weight. Many interests have political assets which can be used to advantage, usually via governments. So, for example, a national pressure group which is closely linked with a party in government may be able to get a minister to virtually act on its behalf in the Council of Ministers. At a broader level, electoral factors can be important, with ministers in the Council not usually anxious to support anything which might upset key voters – especially if an important national or local election is looming. Farmers' organisations in France, Italy, Germany and elsewhere are the best examples of interests which have benefited from having electoral significance.

Genuine representational claims. National pressure groups and Euro-groups which genuinely represent a sizeable proportion of the interests in a given sector are naturally in a stronger position than those which do not.

Cohesion. Some interests find it difficult to put forward clear and consistent views and are thereby weakened. As was noted in the previous section this often applies to Euro-groups, especially umbrella Euro-groups, because of their varied membership and their loose confederal structures.

Access to decision-makers. Most of the characteristics just described play some part in determining which interests enjoy good access to decision-makers and which do not. Clearly, those interests which do have good access – especially if it is at both national and Community levels – are more likely than those which do not to be fully aware of thinking and developments in decision-making circles, and to be able to present their case to those who matter. At the Community level, COPA is the most obvious example of such an 'insider' interest, while at national levels COPA affiliates usually also enjoy advantageous positions. Of course, the closer the relations a national interest has with its own government the less it may seek insider status, or need to lobby, in Brussels. The UK Central Electricity Generating Board, for example, has had considerable success in opposing Commission proposals for a tightening-up of Community legislation on the amount of pollution that can be emitted from large industrial plants like power stations. The success of the Board stems almost entirely from its close working relationship with the UK government and the acceptance by the government of its argument that the capital investment implied by the proposals is too high – an argument and a position which UK representatives have consequently adopted in the Council of Ministers.

Concluding Comments

There are both positive and negative aspects to the involvement of interests in Community processes. Of the positive aspects, two are especially worth emphasising. First, interest activity broadens the participatory base of the Community and ensures that policy and decision-making is not completely controlled by politicians and officials. Second, interests can provide Community authorities with information and viewpoints which improve the quality and effectiveness of their policies and decisions. Of the negative aspects, the most important is that some interests are much more important and influential than others. This lack of balance raises questions about whether interests unduly, perhaps even undemocratically, tilt Community policy and decision-making in certain directions – towards, for example, producing a legislative framework which tends to favour producers more than such 'natural' opponents as consumers and environmentalists.

But whether interest activity is judged to be, on the whole, beneficial or not, its importance is clear. Interests are central to many key information flows to and from Community authorities, and they bring considerable influence to bear on policy and decision-making processes from initiation right through to implementation. There are few, if any, Community policy sectors where interests of at least some significance are not to be found.

PART THREE

Policies and Policy Processes of the Community

Introduction

Part Three examines what the Community does and how it does it. Chapter 9 looks at Community policies. The origins, the range, and the context of the policies are all considered. Particular themes of the chapter are the breadth and diversity of Community policy interests, and the less than complete nature of many of the policies.

Chapter 10 focuses on patterns, practices and features of the Community's policy-making and decision-making machinery. Having examined the Community's institutions and political actors in Part Two, this chapter considers how the various pieces fit together. What sort of policy and decision-making system are they part of and have they helped to create? A central concern of the chapter is to emphasise that even the most general statements about how the Community operates normally have to be qualified. For one of the few things that can be said with certainty about Community processes is that they are many, complex, and varied.

In Chapter 11 the Community budget is examined. Where does the Community get its money from and what does it spend it on? The budgetary decision-making process, which in several important respects is distinctly different from the processes which apply in policy areas, is also examined.

Chapter 12 considers one particular policy area in depth. As such, the chapter offers something of a contrast to the necessarily rather general approach of Chapters 9 and 10. Agriculture has been selected for this special examination not because of any suggestion that it is typical – the variability of the Community's policy processes precludes any policy area being described as such – but simply because of its importance in the Community context.

Finally, Chapter 13 focuses on one of the most important, and certainly one of the most distinctive, features of Community processes: the mechanisms and arrangements used by the member states to control their relations with the Community and, insofar as it is possible, to control the Community itself.

9

Community Policies

The Origins of Community Policies

The origins of Community policies are to be found in a number of places. At a general level, the changed post-war mood in Western Europe has played a part. So, also, has the increasingly interdependent nature of the international system which has resulted in national borders becoming ever more ill-matched with political and economic forces and realities. This interdependence has helped to persuade West European states to transfer policy responsibilities to a 'higher' level in an attempt to shape, to manage, to control, to take advantage of, and to keep apace with, the modern world.

At a more specific level, the Treaties are generally seen as key determinants of Community policy. However, their influence is not as great as is commonly supposed. Certainly they are important stimuli to policy development and they also provide the legal base on which much policy activity occurs. So, for example, such 'core' Community policies as the Common Commercial Policy (CCP), the Common Agricultural Policy (CAP), and the Competition Policy find their roots – though by no means all their principles – in the EEC Treaty. Similarly, Community involvement with coal and steel cannot possibly be fully understood without reference to the Treaty of Paris. But Treaty provision for policy development does not guarantee that it will occur. The very limited progress made towards the establishment of a common transport policy, despite it being provided for in Part 2 Title 4 of the EEC Treaty, illustrates this. So, too, does the non-fulfilment of most of the hopes which were held out for Euratom. A third, and in its implications for the nature of the Community

209

crucially important, example of only limited development of Treaty provisions is the very partial implementation of Part 3 Title 2 of the EEC Treaty, under which member states are supposed to regard their macroeconomic policies 'as a matter of common concern' and are to co-ordinate, co-operate and consult with one another on key economic and financial questions. In practice, it is quite clear that although there is co-operation and consultation in these areas – carried out mainly under the Economic and Financial Council of Ministers (Ecofin) by committees of very senior national officials – the states do not work and act as closely together as the Treaty envisaged. Furthermore, one of the key steps towards financial co-operation – the creation in 1979 of the European Monetary System (EMS) which, among other things, fixes maximum and minimum exchange bands for currencies in the system – was created outside the Treaty system because of concern in some quarters about the rigidities that a Treaty-based approach might entail, and also because not all member states (notably the UK) wished to be full participants.

If Treaty provision is no guarantee of policy development nor is lack of provision a guarantee of lack of development. Environmental policy illustrates this. Until it was given constitutional status by the Single European Act, environment was given no specific mention in the Treaties. Yet, from the early 1970s Community environmental policy programmes were formulated and legislation was approved. Legal authority for this was held to lie in the (almost) catch-all Articles 100 and 235 of the EEC Treaty. The former allows the Community to issue directives for the approximation of laws 'as directly affect the establishment or functioning of the common market' and the latter enables it to take 'appropriate measures' to 'attain in the course of the operation of the common market, one of the objectives of the Community'. Environmental policy was, therefore, able to find a tentative constitutional base. However, even the most liberal readings of Articles 100 and 235 cannot stretch to some policy areas, but this has not prevented policy development from occurring. Foreign policy co-operation prior to the SEA illustrates this. Aware that there were no Treaty provisions for such co-operation, and unenthusiastic about subjecting such a sensitive area to the formalities and restrictions of Treaty processes, the states in the early 1970s simply created a new European Political Co-operation (EPC) machinery alongside, but outside the formal framework of, the Treaties.

EPC points to the fact that the really crucial influence on policy development has not been so much the Treaties as the perception of the states of what is desirable, allied with their individual and collective capacities for translating these perceptions into practice.

Regarding the perceptions of the states – or, to be more precise, of national governments – a fundamental pre-condition of successful policy development is a judgement that the advantages of acting together outweigh the disadvantages. The advantages are mainly, though as EPC and recent initiatives on terrorism and drugs show, not entirely, economic in kind: those that stem from having, in an increasingly interdependent and competitive world, a single and protected market, a common external trading position, and some collective action and pooling of resources in particular functional and sectoral areas. The principal disadvantage is the loss of national decision-making powers and sovereignty that transfers of power and responsibilities to the Community inevitably entail. Some states are more concerned about this than others, but even the most pro-integrationists are cautious about ceding powers that may, at a later stage, result in their own national room for manoeuvre being limited in areas that are important to them.

As for the capacities of the states to operationalise their perceptions of what is desirable, there are many problems. At the individual state level, a government may be favourably disposed towards a Community initiative but be inhibited from supporting it in the Council of Ministers because of opposition from a powerful domestic interest or because it could be electorally damaging. Following this through to the Community level, opposition from just one state, whether it is principled or pragmatic, can make policy development very difficult to achieve, given the preference for progress through consensus, and the custom, on major issues, of advancing only on the basis of unanimous agreements.

The Community's Policy Interests and Responsibilities

The Community's main policy interests and responsibilities can be grouped under five headings: establishing the Common Market; general economic and financial policies; functional policies; sectoral policies; and external policies.

Establishing the Common Market

The continuing process of establishing the Common Market rests on four main pillars.

The first is the guarantee of *free movement of goods, persons, services and capital between the member states.* Of these, the free movement of goods has received the greatest attention. It is a freedom which, it might be thought, could be fairly easily realised: all barriers to trade must be dismantled according to the guiding principles of the EEC Treaty which states that customs duties, quantitative restrictions, and measures having equivalent effect are not permitted. Great steps were quickly made in the 1960s with the first two of these and by 1968 customs duties and quantitative restrictions were removed. Measures having equivalent effect, however, have been more difficult to deal with and have frequently acted, and been used, as obstacles to trade. Attempts to eliminate such measures have generated a considerable amount of secondary legislation and also much activity in the Court of Justice (see below and Chapter 6).

In seeking to establish the conditions for the free movement of persons, the Treaty provides for both the employed and the self-employed. The free movement of the former is to be attained by 'the abolition of any discrimination based on nationality between workers of the Member States as regards employment, remuneration and other conditions of work and employment' (Article 48 EEC). The free movement of the latter is concerned principally with rights of establishment, that is with the right of individuals and undertakings to establish businesses in the territory of other member states, and links up too with the Treaty declaration that restrictions on the provision of services within the Community should be abolished. As with the free movement of goods, secondary legislation and Court rulings have done much to clarify and extend the free movement of persons and of services. They have done so not only by removing legal and administrative obstacles but also by providing key facilitators. Labour mobility, for example, has benefited greatly from the establishment of legal entitlements to education and job training, health care, and social welfare payments. Similarly, the free movement of services has been facilitated by legislation providing for mutual recognition of certain professional and trade qualifications.

Establishing the free movement of capital has been extremely difficult. Treaty provisions partly explain this, since the elimination of restrictions on the movement of capital are required only 'to the extent necessary to ensure the proper functioning of the common market' (Article 67 EEC). More importantly, however, and notwithstanding the creation of the European Monetary System in the late 1970s (see below), there was just not, until the late 1980s, the political will that was required to free capital. For many states, control of capital movements is an important economic and monetary instrument and they preferred it to remain largely in their own hands. However, as part of the Community's objective to 'complete' the internal market by 1992, much of this former resistance has now been withdrawn, or at least become less obstructive, and capital markets are due to be greatly liberalised in the early 1990s.

The second pillar of the Common Market involves the *approximation, or harmonisation, of such legal provisions in the member states* as directly affect 'the establishment or functioning of the common market' (Article 100 EEC). The need for harmonisation arises because, as noted above, the dismantling of barriers is not in itself sufficient to guarantee free movement. This is most clearly seen with regard to movement of goods where many non-tariff and non-quantitative barriers exist which inhibit, even prevent, free movement across Community borders. These barriers have, in the words of the Treaty, the 'equivalent effect' of tariffs and quantitative restrictions, and as such are obstacles to the creation of a market based on free and open competition. They tend, moreover, to be barriers of a kind that cannot be removed simply by issuing general prohibitions. Many take the form of different national standards, requirements, provisions and practices that have been adopted over the years, sometimes for perfectly good reasons, but sometimes as a deliberate attempt to protect a domestic market from unwanted competition without actually infringing Community law. Whatever the intent, the effect is often the same: producers in one member state cannot compete on an equal basis with producers in another state. Examples of non-tariff barriers include different health and safety standards, charges for inspections on categories of imported goods, and taxes which though nominally general in their scope are discriminatory against imported goods in their effect.

Harmonisation is concerned with the removal of barriers of this type, and as such is vital if free movement across national boundaries is to be achieved. Council directives are the main instrument for achieving harmonisation, although Court of Justice rulings have also been supportive and helpful. Most harmonisation law is naturally to be found in relation to the free movement of goods, and consists largely of matters such as the setting of common standards on technical requirements, design specifications, product content, and necessary documentation. Critics of the Community often present such measures as harmonisation for harmonisation's sake, and from time to time proposals do indeed appear to smack of insensitivity to national customs and preferences. Sight should not be lost, however, of what harmonisation is all about: creating conditions which will allow, encourage and increase the uniform treatment of persons, goods, services and capital throughout the Community.

Competition policy is the third pillar. The basic rules on competition are outlined in Articles 85–94 of the EEC Treaty. They have three principal aspects to them. First, under Article 85 'all agreements between undertakings, decisions by associations of undertakings and concerted practices which may affect trade between Member States and which have as their object or effect the prevention, restriction or distortion of competition within the common market are prohibited'. Second, under Article 86: 'Any abuse by one or more undertakings of a dominant position within the common market or in a substantial part of it shall be prohibited or incompatible with the common market insofar as it may affect trade between Member States.' Third, under Article 92, state aid, 'which distorts or threatens to distort competition by favouring certain undertakings or the production of certain goods shall, insofar as it affects trade between Member States, be incompatible with the common market'.

All of these Treaty prohibitions – on restrictive practices, dominant trading positions, and state aids – have been clarified by subsequent Community law, mainly in the form of Council legislation and Court judgements. It has been established, for example, that a 'dominant position' cannot be held to apply on the basis of an overall percentage market share, but only in relation to factors such as the particular product, the structure of its market, and substitutability. Similarly, exemptions to state aid prohibitions, which are only generally referred to in the Treaty, have been confirmed as legally permissible if they are for purposes such as regional development, retraining, and job creation in potential growth industries. Much of the work and time of DGIV (Competition) is taken up examining allegations of breaches in competition law and considering applications for exemptions.

Since 1986–7 the policy attentions of the Community have been much taken up with these first three pillars of the Common Market. This is because Article 8A of the Single European Act, which is incorporated into the EEC Treaty, includes the following:

> The Community shall adopt measures with the aim of progressively establishing the internal market over a period expiring on 31 December 1992 . . . The internal market shall comprise an area without internal frontiers in which the free movement of goods, persons, services and capital is ensured in accordance with the provisions of this (the EEC) Treaty.

The Commission is anxious that, as far as possible, the 1992 deadline is met and to this end has forwarded many proposals to the Council with a view to removing the remaining obstacles to genuine free movement. (In its 1985 White Paper on the internal market the Commission identified 300 measures which were necessary for the market's completion). Not all the proposals are being acted upon as quickly as the Commission would like, and doubtless some impediments to complete free movement will still be in place by the end of 1992, but progress is none the less being made: for instance, thirty-five internal market measures were adopted during the German Council Presidency in the first six months of 1988 – they included a legally binding agreement which will further the aim of establishing a single road haulage sector, harmonising directives on additives in food, on pharmaceutical products, on trademarks and on tractors, and a directive designed to ensure the genuine opening-up of public supply contracts by improving the procedures for awarding them.

The fourth pillar of the Common Market is the *Common Customs Tariff* (CCT), or, as it is also known, the *Common External Tariff* (CET). The purpose of this is to further the course of fair and equal trading by surrounding all the member states with common trade barriers so that goods entering the Community via, say, Liverpool or Rotterdam, do so on exactly the same conditions as they do via Athens or Marseilles. No member state can therefore gain a competitive advantage by having access to cheaper raw materials and none can make a profit from exporting imported goods to a Community partner. The CCT takes the Community beyond being just a free trade area – where, at best, external tariffs are only approximated – and makes it a customs union.

Establishing the CCT was relatively easily achieved and

maintaining it has not been too difficult. The external tariffs were in place by 1968, to coincide with the removal of the internal tariffs, and since then governments have had no independent legal authority over the tariffs to be charged on goods entering their country. The terms of trade of the member states are established and negotiated on a Community-wide basis via a Common Commercial Policy (CCP). If a member state wishes to seek exemptions from, or changes to, these terms of trade it must go through the appropriate Community decision-making processes. Naturally, there have been frequent disagreements between the states over different aspects of external trade and the CCP – tariff rates, trade protection measures, and alleged dumping are among the issues that have created difficulties – but the existence of a clear and binding legal framework has ensured that, for the most part, the external protection and common front system has worked.

General Economic and Financial Policies

Notwithstanding certain EEC Treaty provisions, and despite declarations by the Heads of Government in 1969 and 1972 that their intention was to establish an economic and monetary union by 1980, only limited progress has been made in approximating the economic policies of the states. Moreover, such progress as there has been has rested more on voluntary co-operation than legal obligation.

So, ministers and senior national officials do regularly convene to consult and to exchange ideas on macroeconomic policy, and at their meetings they periodically consider Commission submissions for the adoption of common guidelines and for short-term and medium-term strategies. But, ultimately, it is up to the states themselves as to what they do. When, for example, the Commission, in its quarterly economic report published in February 1987, stated that Germany had the greatest margin for manoeuvre to stimulate domestic demand, and France and the UK could do more to boost productive capacity, there was no guarantee that national policies would thereby be adjusted. A state may be unwise to fall too much out of step with its partners – as the French government was in 1981–2 when it attempted to stimulate its economy against the general trend – but it is perfectly entitled, and able, to take that decision.

Financial policy (which, of course, in practice, is inextricably linked with economic policy) is also the subject of frequent contacts between the states – at ministerial, official and central bank levels – but, like economic policy, most of what comes out of such exchanges is of an exhortive rather than a directionist nature. That said, however, the existence of the EMS does give to Community financial policy some central structure and some powers, since among its features are: a common reserve fund to provide for market intervention (each country allocating 20 per cent of its reserves to the central pool); the European Currency Unit (Ecu) which acts as a reserve asset and a means of settlement; and fixed – though adjustable when necessary – bands of exchange for nine currencies. (Belgium and Luxembourg share a currency, while Greece, Portugal, Spain and the UK are not, at the time of writing, members of the exchange rate mechanism.)

The Community's general, or macro, economic and financial policies thus have only relatively weak policy instruments attached to them. Attempts to strengthen these instruments, so as to build up a more effective policy framework, have traditionally met with at least four obstacles. First, there have been genuine differences as to which – the economic or the financial – naturally comes first and should be accorded priority. Second, the Community's rather sectionalised policy-making mechanisms have inhibited an overall and co-ordinated approach. Third, different aspects of economic and monetary integration have different implications for the states, which has resulted in their being viewed with different degrees of enthusiasm. Fourth, for some states the possibility of ceding key macroeconomic and financial powers to the Community raisess fundamental sovereignty questions.

But notwithstanding the many obstacles in the way of policy development it is likely that the present situation, in which there is a shortage of effective general economic and financial policies aimed at broadening the EC out into a genuine community, will gradually change in the future. One reason for this is that there will be many who will seek to take advantage of the provisions in the SEA which explicitly call for a greater convergence between the states in their economic and monetary policies. Another reason is that convergence, especially in financial matters, may well be forced upon even the most reluctant states as a result of developments elsewhere. It is, for instance, clear that the internal market momentum, and particularly moves to liberalise capital movements, is generating pressures to strengthen monetary co-operation via developments such as making the Ecu a full and proper Euro-currency, and establishing a European Central Bank with powers to intervene in financial markets.

Functional policies

The Community has interests and responsibilitises in many functional policies: policies, that is, which have a clear functional purpose, and which are more specific in nature than the policies considered under the previous heading.

The best known of the Community's functional policies, and in budgetary terms by far the most important, are the regional policy – which is financed by the European Regional Development Fund – and the social policies – which are mainly financed by the European Social Fund. (There is some discussion of these funds in Chapter 11.) Less prominent functional policies include educational policies, cultural policies, and consumer protection policies. Since it is not possible to examine all of the Community's functional policies here, three examples will be briefly considered to illustrate the range, and varying depth, of Community involvement in different functional areas.

Energy policy. Given the existence of the ECSC and Euratom Treaties, given the centrality of energy to any modern economy, and given the disruption and damage that was caused by oil price increases in the 1970s, the very limited progress that has been made towards a common energy policy – as opposed to policies for particular energy sectors – must be ranked as one of the Community's major failures. The member states, which have very different domestic energy resources, and consequently very different energy requirements, have preferred essentially national solutions. Gradually recognising this, the Commission has switched the focus of Community energy policy away from attempts to achieve market integration towards a more pragmatic and less compulsory approach based on the identification of objectives around which national policies can converge. These objectives include the very general aims of promoting efficiency, slowing the growth in total energy consumption, and reducing the Community's dependence on imported energy.

Research policy. From its earliest inception with the ECSC, the Community has sponsored research, though until the 1980s in only a very small way. In recent years, however, a more ambitious approach has been taken, principally in order to enable the Community to compete effectively in new growth sectors such as electronics, communications, and information technology. Research activity has been grouped into general framework programmes so as to give them a coherence and to maximise their effectiveness, but funds have been consistently tight. In the industrial field the principal programmes are ESPRIT (information technology), BRITE (industrial technology), RACE (advanced telecommunications), and continuing research into nuclear fission, nuclear fusion, and other energy sources. Apart from its still limited scope and funding base, the principal problem with this research, from the viewpoint of its contribution to the Community's industrial efficiency and competitiveness, is that it is not followed through in any co-ordinated way when it comes to development and marketing. Beyond the basic research stage companies and states tend to be reluctant to share ideas and pool resources, with disadvantageous effects in world markets.

Environmental policy. Protection of the environment was not mentioned in the EEC Treaty and might be thought to be hardly a Community concern. Yet by 1988 well over 100 legal instruments had been adopted, most of them designed to give effect to the four Environmental Action Programmes that the Community has adopted since 1973. Community environmental law now covers matters as important as water and air pollution, disposal of chemicals, waste treatment, and protection of species and natural resources. The inclusion of a separate chapter on the environment in the SEA has consolidated the position of environmental issues and seems likely to lead to a continued expansion of Community evironmental law.

Sectoral Policies

Some Community policies are directed towards specific economic sectors. A few such policies were explicitly provided for in the Treaties. Others have their origins in a combination of factors: difficulties in adjusting to changed trading conditions, rapid sectoral decline, and effective political lobbying by interested parties.

The most obvious example of a sectoral policy is the Common Agricultural Policy which consumes by far the largest proportion of Community expenditure and where most policy-making responsibilities have been transferred from the states to the Community. (The

CAP is examined in some detail in Chapter 12.) Other – though more modest and less comprehensive – examples of sectoral policies include atomic energy, where important work is undertaken in areas such as research and safety standards, and shipbuilding, where a code of practice includes specified instructions on national aids.

Two important sectoral policies will be taken to illustrate Community sectoral activity.

Fishing. Following years of discussion, and the periodic issuing of laws from 1970 regulating aspects of the industry, a legally enforceable Common Fisheries Policy (CFP) was eventually agreed in 1983. There are four main aspects to it. First, all waters within the Community's 200 mile zone are open to all Community fishermen, but within a 12 mile limit of their own shores member states may reserve fishing to their own fishermen and to those with traditional rights. Atlantic and North Sea fish stocks are controlled by the setting of total allowable catches that are divided into national quotas. All conservation measures are agreed at Community level. Second, there is a market organisation for fish covering a price system, marketing arrangements, and an external trade policy. Third, structural measures provide for matters such as processing and market development projects, conversion and modernisation schemes, and redeployment. Fourth, international negotiations – which mostly concern access to waters and conservation of fishing stocks – are conducted by Community representatives on behalf of all member states.

Steel. The Treaty of Paris is essentially based on a liberal economic philosophy in the sense that it is principally concerned with the removal of barriers to trade. So, for the products falling within its jurisdiction it provides for the removal of internal tariffs, quantitative restrictions and most state aids, and it also forbids, subject to certain exemptions, price discrimination and cartels. However, some direct intervention is also permitted and powers are given to the Community authorities to grant loans for capital investment, to finance research and development, and, above all, to set mandatory minimum prices and production quotas when a 'manifest crises' is deemed to exist. These policy instruments, developed and clarified by secondary legislation, do not add up to a comprehensive Community legal framework for steel – key decisions on individual enterprises, for example, are still taken primarily at national levels – but they do constitute a very important part of the sectoral law. The Community authorities have, indeed, greater powers of intervention on steel than in any other sector apart from agriculture and fishing, and, from the mid–1970s, they used these powers to some effect to try and manage the Community's response to problems of falling demand. Initially the response relied mainly on voluntary measures, but from 1980 to 1988, during which a 'manifest crisis' was declared to exist, all producers were subject to mandatory price and quota restrictions. The purpose of these draconian powers was to effect a general restructuring of the industry.

External Policies

There are many different aspects to the Community's external relations and policies. Three are particularly important.

Trade policy. As was briefly noted above, in the examination of the pillars of the Common Market, the Community states present a common external front to the world in respect of international trade. If they did not do so a unified internal market would not be possible. The main foundations of the common external front are the Common Customs Tariff and the Common Commercial Policy which enable, indeed oblige, the member states to act as one on matters such as the fixing and adjusting of external customs tariffs, the negotiation of customs and trade agreements with non-member countries, and the taking of action to impede imports – this being especially likely where unfair trading practices, such as dumping and subsidies, are suspected.

The Community negotiates on trade both in international forums – which are mostly held under the auspices of the General Agreement on Tariffs and Trade (GATT) or the United Nations Conference on Trade and Development (UNCTAD) – and bilaterally. In such negotiations the twelve states, acting through the Commission, can bring considerable influence to bear since, together, they constitute the world's largest economy (accounting for over 20 per cent of world gross domestic product), and they are also the world's largest trader (accounting for around 18 per cent of world trade, compared with 13 per cent for the USA and 11 per cent for Japan).

For the most part, this economic and commercial weight is used in the interests of a liberal trading policy, in which customs duties are set as low as possible and non-tariff barriers to trade are removed. It is a policy, however, which is not always pursued with complete consistency, especially where economic circumstances or political pressures suggest a dose of protectionism. For instance, Community agriculture has long been sheltered from external competition – a fact that has strained trading relations with the USA. And special protection measures, often in the form of export restraint agreements with cheaper competitors, have been sought and obtained in respect of certain Community industries (notably textiles and steel) experiencing difficulties.

Development policy. The Community is actively engaged in helping to promote economic development in the Third World. Its reasons for being so engaged are a mixture of the moral: the belief that something should be done about world poverty and hunger; and the economic: the Community is highly dependent on the Third World for products such as rubber, copper and uranium, and also for markets – Third World countries account for around 35 per cent of Community exports.

Some of the forms of assistance made available by the Community apply to the whole of the Third World. Among these are:

1. Generalised preferences. All developing countries can export their industrial products to the Community without paying tariffs (subject to volume limits for some products). Additionally, many agricultural products can also be exported free of duty.
2. Food aid. Foodstuffs are sent to countries with serious food shortages.
3. Emergency aid. Aid of an appropriate sort is made available to countries stricken by natural disasters and other crises.
4. Aid to non-governmental organisations. The Community makes available aid to projects sponsored by non-governmental organisations in a number of Third World countries.

In addition to these general forms of assistance, the Community makes additional assistance and aid available to countries with which it has entered into special relationships. Most of these special relationships take the form of economic, trade, industrial, technical, and financial co-operation agreements. The most important, and most wide-ranging, co-operation agreement is the Lomé Convention which links the Community with African, Caribbean and Pacific countries (the ACP countries) with which some member states have historical links. Lomé III (covering the years 1985–90) was signed in 1984 by 66 ACP states and contains among its main features: duty-free access to the Community market for virtually all ACP exports; a stabilisation of export earnings scheme (Stabex) which guarantees a minimun revenue to ACP countries from their exports of 48 basic commodities to the Community; and the European Development Fund (EDF) which has as its main purpose financially assisting, on the basis of concerted programmes, the development of ACP countries, especially as regards rural development, industrialisation, and economic infrastructure.

It should be stressed that these Community policies do not constitute the sum total of the Community's overall contribution to Third World development. This is because, unlike with trade policy, the Community itself does not enjoy exclusive policy competence in the development field but rather shares it with the member states. In some respects the Community takes the leading role, in other respects it aims to supplement, complement, and co-ordinate national development policies. So, the trade aspects of development policy are necessarily the Community's responsibility, but the states are much more prominent in respect of financial assistance – as is seen in the fact that the Community's own financial aid represents only about 13 per cent of the combined efforts of the member states. (In 1986 the Community's own aid totalled about 2.2 billion Ecu – 1.1 billion financed by the Community budget, 0.8 billion financed by the EDF which is funded by special contributions from the member states, and 0.3 billion in the form of EIB loans.)

Foreign policy. There are many obstacles in the way of a developed, let alone a common, Community foreign policy. Among these obstacles are the following: many member states, especially those larger ones which have long histories of being influential on the world stage in their own right, prefer, at least in certain key areas, to conduct their own foreign policies; some member states have traditional and special relationships with particular parts of the world which they are anxious to maintain; important differences between the states on foreign policy questions arise from the ideological orientations of the national governments – differences, for example, over South Africa, over 'liberation'/'revolutionary' movements in South America, and over relations with the USA; and, finally, defence, which of course is inextricably linked with foreign policy, is largely outside the Community framework – and seems likely to remain so given the role and importance of NATO, and given too the doubts that some states (such as Ireland because of its traditional policy of neutrality) have of the wisdom of putting defence questions on the Community agenda.

But notwithstanding these obstacles important developments have occurred. Since 1970, when foreign policy co-operation, under the name European Political Co-operation, was first launched (following a request from the 1969 summit of national leaders at the Hague), the states have consulted with one another on virtually all important foreign policy issues. The consultations occur at European Council level, where time is invariably set aside for an EPC discussion, and, as described in Chapter 10, at Foreign Minister and senior national official levels, where EPC meetings are both regular and institutionalised.

These consultations are undoubtedly facilitating Community foreign policy co-operation and are assisting in the emergence of a distinctive European political voice. In at least four ways. First, the member states have a better understanding of their partners' foreign policy stances. Second, the ability of the twelve to take a united approach in other international organisations and forums – such as the United Nations and its agencies – is improved. Third, the Community is increasingly in a position to engage in a political dialogue with non-Community states and organisations – as, for example, it does in periodic ministerial conferences with the countries of Central America and of the Contadora Group. And, fourth, the Community frequently is able to adopt common positions on international issues of contemporary importance. Many of these common positions are, it must be said, rather vague and fudged, but by no means all. In recent years, for instance, important joint statements and declarations, which have differed in important respects from the position of the major Western power, the USA, have been issued on subjects such as the Arab-Israeli conflict, the Falklands war, Poland, and arms control negotiations.

It seems likely that EPC will continue to develop and will become more effective in the future. One reason for this is that some of the obstacles mentioned above – such as the importance of special national relationships with particular parts of the world – may well become less problematic as ties are loosened. A second reason is that there appears to be a growing desire on the part of at least most of the states to improve the links, and where possible the match, between external economic relations and external political relations. And a third reason is that EPC, which of course was not mentioned in the founding Treaties, was accorded its own section (Title III) in the Single European Act. Title III is not incorporated into the Treaties, but it does none the less formalise and give a clear impetus to foreign policy co-operation with its clearly stated intention: 'The High Contracting Parties (i.e. the member states), being members of the European Communities, shall endeavour jointly to formulate and implement a European foreign policy'.

Characteristics of Community Policies

Three features of Community policies are particularly striking.

The Range and Diversity of Community Policies

The Community is often referred to as 'The Common Market'. It is so because, as was shown in the previous section, many of its policies and its laws centre on the promotion and defence of an internally free and externally protected market. So, there are the policies that are designed to encourage the free movement of goods, persons, services, and capital; there is the competition policy that seeks to facilitate fair and open competition within and across the borders of the member states; there is the common external tariff; and there is the common external trading policy. In practice, however, not all of these policies are complete or are wholly successful. There are, for example, many barriers to open tendering for public contracts, and, despite strenuous activity on harmonisation, many non-tariff barriers to internal trade still exist. In consequence, the Community is, in some respects, less than the Common Market it is commonly supposed to be.

But, in other respects, it is more than the Common Market in that many of its policy concerns range far beyond matters that directly, or even indirectly, are part and parcel of a common market's requirements. Most of these policies still have a strong economic focus, although they are not necessarily of the non-interventionist/ *laissez-faire* kind that is usually thought of as providing the ethos, the ideology even, of the Community. In some spheres indeed the

Community tends very much to interventionism/managerialism; state capitalism, some would say. These 'non-common market' economic policies take a number of different forms. Some, for instance, are designed to encourage economic and financial co-operation at the macro level. Others are more narrowly based, such as the sectoral policies which have a number of purposes: improving the efficiency of the Community market, as with aspects of the CAP and of the policies for steel and shipbuilding; making good market inefficiencies and failings, as with the emphasis in the Common Fisheries Policy on preservation of stocks, and the Community's increasing involvement in advanced research; and softening nationally unacceptable or socially inequitable market consequences, as with the regional and social policies, to an extent overseas aid policy, and much of the CAP.

Of the Community's non-economic policies the most obvious are those falling within the EPC framework, where the states consult and attempt to co-ordinate their positions on key foreign policy questions. But in addition to EPC, there are also other areas, initially thought of as not being the Community's concern because of their non-economic nature, where important developments have occurred. A particularly graphic example of this was seen in December 1986 when the Heads of Government, at the end of their summit meeting, issued a communiqué that was much taken up with joint action they were proposing to combat terrorism, illegal immigration, and drug trafficking, and also with the co-ordination of public health campaigns on Aids and cancer.

The Differing Degrees of Community Policy Involvement

The Community's responsibility for policy-making and for policy-management varies enormously across its range of policy interests. In those spheres where significant responsibilities are exercised, arrangements are usually well established, and effective policy instruments – legal and financial – are usually available. Where, however, Community involvement is marginal, policy processes may be confined to little more than occasional exchanges of ideas and information between interested parties, whilst policy instruments may merely be of the exhortive and persuasive kind such as are common in many international organisations.

Examples of high Community involvement are the CCP, the CAP, and the CFP. Here, most major policy decisions, such as on external tariffs, agricultural prices, and fishing quotas, are taken at the Community level, while their detailed and supposed uniform implementation is left to the states acting as agents of the Community. In areas where these so-called common policies are not, in reality, totally common – and both the CAP and the CFP allow ample room for governments to provide national aids and assistance – decisions of any significance normally require at least clearance from Brussels.

Moving along the spectrum of Community policy involvement there are many spheres in which the Community's interests and competence, though less comprehensive than in the examples just given, remain significant, and complement and supplement the activities of the states in important ways. Competition policy is an example. It seeks to encourage free and open competition throughout the Community by, for instance, setting out conditions under which firms can make and sell their products, by laying down conditions under which national authorities may assist firms, and by imposing restrictions on certain types of company merger. Social policies provide another example. Much of their concern is with job training and re-training, labour mobility, working conditions, and the general promotion of employment.

Turning, finally, to policy spheres where the Community's involvement is, at best, very limited, examples include education, health, and – a qualitatively different case – national defence. Interestingly, however, if one looks back to say, 1970, many issues which would have been listed then as being in this category of very limited Community involvement – such as environment and foreign policy – are now no longer so marginal. As has already been indicated, environment has spawned policy programmes and legislation, foreign policy has evolved its own machinery and has seen some co-ordinated policy development, while both have been awarded constitutional recognition via the SEA. At the same time, some policy spheres which, in 1970, the Community would have been thought of as having no competence in at all, have crept onto the agenda. One such example is seen in the semi-secret Trevi process under which, since the mid-1970s, Interior and Justice officials, senior police and intelligence officers, and lately ministers, have met to exchange information and further co-operation (often the first steps in policy development) on terrorism, drug trafficking and organised crime.

The Patchy and Somewhat Unco-ordinated Nature of Community Policies

Although the Community was given as one of its tasks in the EEC Treaty the promotion of 'a harmonious development of economic activities', the Community's overall policy framework lacks any obvious pattern or coherence. Certainly, it can hardly be said to be modelled around, or progressing towards, any clear vision of an integrated policy community based on consistent and mutually reinforcing principles. Whatever idealism there may have been in the early post-war years has almost completely disappeared. In a Community which now has much greater national and political divisions between its members, and in a world where rapid economic growth can no longer be assumed, policy development is usually only possible if some difficult questions are answered to the satisfaction of a large number of Community actors. From the states' viewpoint these questions include: is the national (or at least government) interest being served? Is the co-operation and integration that the development involves politically acceptable? And, if the policy sphere does require closer relations with other states, is the Community the most desirable arena in which it should occur? As the Community's extensive range of policies demonstrates these questions have often been answered in the affirmative, though normally only after being subject to caveats and reservations which sit uneasily beside, and sometimes clash with, one another. But often, too, the responses have been in the negative, or at least have been so on the part of a sufficient number to prevent progress.

Policy development has consequently been as much about what is possible as what is desirable. In the absence of a centre of power with the authority and internal coherence to take an overall view of Community requirements and impose an ordered pattern, policies have tended to be the outcome of complex and laboured interactions where different, and often contrasting, requirements, preferences, reservations, and fears have all played a part. As a result, the Community's overall policy picture is inevitably patchy and rather ragged. A few spheres – such as the CAP and, increasingly, the operation of the internal market – are well developed. Other spheres, however, which might have been expected to be developed, are either developed only in unco-ordinated and partial ways, or are barely developed at all.

Industrial policy is a prime example of just such an unco-ordinated and underdeveloped policy. With industry employing 35 per cent of the Community's active population and accounting for 40 per cent of the gross value-added of the Community's economy, and with industrial growth in the Community lagging behind competitors (between 1972 and 1984 the index of industrial production rose by 20 per cent in the Community, as against 36 per cent in the United States and 58 per cent in Japan), it might be expected that an industrial policy would be at the very centre of Community policy concerns. In practice, an industrial policy as such can hardly be said to exist. What do exist are large number of policies, themselves usually only partially developed, which affect industry, but which do not in any sense constitute an integrated industrial framework with clear and consistent goals. Without listing them all, these policies include the policies promoting the free movement of goods, persons, services and capital throughout the Community, the competition policy, the research policy, aspects of the regional policy, and specific policies for some expanding and some contracting sectors.

Concluding Comments

A principle theme of this chapter has been the range and diversity of the Community's policy responsibilities and interests. There are now few policy areas with which the Community does not have at least some sort of involvement.

But another theme has been that there are many deficiencies in Community policies. Economic and monetary policy, industrial policy, energy policy, and regional policy are but four examples of key policy areas where there are not, if Community effectiveness is to be maximised, sufficiently strong or integrated policy frameworks with clear and consistent goals. They are too partial and too fragmented. They are also, in general, under-funded.

Of course, similar critical comments about underdevelopment and lack of cohesion can also be levelled against many national policy frameworks. But not, usually, to the same extent, for at individual state level, there is, even when the political system is weak and decentralised, more opportunity than there is in the Community for direction from the centre. This is partly because national decision-makers have access to more policy instruments than do Community decision-makers. It is mainly, however, because at state level there is normally some focus of political authority capable of imposing a degree of order: a Head of Government perhaps, a Cabinet or Council of Ministers, a Ministry of Economics or Finance, or a dominant party group. In the Community, the Council of Ministers and the European Council are the main foci of political authority, but neither is constituted or organised in such a way as to enable them to forge an overall policy coherence or specify a clear policy direction.

10

Policy Processes

Variations in Community Policy Processes

There can hardly be said to be a 'standard' or a 'typical' Community policy-making or decision-making process. A multiplicity of actors interact with one another via a myriad of channels.

The Actors

There are three main sets of actors: those associated with the Community institutions, the member governments, and Euro and national interests. As has been shown in previous chapters, each of these has responsibilities to fulfil and roles to perform. But so variable and fluid are Community policy processes that the nature of the responsibilities and roles may differ considerably according to circumstances. For instance, in one set of circumstances an actor may be anxious to play an active role and may have the power – legal and/or political – to do so. In a second set of circumstances an actor may not wish to be actively involved, perhaps because there are no direct interests at stake or because prominence may be politically damaging. And, in a third set of circumstances, an actor may wish for a leading part but not be able to attain it because of a lack of appropriate power resources.

The Channels

The channels vary in four principal respects.

In their complexity and exhaustiveness. Some types of decisions are made fairly quickly by a relatively small number of people using procedures that are easy to operate. By contrast, others are the subject of complex and exhaustive processes in which many different sorts of actors attempt to determine and shape outcomes.

In the relative importance of Community level processes and member state level processes and in the links between the two levels. One of the Community's major structural difficulties is that it is multi-layered and there are often no clear lines of authority or of hierarchy between the different layers or levels.

In their levels of seniority. This is seen in the many different forums in which the member states meet: Heads of Government in the European Council; Ministers in the Council of Ministers; Permanent Representatives and their deputies in COREPER; senior officials and national experts in working groups, management committees and expert groups.

In their degrees of formality and structure. By their very nature the fixed and set-piece occasions of Community policy processes – such as meetings of the Council of Ministers, plenary sessions of the EP, Council of Ministers–EP delegation meetings called to resolve legislative and budgetary differences – tend to be formal and structured. Partly because of this, they are often, in themselves, not very well equipped to produce the trading, the concessions, and the compromises that are so often necessary to build majorities, create agreements, and further progress. As a result they have come to be supported by a vast network of informal and unstructured channels between Community actors. Examples of such channels are everywhere and range from the after dinner discussions that are held at European Council meetings to the continuous rounds of soundings, telephone calls, lunches, lobbying opportunities, and pre-meetings that are such a part of Community life in Brussels, Strasbourg, Luxembourg and national capitals.

An Illustration of Variations: External Relations

It is worth illustrating and reinforcing the central point made in the previous section, about the multifaceted nature of Community processes, with a brief example. An outline sketch of some of the key policy and decision-making features involved in external relations will be taken.

External *commercial* relations involve the Community acting as a single unit in international trading relations. Policies are developed and decisions are taken by the Council and the Commission working – usually – closely with each other. The former agrees negotiating mandates and then the latter, on the basis of the mandates and under the watchful eye of the Ministers and senior national officials in the Article 113 Committee, negotiates on behalf of all twelve Community states with non-member states, groups of states, and in international forums (notably GATT). The relationship between the Council and the Commission can thus be very delicate: with the Council wanting to ensure that the Commission remains under its control, and the Commission needing enough manoeuvrability to enable it to be an effective negotiator.

External *political* relations – in the form of European Political Co-operation (EPC) – are centred on a network of co-operative activity between the member states. The activity includes: regular exchanges of information; consultations and meetings at official and ministerial levels (during a six-month Council Presidency there might be three meetings of Foreign Ministers, six of political directors, and thirty or so of working groups); and, where possible, the issuing of joint statements by Foreign Ministers. Because EPC developed largely outside of the formal Community framework, because of the politically sensitive nature of much of its subject matter, and because it does not directly require Community legislation, policy and decision-making processes have rather by-passed other Community institutions and have been based on inter-governmental – and in particular inter-Foreign Office – arrangements. It is possible that this emphasis may change a little in the future: under the Single European Act the Commission is to be 'fully associated', and the European Parliament is to be 'closely associated', with EPC, and a permanent Secretariat based in Brussels has been established.

As part of its policy on *development co-operation* the Community has concluded numerous agreements with most of the countries of the Third World. As was shown in Chapter 9, the Lomé Convention is the most important of these agreements. The Convention has its own institutional structure which is made up of three principal bodies. The first is the ACP–EEC Council of Ministers, which is composed of the members of the Council of Ministers of the Community, a member of the Commission, and a member of the government of each ACP country. The Council meets at least once a year and takes the major political and policy decisions that are necessary during the life of a Convention. The second body is the Committee of Ambassadors, which is composed of a representative of each Community state, a representative of the Commission, and a representative of each ACP state. The Committee meets at least twice a year and is charged with assisting and advising the Council of Ministers, monitoring implementation of the Convention and progress towards achieving the objectives, and generally supervising and co-ordinating the work of the many committees and subsidiary bodies that exist under the general umbrella of the Convention. Finally, there is the Joint Assembly, which is made up of equal numbers of MEPs and ACP members of parliament or national representatives. It meets once a year and acts as a general advisory and deliberating body.

Factors Determining Community Policy Processes

A number of factors can be identified as being especially important in determining the particular mix of actors and channels in Community policy-making and decision-making processes. (Factors applying to budgetary decision-making are not included in the following analysis as there is a separate chapter on the budget.)

The Proposed Status of the Matter Under Consideration

As a general rule, procedures tend to be more fixed when Community law is envisaged than when it is not. They are fixed by such factors as the Treaties (the requirement that a Commission proposal is needed), Court interpretations (the obligation on the Council to wait for the EP's Opinion), and conventions (the right of a state to invoke a veto even where majority voting is constitutionally permissible).

As for different types of Community law, Commission legislation is usually subject to much less review and discussion than Council legislation. The reason for this is that Commission legislation is normally of an administrative kind, more technical than political.

Much of it, indeed, consists of updates, precisions, or amendments to already existing legislation – usually in the sphere of external trade or the CAP. As a result, Commission legislation, prior to being introduced, is often only fully discussed by appropriate officials in the Commission, and perhaps by national officials in an experts' committee or a management committee. Council legislation, on the other hand, especially directives because of their normally broader scope, usually becomes the subject of representations and pressures from many interests, is assessed by the EP and the ESC, and is scrutinised in detail in national capitals and in Council forums in Brussels.

Where policy activity does not involve law making, considerable discretion is available to key decision-makers, especially governments, as to what policy processes will be used and who will be permitted to participate. A common procedure when states wish the Community to do something, but do not wish for it necessarily to involve making new law (which may be because there is no agreement on what the law should be or because, as with foreign policy pronouncements, law is inappropriate), is to issue Council resolutions, declarations, or agreements. These can be as vague or as precise as the Council wishes them to be, and often they can have a very useful policy impact, even if it is just to keep dialogue going. But, because they are not legal instruments, they are not normally as subject as most Council legislation to examination and challenge by other Community institutions and actors.

The Degree of Generality or Specificity of the Policy Issue

At the generality end of the scale, Community policy-making may consist of little more than exchanges of ideas between interested parties to see whether there is common ground for policy co-ordination, for the setting of priorities, or for possible legislation. Such exchanges and discussions take place at many different levels on an almost continuous basis, but the most important, in the sense that their initiatives are the ones most likely to be followed up, are those which involve *les grands messieurs* of the Commission and the member states. At the other end of the scale, are included the mass of highly detailed and technical regulations that make up the great bulk of the Community's legislative output. Senior Community figures, especially ministers, are not normally directly involved in the processes which lead to such legislation. There may be a requirement that they give the legislation their formal approval, but it is Commission officials, aided in appropriate cases by national officials, who do the basic work.

The Newness, Importance, Controversiality or Political Sensitivity of the Issue in Question

The more these characteristics apply, and they may well not do so uniformly – what may be a technical question for one may be politically charged for another – the more complex policy processes are likely to be. If, for example, it seems likely that a proposal for a Council directive on some aspect of animal welfare will cause significant difficulties for farmers, it is probable that the accompanying decision-making process will display all or most of the following features: particularly extensive pre-proposal consultations by the Commission; the raising of voices from many sectional and promotional interest groups; very careful examination of the proposal by the EP and the ESC; long and exhaustive negotiations in the Council; considerable activity and manoeuvring on the fringes of formal meetings, and in between the meetings; and, overall, much delay and many alterations *en route* to the (possible) eventual adoption of the proposal.

The Balance of Policy Responsibilities between Community and National Levels.

Where there has been a significant transfer of responsibilities to the EC – agriculture and external commercial policy are the most obvious examples – Community-level processes are naturally very important. In such policy spheres, Community institutions, and the Commission in particular, have many tasks to perform: these include, monitoring developments, making adjustments, and ensuring existing policies and programmes are replaced when necessary. On the other hand, where the Community's policy role is at best supplementary to that of the states – fiscal policy and transport policy are examples – most significant policy and decision-making activity continues to be directed through the customary national procedures.

Circumstances and the Perceptions of Circumstances

This is seemingly rather vague, but it refers to the crucially important fact that policy development and decision-making processes in the Community are closely related to prevailing political and economic circumstances, to the perceptions by key actors – especially states – of their needs in the circumstances, and to perceptions of the potential of the Community to act as a problem solving organisation in regard to the circumstances. Do the advantages of acting at Community level, as opposed to national levels, and of acting in the Community in a particular way as opposed to another way, outweigh the disadvantages?

It is best to explain this point about circumstances with a specific example. Steel will be taken because it shows in a particularly clear manner how changing circumstances may bring about related changes in Community processes.

As was explained in Chapter 2 the Treaty of Paris gave considerable powers to the High Authority (later Commission). Until the mid-1970s these powers were used primarily to liberalise the market, with the High Authority/Commission expending much of its time and energy attempting to ensure that internal barriers were removed and cartels were eliminated. From 1974, however, market conditions began to deteriorate as a result of falling internal and external demand, reduced profit margins, and cost increases. This led the Commission to look more towards its hitherto largely neglected interventionist powers. Initially a largely voluntarist path was preferred, but when this proved to be ineffective a stronger approach was taken. By the end of 1980 an assortment of highly *dirigiste* policy instruments, some of which were mandatory, were in place. These included common external positions in the form of price agreements and export restraint agreements, strict controls on national subsidies, restrictions on the investment decisions of individual firms, and compulsory quotas (which became possible following the declaration by the Council of a 'manifest crisis' in October 1980).

The emphasis of Community steel policy thus switched between 1974–80, from promoting the freedom and efficiency of the market, to managing the market. This switch had very important implications for steel policy and decision-making processes. Four of these implications are particularly worth noting. First, there was now more policy responsibility and activity at Community level than previously. As a result of this, the overall policy picture as regards steel became a complicated mixture of Community and national processes, with not all of them pulling in the same direction. Second, the assumption by the Community of new and important policy powers, many of which had direct distributional consequences, inevitably created tensions in the Council. At the same time, it also resulted in the Council, as a collective body, taking greater care to ensure that on key decisions the Commission acted under its direction (although this did not stop governments from using the Commission as a useful device for deflecting the blame for necessary, but unpopular, decisions away from themselves). Third, the Commission, notwithstanding its obligation to work within a Council-approved framework, extended its roles and functions in several important respects: as an initiator and proposer of policy; as a mediator among national and corporate interests (by, for example, putting together complicated production quota packages for the different types of steel product); as the Community's external negotiator (the Treaty of Paris did not establish a customs union and it was not until the late 1970s that the states began to adopt common external positions); and as a decision-maker (the Commission assumed more powers to act directly – for example, on investment aids subsidies). Fourth, non-institutional and non-governmental interests inevitably sought to become much more involved in decision-making, as the Community developed policies with a very obvious and very direct impact on output, prices, profits, and employment. A striking illustration of this was the way in which EUROFER – the European Confederation of Iron and Steel Industries, which represents about 60 per cent of Community steel capacity – negotiated with the Commission on production quotas.

The Making of Community Legislation

Having established that there are considerable variations in Community policy and decision-making processes, it is necessary now to look at common, shared, and recurring features. For, except in the narrowest of senses, not every policy is formulated nor every decision taken, in a manner that is unique to it alone.

This is no more clearly seen than in relation to the making of Community legislation. Most legislation takes one of three 'set routes'.

1. Administrative/management/regulatory legislation is issued mainly in the form of Commission regulations and decisions. As has previously been explained (notably in Chapter 3) the basic work on this type of legislation is undertaken by officials in the relevant Directorate General. Commissioners only discuss such legislation themselves when it is not straightforward or someone requests it. Where appropriate, and when time permits, national officials and sometimes sectional interests are consulted.

   Some of this type of legislation is issued as Council legislation, which results in national officials playing a more active role and formal Council approval being required.

2. Much of the legislation that is enacted in connection with the Community's external economic policies is based on agreements with third countries and is, therefore, subject to special procedures. An indication of some of these procedures was given above. Among the distinctive features are: the Commission usually acts as the Community's main negotiator in economic negotiations with third countries; the Council seeks to control and monitor what the Commission does during negotiations; the EP does not normally exercise much influence – except, following provisions included in the Single European Act, with regard to agreements establishing special relations negotiated under Article 238 of the EEC Treaty (see Chapter 5); legislation produced as a result of negotiations, including virtually all framework legislation, is usually enacted in the form of Council regulations and decisions and therefore requires formal Council approval.

3. Most of what remains consists of Council legislation that is deemed to require examination via a full legislative process. There are no hard and fast rules for deciding when proposals fall into this category, but, in general, they are those thought to be significant or concerned with establishing principles. The broader in scope they are, the more likely they are to be in the form of directives.

   Because of its obvious importance, this full legislative process needs to be examined here. However, since much of the detail of how the Community institutions exercise their particular responsibilities has already been set out in Part Two, a comprehensive account is not attempted in what follows.

Attention is restricted merely to highlighting the principal features of each legislative stage.

Initiation

The starting point is when somebody somewhere suggests that the Community should act on a matter. Most likely this will be the Commission or the Council: the Commission because in most cases it is the only body with the authority formally to table a legislative proposal, and also because of its special expertise in, and responsibility for, Community affairs; the Council because of its political weight, its position as the natural conduit for national claims and interests, and its unique legal power to request the Commission 'to undertake any studies the Council considers desirable for the attainment of the common objectives, and to submit to it any appropriate proposals' (Article 152 EEC).

Beyond the Commission and the Council there are many other possible sources of Community legislation, but little progress can be made unless the Commission decides to take the issue up and draft proposals. Many circumstances may result in its deciding to do so, but often it is very difficult, in looking at specific proposals, to discover just why it decided to act and to identify precisely from where the initiative originated. For example, a Commission proposal that may seem to be a response to a Council request may, on inspection, be traced back beyond the Council to a national pressure group influencing a minister, who then gradually and informally introduced the issue into the Council as an option to be considered. Similarly, a Commission proposal may seem to be a response to an EP own initiative report or to representations from European-wide interests, but in fact the Commission may itself have dropped hints to the EP or to interests that they should look at the matter, (thus reinforcing the Commission's own position *vis-à-vis* the Council).

Preparation of a Text

Once it has been decided to produce a proposal (a decision that is usually taken at a senior level within the most relevant Directorate General), a text is prepared. The standard way in which this is done is as follows: junior officials in the appropriate DG write the initial draft; the draft is passed upwards through superiors; as it is passed upwards the draft is discussed with all DGs and specialised Commission services which have an interest; when all directly involved Commission interests have given their approval, the draft is sent to the *cabinet* of the Commissioner responsible for the subject; the *cabinet* may re-work the draft before submitting it to the Commissioner for his approval; when the Commissioner is satisfied, he asks the Secretariat General to submit the draft to the College of Commissioners; the draft is scrutinised, and possibly amended, by the *chefs des cabinets* at their weekly meeting; if the draft is judged to be uncontroversial the Commissioners may adopt it by written procedure; if it is controversial the Commissioners may, after debate, accept it, reject it, amend it, or refer it back to the relevant DG for further consideration.

In preparing a text, officials usually find themselves the focus of attention from many directions. Knowing that the Commission's thinking is probably at its most flexible at this preliminary stage, and knowing too that once a proposal is formalised it is more difficult to change, interested parties use whatever means they can to press their views. As for the Commission itself, four factors most affect its approach to consultations at this pre-proposal stage. First, what contacts and channels have already been regularised in the sector and what ways of proceeding have proved to be effective in the past? Second, what political considerations arise and how important is it to incorporate different sectional and national views from the outset? Third, what degree of technical knowledge and outside expertise is called for? Fourth, how do the relevant Commission officials prefer to work?

Assuming, as it is normally reasonable to do, Commission receptivity, there are several ways in which 'external' views may be brought to the attention of those drafting the proposal. The Commission itself may request a report, perhaps from a university or a research institute. Interest groups may submit briefing documents. Professional lobbyists, politicians, and officials from the Permanent Representations may press preferences in informal meetings. EP committees and ESC sections may be sounded out. And use may be made of the extensive advisory committee system that clusters around the Commission and which was described in Chapter 3.

There is, therefore, no standard consultative pattern or procedure. An important consequence of this is that governmental involvement in the preparation of Commission texts varies considerably. Indeed, not only is there a variation in involvement, but there is a variation in knowledge of Commission intentions. Sometimes, governments are fully aware of Commission thinking, because national officials have been formally consulted in expert committees. Sometimes, sectional interests represented on consultative committees will let their governments know what is going on. Sometimes, governments will be abreast of developments as a result of having tapped sources within the Commission, most probably through officials in their Permanent Representations. But sometimes, governments are not aware of proposals until they are published.

The time that elapses between the decision to initiate a proposal and the publication by the Commission of its text naturally depends on a number of factors: (1) is there any urgency? (2) how keen in the Commission to press ahead? (3) how widespread are the consultations? (4) does the Commission want the prior support of all key actors? (5) is there a consensus within the Commission itself? Not surprisingly periods of over a year are common.

The Opinions of the European Parliament and the Economic and Social Committee

On publication, the Commission's text is submitted to the Council of Ministers, which in turn refers it to the EP and, where appropriate, to the ESC, for their Opinions.

The EP is by far the more influential of the two bodies. Though it does not have the full legislative powers of national parliaments it has enough weaponry in its arsenal to ensure that its views are at least taken into consideration, particularly by the Commission. Its representational claims are one source of its influence. The quality of its arguments and its suggestions are another. And it has the power of delay, by virtue of the requirement that Parliament's Opinion must be known before the proposal can become law.

As was shown in Chapter 5, most of the detailed work undertaken by the EP on proposed legislation is handled by its specialised committees and, to a lesser extent, by its political groups. One of their key tasks is to advise MEPs how to vote in plenary. The most usual way in which plenary votes can bring influence to bear is through the use of the requirement that the Commission must state whether or not it accepts Parliamentary amendments to its text in advance of MEPs voting on the draft legislative resolution – which constitutes the EP's Opinion. If the amendments are accepted, a favourable Opinion is issued, and the amended text becomes the text that the Council considers. If they are not accepted, the EP may attempt to exert pressure by not issuing an Opinion and referring the proposal back to the committee responsible. A reference back, and hence delay, can also be made if the whole proposal is judged to be unacceptable. References back cannot normally be for a period exceeding two months.

Observations, suggestions, requests and demands from the EP at this formal consultative stage can often bring about changes not only in the Commission's text but also in the text ultimately approved by the Council. To give just two, very different, examples: in 1985 the Council incorporated EP amendments into directives concerning freedom of establishment for pharmacists; in 1986 it incorporated EP amendments into the sixth directive on state aids to the shipbuilding sector (see Chapter 5 for a general assessment of the EP's legislative influence).

The ESC is, generally, not so well placed as the EP to examine legislative proposals. Part of the problem is that its formal powers are not as great: while it must be consulted on draft legislation in some policy spheres, consultation is optional in others. Furthermore, when it is consulted, the Council or the Commission may lay down a very tight timetable, can go ahead if no Opinion is issued by a specified date, and cannot be frustrated by delays if the ESC wants changes to the text. Other sources of weakness include the part-time capacity of its members, the personal rather than national representational nature of much of its membership, and the perception by many interests that advisory committees and direct forms of lobbying are more effective channels of influence.

Examples of ESC Opinions influencing legislation can be found, but they are relatively few and seldom touch on major points. Even when ESC views do appear to have been taken into account, closer inspection often reveals that the really decisive influence may have come from elsewhere. For example, a Council directive concerned with the implementation of the principle of equal treatment for men and women in occupational social security schemes, which was listed in the 1986 ESC Annual Report as being influenced 'to a large extent' by an ESC Opinion, was also the subject of strong representations by sectional interests and member governments. In the 1987 Annual Report, a similar claim was made for a Council directive on the legal protection of original topographies of semi-conductor products, but on this very same proposal the EP made much the same claim for itself and suggested that the Council had accepted eight of the twelve amendments it had adopted.

Decision-making in the Council

The Council does not necessarily wait on the EP or the ESC before proceeding with a proposal. Indeed, governments may begin preparing their positions for the Council, and informal discussions and deliberations may even take place within the Council itself, before the formal referral from the Commission.

The standard procedure in the Council is for the proposal to be referred initially to a working group of national representatives for detailed examination. The representatives have two principal tasks: on the one hand, to ensure that the interests of their country are safeguarded; on the other, to try to reach an agreement on a text. Inevitably these two responsibilites do not always coincide, with the consequence that working group deliberations can be highly protracted. Progress depends on many factors: the controversiality of the proposal; the extent to which it benefits or damages states differentially; the number of countries, especially large countries, pressing for progress; the enthusiasm and competence of the Presidency; the tactical skills of the national representatives and their capacity to trade disputed points (both of which are dependent on personal abilities and the sort of briefs laid down for representatives by their governments); and the flexibility of the Commission in agreeing to change its text.

Once a working group has gone as far as it can with a proposal – which can mean reaching a general agreement, agreeing on most points but with reservations entered by some countries on particular points, or very little agreement at all on the main issues – reference is made upwards to COREPER or, in the case of agriculture, to the Special Committee on Agriculture. At this level, the Permanent Representatives (in COREPER II), their deputies (in COREPER I), or senior agriculture officials (in the SCA) concern themselves not so much with the technical details of a proposal as with its policy and political implications. So far as is possible differences left over from the working group are sorted out. Where this cannot be done, bases for possible agreement may be identified, and the proposal is then either referred back to the working group for further detailed consideration, or forwarded to the ministers for political resolution.

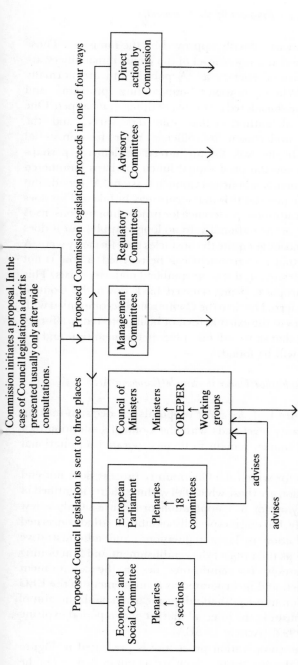

Commission initiates a proposal. In the case of Council legislation a draft is presented usually only after wide consultations.

Proposed Council legislation is sent to three places

Proposed Commission legislation proceeds in one of four ways

| Economic and Social Committee | European Parliament | Council of Ministers | Management Committees | Regulatory Committees | Advisory Committees | Direct action by Commission |

Economic and Social Committee

Plenaries ← 9 sections

European Parliament

Plenaries ← 18 committees

Council of Ministers

Ministers ← COREPER ← Working groups

advises

advises

Legislation is adopted in three forms:
1. *regulations*, which are directly binding on member governments and citizens of member states;
2. *decisions*, which are binding on those to whom they are addressed;
3. *directives*, which are binding on member governments, but which require intervening national measures to take effect.

National governments, under the watching eye of the Commission, carry the main responsibility for implementing legislation.

Note: This figure does not include stages which apply under the co-operation procedure (see Fig. 10.2).

Figure 10.1
Main community legislative stages

All proposals must be formally approved by the ministers. Those that have been agreed at a lower level of the Council machinery are placed on the ministers' agenda as 'A points' and are normally quickly ratified. Where, however, outstanding problems and differences have to be considered a number of things can happen. One is that the political authority that ministers carry, and the preparatory work undertaken by officials prior to ministerial meetings, may clear the way for an agreed settlement: perhaps reached quickly during the pre-Council lunch, perhaps hammered out in long and frequently adjourned Council sessions. A second, and increasingly utilised, possibility is that a vote may be taken. This does not mean that the traditional preference for proceeding by consensus or the potential use of the national veto no longer apply, but it does mean that they are no longer quite the obstacles they formerly were. A third possibility is that no agreement can be reached, a vote is not judged to be appropriate, or, if it is, no qualified majority exists. This may lead to the proposal being referred back down the Council machinery, being referred back to the Commission accompanied with a request for changes to the existing text, or being referred to a future meeting in the hope that shifts will take place in the meantime and the basis of a solution will be found.

Additional Stages Established Under the Single European Act

As is shown in Figure 10.1, for most proposals the decision-making process at Community level ends with the Council's adoption of a text. Directives, of course, remain to be incorporated into national law.

Those proposals for which the Community process does not end with Council adoption are those which fall within spheres identified in the SEA as qualifying for a 'co-operation procedure'. Only a few spheres do so qualify, but one is especially significant – that concerned with the harmonisation of laws, regulations, and administrative actions which have as their object the establishment and functioning of the internal market. Its significance lies in the commitment contained in the Act, and incorporated as a supplement to the EEC Treaty, that the Community 'shall adopt measures with the aim of progressively establishing the internal market over a period expiring on 31 December 1992' (Article 13 SEA).

An outline of the co-operation procedure is presented in Figure 10.2. The details of the procedure, which are set out in Article 7 of the

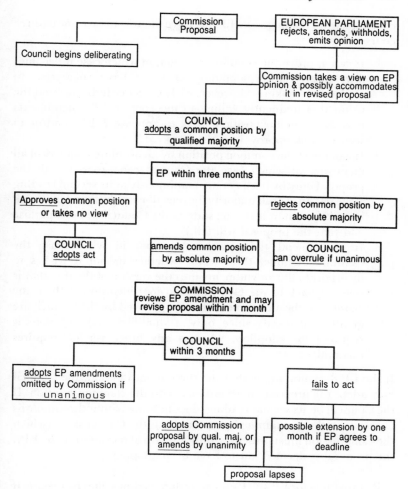

Source: J. Lodge, 'The Single European Act and the New Legislative Cooperation Procedure: A Critical Analysis', *Journal of European Integration*, XI (1) (Autumn 1987).

FIGURE 10.2
The co-operation procedure

SEA and which are incorporated into a new Article 149 of the EEC Treaty, are as follows.

The Council, after obtaining the EP's Opinion on a proposal, adopts a common position by a qualified majority vote.

The common position is communicated to the EP for what is, in effect, a second reading. The EP has three months to take one of three courses of action:

1. It can approve the common position, in which case it becomes law. (This hardly amounts, as some have suggested, to co-decision making. However, early evidence indicates that the Council is frequently willing to incorporate EP amendments into the common position so as to appease MEPs and/or to secure quick approval for the proposal.)
2. It can reject the common position by an absolute majority of all members, in which case the Council can proceed with the proposal only by itself acting unanimously at its second reading stage. (If an overall majority for rejection can be found in the EP it is likely that at least one state in the Council will sympathise and that the proposal will fall.)
3. It can amend the common position, in which case the Commission must then decide whether or not it wishes to incorporate the amendments into the version of the text that is referred back to the Council. If it does incorporate them the chances of the amendments being approved by the Council are greatly enhanced, since only a qualified majority vote is required for adoption, whereas any other version requires unanimity.

If the EP does nothing within the three-month period, the Council may adopt the proposal in accordance with the common position. If the Council, on its second reading, does nothing within three months of receiving the re-examined proposal from the Commission (which the Commission must present within a month of receipt from the EP), the proposal is deemed not to have been adopted.

By providing for EP and Council second readings, and by making it difficult – though by no means impossible – for the Council to ignore a majority Parliamentary view, the co-operation procedure increases the potential influence of the EP. Early evidence indicates that this potential is being realised, with more EP amendments being accepted by the Council where the procedure applies than is the case where there is only a single reading. To give just one specific example of EP influence being exercised under the procedure: when, in April 1988, the Council reached its common position on the Commission's hi-tech programme for road transport (DRIVE), it incorporated EP amendments made at the first reading relating to cross-frontier co-operation, greater involvement of small and medium-sized companies, and more sharing of costs. It must be emphasised, however, that the co-operation procedure applies in only limited spheres. In most cases where the Council rejects the EP's Opinion the procedure does not apply and the best Parliament is able to hope for are conciliation meetings with the Council. As was explained in Chapter 5, these do not usually achieve very much, mainly because the Council has no wish to re-open questions which may put at risk its own, often exhaustively negotiated, agreements.

Characteristic Features of Community Policy Processes

A number of general features are characteristic of much Community policy and decision-making. They include compromises and linkages, difficulties in effecting radical change, tactical manoeuvring, and protracted processes.

Compromises and Linkages

The diversity of competing interests across the twelve member states, coupled with the nature of the Community's decision-making system, means that successful policy development is usually heavily dependent on key actors, especially governments, being prepared to compromise. If they are not so prepared, effective decision-making becomes all but impossible.

As part of the process wherein compromises provide the bases for agreements, deals are frequently formulated in which different, and sometimes seemingly unrelated, policy issues are linked. Linking issues together in 'package deals' can open the door to agreements by ensuring that there are prizes for everybody and not, as might be the case when only a specific issue is taken, for just a few.

The European Council has been instrumental in formulating some of the Community's grander compromises and linked deals. For example, it was centrally involved in the bargain which, in 1978, saw Ireland and Italy extract a range of 'compensating' resource transfers in exchange for their agreeing to join the European Monetary System. Again, in 1984, at the Fontainebleau summit, it put together the package that included increasing the Community's budget revenue, decreasing the UK's budgetary contribution, and establishing budgetary discipline guidelines.

One of the reasons the European Council has become involved in the construction of overarching deals of the kind just described is that other Community institutions and actors, and Community processes as a whole, are ill-adapted to linking different policy areas and constructing complex package deals. The Foreign Ministers have a theoretical potential in this regard but, in practice, they tend not to have the political authority or status to impose global solutions on sectoral Councils. As for the sectoral Councils, they do not normally become involved in discussions beyond their immediate policy concern, and they certainly do not have the effective means – except perhaps occasionally in joint Councils – of linking difficulties in their own areas with difficulties being experienced by other ministers elsewhere.

Much Community policy and decision-making thus tends to be rather compartmentalised, and it is within, rather than across, policy compartments that the trading, bargaining, linkaging and compromising that is so characteristic of Community processes are mainly to be found. At Council working group level, trading may consist of little more than an official conceding a point on line 8 of a proposed legal instrument in exchange for support received on line 3. At ministerial level, it may result in a wide-ranging and interconnected package, such as is agreed annually between Agriculture Ministers to make up the farm price settlement.

Difficulties in Effecting Radical Change

Partly as a consequence of the prevalence of compromise, much Community policy and decision-making displays a deep gradualism and incrementalism. It is just not possible for the Commission, the Council Presidency, a national government, or anyone else, to initiate a clear and comprehensive policy proposal, incorporating bold new plans and significant departures from the *status quo*, and expect it to be accepted without being modified significantly – which usually means being watered down. Ambitious proposals customarily find themselves being smothered with modifications, escape clauses, and long transitional periods before full implementation.

The obstacles to innovation and radical change are powerful, and some of them have increased in force over the years. They have done so for four principal reasons. First, the way forward is not as clear as it was in the 1960s, when specific Treaty obligations were being honoured and 'negative integration' (that is, the dismantling of barriers and the encouragement of trade liberalisation) was generally accepted as the main policy priority. Second, the international economic recession that began in the early 1970s has made states more reluctant to cede decision-making powers to the Community. It has also exacerbated the pre-existing tension between a Community founded on an essentially liberal model of integration and states that have traditionally sought to regulate economic life by intervention. Third, the Community is now more politically and ideologically heterogeneous. This is partly because of enlargement and partly because the broad Keynesian consensus on social and economic policy that existed in most Western European countries until the mid-1970s has been called into question by high rates of inflation, high unemployment, and low economic growth. Finally, policy development has inevitably created and attracted interests which have a stake in the *status quo*. This is most obviously the case in agriculture, where Commission proposals for reform invariably produce protests from powerful sectional groups and from electorally sensitive governments. The ability of the farmers' lobby to defend its interests has helped agriculture to dominate the Community budget, which in turn – given the determination of some governments to restrain overall expenditure – has seriously limited policy development in other fields.

Tactical Manoeuvring

Tactical manoeuvring and jockeying for positions are universal characteristics of policy and decision-making processes. However, they are especially apparent in the Community as a result of the multiplicity of its actors and channels and the diversity of its interests.

It is not possible to attempt a comprehensive catalogue of tactical options here, but a sample of the questions that often have to be considered by one category of key Community actors – national representatives in the Council – will serve to give a flavour of the intricacies and potential importance of tactical considerations:

● Can a coalition be built to create a positive majority or a negative minority? If so, should it be done via bilateral meetings or in a Community forum?

● Is it necessary to make an intervention for domestic political purposes? (Although Council meetings are not open to the public or the media most of what goes on – especially in ministerial meetings – gets reported back.)

● Is it possible to disguise an opposition to a proposal by 'hiding' behind another state?

● Should concessions be made in a working party or in COREPER to ensure progress, or should they be held back until the ministers meet in the hope that this will be seen as conciliatory and reap dividends elsewhere?

● How is the necessary balance to be struck between being seen to be tough in the defence of the national interest and being seen to be Community minded and ready to compromise? (Often, on a particular issue, some states have a vested interest in an agreement being reached, while the interests of others are best served by the absence of any agreement and, as a result, the absence of Community obligations).

Protracted Processes

Community processes are often criticised for being cumbersome and slow. Unquestionably, they can be, but it should be recognised that they are not always so. Procedures exist that allow certain types of decisions to be made as and when they are necessary. So, farm price and budgetary decisions are made (more or less) according to a predetermined annual timetable; Commission legislation can be issued almost immediately; and Council regulations and decisions can be pushed through via urgent procedures if the circumstances require it.

The problems arise principally with issues which, for whatever reason, cause difficulties for a state or states, and which are not subject to the dictates of a timetable. In such cases, it may take years for an idea, or even a formally tabled Commission proposal, to achieve legislative status. This is because the Council is, in many respects, weak in its decision-making capability. If just one state decides to dig in its heels against a proposal it can be very difficult for progress to be made. There may not even be much of a concerted attempt to force progress if it is felt that the minority state genuinely has difficulties with the proposal, for governments tend to be very sensitive to one another's needs – not least because they are aware that they themselves may be in a minority one day.

The increasing use of majority voting is quickening the pace in some policy areas. However, speedy and decisive decision-making across the whole policy spectrum will be possible only when it is generally accepted that effective decision-making is as much about the making of decisions as it is about accommodating and safeguarding national interests.

The Efficiency of Community Policy Processes

The Community lacks a fixed, central authoritative point where general ·priorities can be set out and choices between competing options can be made. In other words, there is no adequate framework or mechanism for determining and implementing an overall policy view in which the requirements of agriculture, industry, the environment, etc., are weighed and evaluated in relation to one another and in relation to resources. The Commission, it is true, produces general programmes but it does not itself have the decision-making power to carry them through. In the Council of Ministers, incoming Presidencies set priorities, but these are essentially short-term in nature and are not part of a properly integrated long-term programme. As for the European Council, it has had some limited success in co-ordinating policies, notably at the 1988 Brussels summit when a five-year reference framework for expenditure was agreed (see below and Chapter 11), but it has never attempted to set out anything like a comprehensive Community policy programme.

Within individual policy sectors, there are, as has been shown, many obstacles to coherent and properly ordered policy development. For example, resistance by states to what they regard as an excessive transfer of powers to the Community has undoubtedly resulted in many policy spheres being less integrated and comprehensive in their approach than is – from a policy efficiency perspective – ideally desirable. Regional policy, industrial policy, taxation policy, and policy on social security systems are cases in point: policy responsibilities are shared between the Community and the states – with the former usually in a junior role – and very frequently the activities of the two levels are not properly co-ordinated, and sometimes are not even mutually complementary.

Community policy thus tends not to be the outcome of a rational model of decision-making. That is to say, policy is not normally made via a procedure in which problems are identified, objectives are set, all possible alternatives for achieving the goals are carefully evaluated, and the best alternatives are then adopted and proceeded with. Rather are other models of decision-making often more useful for highlighting key features of Community processes. For example:

The political interests model of decision-making draws attention to the interaction of competing interests in the Community, to the variable power exercised by these interests in different decision-making situations, and to the ways in which decisional outcomes are frequently a consequence of bargains and compromises between interests.

Political elite models highlight the considerable concentrations of power, at official and political levels, that exist across the Community's decision-making processes. Concentrations are especially marked in areas such as monetary and foreign policy, where processes are more secret and more closed than they are, for example, in steel or agriculture. Political elite models also draw attention to the absence of mechanisms available to Community citizens for exercising direct accountability over Community decision-makers.

The organisational process model of decision-making emphasises how the rules and understandings via which decisions are made does much to shape the nature of the decisions themselves. Organisational processes, that is to say, are not neutral. So where, to use Jacques Delors' phrase, policy can only 'make progress twelve abreast', and where every conceivable national, regional and sectional interest is entitled to be consulted before policy can be developed, progress is frequently slow and outcomes are often little more than lowest common denominators. Where, on the other hand, processes are more streamlined – and permit, for example, majority voting in the Council of Ministers, or the Commission to disburse funds directly – then decision-making is likely to be more decisive and, perhaps, more coherent.

Having identified weaknesses in the quality of Community policy and decision-making processes, some re-balancing is now in order lest the impression be left of a system that is wholly and uniquely disordered and undemocratic. There are three main points to be made.

The first point is that, in many respects, Community policy and decision-making processes are not *so* different from national processes. That is not to say that differences do not exist. The international nature of the Community, for example, makes for more diverse and more powerful opposition to its initiatives than customarily exists within states. It is also the case that Community decision-makers are less directly accountable than are national decision-makers to those who are subject to their decisions: the power of the European Council, the Council of Ministers, and the Commission, on the one hand, and the comparative weakness of the EP on the other, does make, as many have observed, for a 'democratic deficit' in the Community. Another difference is that the Community's institutions, taken collectively, are much weaker than their national counterparts. But recognition of these and other differences should not obscure similarities of type – if not perhaps intensity – between Community and national processes: political interest, political elite, and organisational process models of decision-making can throw light on features of the latter, as well as the former. So, for example in all member states, especially those where there are coalition governments (which is the norm in most Community states) political accommodations are an everyday occurrence and policy trimming is common. Furthermore, in those countries where there is a considerable geographical decentralisation of power (as, for example, there is in Germany's quasi-federal system), tensions between levels of government over who does what, and who pays for what, are by no means unusual. In short, many of the Community's decision-making 'problems' – such as the prevalence of incrementalism, of 'irrationality', and of policy slippages – are by no means unknown in national political systems.

The second point is that not all Community policy and decision-making processes are completely a matter of cobbling together deals which can satisfy the current complexion of political forces. These certainly are crucially important features, but they do not amount to the complete picture. In recent years, greater efforts have been made, especially by the Commission, to initiate rather than just to react, to look to the medium-term rather than just tomorrow, and to pull at least some of the pieces together into co-ordinated programmes.

At the level of over-arching policy co-ordination, progress in the direction of more forward-looking and more co-ordinated policy planning has, it must be said, been only modest. But there have been some potentially significant developments. Most notably, the Commission's 1987 document *The Single Act: A new frontier* (see Chapter 3) made recommendations for dealing with what it saw to be the Community's central priorities over the period up to 1992. The programme outlined in the document became the subject of exhaustive Council and European Council negotiations. These negotiations led, at the 1988 Brussels summit, to a package deal which, though the outcome of the usual political trading, did at least address, in an inter-linking five-year financial programme, some, though by no means all, of the Community's most pressing problems (see Chapter 11). Whether the Brussels summit agreement will prove to be a first step in the direction of proper co-ordinated policy development at the general Community level remains to be seen. Given, however, that it was only agreed in circumstances of mounting budgetary and agricultural crises, and given too that it was prefaced by tremendous haggling between the states, the prospects, in the foreseeable future at least, are not too bright.

But if there is a shortage of over-arching policy co-ordination, within certain policy sectors clear medium to long-term policy objectives and rounded programmes are to be found. These are drawn up by the Commission, usually in consultation with appropriate advisory committees and expert groups, and have to be approved by the Council. They appear in various forms: policy documents (for example, 'A future for Community agriculture' which was approved by the Council in December 1985); White Papers (for example, the 1985 Paper that contained detailed proposals for the completion of the internal market); framework programmes (for example, the 1987–91 programme setting out proposed action in the field of research and technological development); and action programmes.

It is worth saying a little about action programmes to illustrate how, within specified fields of activity, a measure of co-ordinated development over a planned medium-term period is possible. Action programmes vary in nature, from the broad and general to the highly specific. The broad and general typically include measures for improving the monitoring and supervision of existing legislation, ideas for new legislation, and spending programmes. Such an action programme, aimed at improving 'equal opportunities for girls and boys in education' was approved by the Education Ministers in June 1985. The ten-point programme was rather modest, as it had to be to attract the support of those governments which are not especially committed to such concerns and/or have little national legislation in the sphere themselves, but the provisions were not without significance. They included: educational and vocational guidance to be provided as a service to all pupils to encourage girls and boys to diversify their career choices; opening schools to working life and the outside world; eradicating persistent stereotypes from school textbooks, teaching materials in general, and guidance and assessment materials; and special measures to help the underprivileged. By contrast with the broad and general action programmes, the specific action programmes are naturally much more specialised in their areas of concern and tighter in their provisions. Examples are the ECSC social research programmes which are given appropriations for a specific period and which provide up to about 60 per cent of the costs of approved research projects. Among such programmes approved in the 1980s was one on safety in mines, which was given a total appropriation of 12.5 million Ecu spread over five years, and one on industrial hygiene in mines, which was allocated an appropriation of 11 million Ecu over five years.

The third, and final, 're-balancing' point to be made about Community processes is that critical judgements about how the Community functions ought to be placed in the context of the considerable degree of co-operation and integration that has been achieved. There is no comparable international development where individual states have voluntarily transferred so many policy responsibilities to a collective organisation of states and, in so doing, have surrendered so much of their national sovereignty. It is hardly surprising, given the enormity of the exercise, that pressures and desires for co-operation and integration should so often be challenged, and held in check, by caution, uncertainties, conflicts, and competition.

11

The Budget

The Community raises and spends money in many different ways. Mostly it does so within the framework of the annual budget, and it is with the budget that this chapter is concerned.

Before examining the budget, however, the Community's non-budgetary revenue raising and spending operations will be outlined. This will enable a full picture of the Community's financial instruments and activities to be presented. The non-budgetary revenue raising and spending operations fall into four main categories:

● The Community borrows sums on capital markets which are then made available, in the form of loans, to both public and private undertakings for investment. The European Investment Bank, which is the principal source of Community investment finance, has already been discussed in this connection (see Chapter 8). Borrowing and lending operations, to assist projects of many different sorts, are also conducted in respect of the ECSC, Euratom, and the New Community Instrument (NCI) which has as its general purpose assisting the financing of investments which make for greater convergence and integration in member states' economic policies.

● Borrowing and lending activities, of a different sort, are also undertaken to enable member states to cope with balance of payments difficulties. The Community Loan Instrument was established for this purpose in 1975, and in 1979 standby arrangements between the Central Banks were created within the framework of the European Monetary System.

● The European Development Fund, which finances aid to the African, Caribbean and Pacific countries under the Lomé Convention, is not resourced from the budget but from direct contributions by the member states.

● The ECSC is resourced from its own funds, the principal component of which is a levy on coal and steel production.

Turning now to the Community budget, one point needs to be emphasised at the outset: despite the considerable attention it has received over the years, and despite the enormous amount of political acrimony it has generated, the budget is, in fact, relatively small. In 1988 it amounted to 43.6 billion Ecu: about £28.6 billion and $53.2 billion at May 1988 exchange rates. This represented only about 1.15 per cent of the Gross Domestic Product of the member states and about 3.0 per cent of the total of their national budgets.

The modesty of these figures should be borne in mind when assessing the financial and policy impact of the budget. Clearly there can hardly be said to have been a major transfer of financial resources from national exchequers to the Community.

The Composition of the Budget

Revenue

Following a decision taken by the member governments in 1970, the funding of the Community's budget was changed between 1970 and 1975 from a system based on national contributions to one based on 'own resources'. A major reason for bringing about this change was that it would give to the Community an increased financial independence. The member states would determine the upper limit of the own resources, but the resources themselves would belong to the Community and not the states.

At the time of the introduction of the new arrangements the own resources consisted of customs duties, agricultural levies, and a proportion of Value Added Tax (VAT) up to a 1 per cent ceiling. At the beginning of the 1980s, however, it became apparent that these resources were not capable of generating enough income to meet the Community's increasing financial obligations. The member states could, in theory, have resolved this problem easily enough by raising the own resources limit, but some states – the UK in particular – were reluctant to do this. The consequence was that the Community experienced a series of budgetary crises in the early 1980s. These crises led, eventually, to the conclusion of a complicated deal at the 1984 Fontainebleau European Council. Key elements of the deal included new rules on budgetary discipline, a formula for reducing UK budgetary contributions (which were generally recognised as being excessive), and an expansion of own resources through the setting of a new 1.4 per cent ceiling for VAT from 1986. The Fontainebleau agreement was, however, too little too late, in that no sooner had the 1.4 per cent ceiling been introduced in 1986 than it was exhausted and the Commission was forced to open a new campaign for a further expansion of the revenue base.

That campaign culminated in the 1988 Brussels summit which saw a further – but as compared with Fontainebleau, much more radical – package deal designed to resolve the Community's recurring budgetary difficulties. Included in the deal were provisions for expanding certain categories of expenditure, a continuation of special arrangements for the UK, a much tighter framework for ensuring budgetary discipline, and a significant expansion of own resources through the creation of a new own resource.

A financial perspective for the years 1988 to 1992 was agreed as part of the Brussels package, and it is within the context of this perspective that the expansion of own resources is to occur. Own resources are to be linked to an expanding spending programme, subject to the limitation that the total amount of own resources for any one year may not exceed the following percentages of the total GNP of the Community for the year in question – 1988: 1.15; 1989: 1.17; 1990: 1.18; 1991: 1.19; 1992: 1.20

The creation of the new resource at the Brussels summit means that the own resources now consist of the following:

● *Common Customs Tariff duties and other duties* which are collected in respect of trade with non-member countries.

● *Agricultural levies, premiums and other duties* which are collected in respect of trade with non-member countries within the framework of the CAP. These differ from customs duties in that they are not fixed charges on imports, but are fluctuating charges designed to have the effect of raising import prices to Community levels. There are also certain internal agricultural levies and duties, notably within the framework of the common organisation of the market in sugar, which have as their purpose limiting surplus production.

● *The application of a 1.4 per cent rate to the VAT assessment base* which is determined in a uniform manner for member states. So as to protect countries whose VAT base is high, the assessment base for VAT may not exceed 55 per cent of the Gross National Product at market prices. (It should be emphasised that these VAT rules still allow countries to vary their specific national VAT rates – though the Commission is pressing for these to be harmonised around two bands.)

● *The application of a rate to a base representing the sum of member states' Gross National Product at market prices.* This is the Brussels-agreed fourth own resource. The rate is determined under the budgetary procedure in the light of the total of all other revenue and the total expenditure agreed. Since this resource is very much like a national contribution, it has been suggested by many observers that it does not have quite the own resource character of the other resources.

The four resources constituted the following proportions of budgetary revenue in respect of the 1988 budget – VAT: 56.9 per cent; customs duties: 20 per cent; the new fourth resource: 16.5 per cent (initially paid in the form of national contributions in 1988 since the new own resource arrangements could not come into effect until all national legislatures had ratified the relevant Council decision); and, agricultural and sugar levies: 6.6 per cent. Relative proportions in the 1989 draft budget were almost identical.

Expenditure

The Community makes a distinction between expenditure which is a direct result of Treaty application or acts adopted on the basis of the Treaties – called compulsory (or obligatory) expenditure – and that which is not – called non-compulsory (or non-obligatory) expenditure. The former has regularly taken up between two-thirds and three-quarters of the total budget – and, of this, over 90 per cent has gone on farm price guarantees. Two main factors account for this dominance. First, agriculture has seen a greater transfer of financial responsibility from national budgets to the Community budget than any other major policy area. Secondly, as is shown in Chapter 12, an agricultural price guarantee policy has been pursued that has kept Community prices well above world prices, and in a number of product sectors this has resulted in production levels well in excess of the capacity of the market. In consequence, the Community has had to pay for agricultural produce it does not require: by buying up surplus production; by storing it; by selling it at subsidised rates on domestic and world markets; and by converting it into animal feed.

On a 'rational' and 'commonsense' basis this can hardly be justified. Agriculture is clearly over-funded, whilst policy areas drawing on non-compulsory expenditure – which, as Table 11.1 shows, includes such key policies as regional policy, social policy, and energy policy – have access to only very limited resources. However, budgetary expenditure, like budgetary income, is not determined by 'objective' criteria but by political interplay. And in that interplay there are many powerful forces which wish to maintain high levels of spending on agriculture: governments anxious to receive farmers' votes do not normally wish to upset this often volatile section of the electorate, and net beneficiaries of the CAP (both states and sectional interests) are not inclined voluntarily to surrender their gains.

However, notwithstanding these obstacles to reform, the pressures for radical change were becoming intense by the mid to late 1980s: previous schemes for reducing agricultural expenditure were having only a marginal effect; ever-larger surpluses for some products were being predicted; and some states were becoming increasingly anxious to increase non-agricultural spending. As a result, important measures designed to bring about a gradual shift in the Community's pattern of expenditure were agreed to as part of the 1988 Brussels package deal.

Central to these expenditure measures was a five-year programme for reducing agricultural spending on the one hand (see Chapter 12 for details), and a programme for doubling spending on the structural funds (mainly the Regional Fund and the Social Fund) by 1993 on the other. These programmes were given added force when, in June 1988, the Presidents of the Council of Ministers, the Commission, and the European Parliament, signed, on behalf of their respective institutions, the *Interinstitutional Agreement on Budgetary Discipline and Improvement of the Budgetary Procedure* (see Document 11.1). The importance of the *Interinstitutional Agreement* is that it contains a formal commitment by all three Community institutions to the framework of the financial perspective for the years 1988 to 1992 that is attached to the Agreement. The financial perspective is based on the Brussels agreement and envisages the proportion of agricultural expenditure over the period of the perspective being reduced to around 60 per cent of total budgetary expenditure, and the proportion of expenditure on structural operations being almost doubled.

TABLE 11.1

The Community Budget 1988

	Commitment appropriations*	Payment appropriations*
1 *European Agriculture Guidance and Guarantee Fund – Guarantee*	27,500	27,500
2 *Structural Policies*		
European Agriculture Guidance Guarantee Fund – Guidance	1,130	1,151
Fisheries	339	281
European Regional Development Fund	3,684	2,980
Mediterranean Policies	134	86
Specific Agricultural Activities	68	61
Other Regional Activities	126	66
Transport	65	65
Social Fund	2,865	2,600
Social Miscellaneous	83	81
Education, Information, Communications and Culture	89	89
Environment and Consumers	28	29
Total 2	8,620	7,499
3 *Research, Energy, Industry*		
Energy Policy	127	108
Research and Investments	1,016	910
Information and Innovation	20	21
Industry and Internal Market	90	67
Financial Engineering	7	7
Total 3	1,262	1,114
4 *Repayments and Reserves*	4,726	4,726
5 *Development and Third Country Co-operation*		
Food Aid	374	320
Co-operation with Latin-American and Asian Developing Countries	307	262
Specific and Occasional Activities	144	139
Co-operation with Mediterranean Countries	140	71
Miscellaneous	34	34
Total 5	1,001	827
6 *Personnel and Operating Funding*	1,965	1,965
GRAND TOTAL	45,125	43,633

NB 1. The financial year runs from 1 January to 31 December.
 2. Payment appropriations cover expenditure during the financial year. Commitment appropriations cover expenditure during the financial year plus liabilities extending beyond the year.

Note
*In millions of Ecu. The value of the Ecu in May 1988 was: 1 Ecu = £0.65 = $1.23.

DOCUMENT 11.1

Extracts from the
INTERINSTITUTIONAL AGREEMENT

ON BUDGETARY DISCIPLINE

AND IMPROVEMENT OF THE BUDGETARY PROCEDURE

I. BASIC PRINCIPLES OF THE AGREEMENT

1. The main purpose of the Interinstitutional Agreement is to achieve the objectives of the Single European Act, to give effect to the conclusions of the Brussels European Council on budgetary discipline and accordingly to improve the functioning of the annual budgetary procedure.

2. Budgetary discipline under the Interinstitutional Agreement covers all expenditure and is binding on all the institutions involved for as long as the Agreement is in force.

3. This Agreement does not alter the respective budgetary powers of the various institutions as laid down in the Treaty.

4. The contents of the Interinstitutional Agreement may not be changed without the consent of all the institutions which are party to it.

II. BUDGET FORECASTS: FINANCIAL PERSPECTIVE 1988 to 1992

A. Contents

5. The financial perspective 1988 to 1992 constitutes the reference framework for interinstitutional budgetary discipline. Its contents are consistent with the conclusions of the Brussels European Council; it forms an integral part of the Agreement ....

B. Nature

7. The European Parliament, the Council and the Commission recognize that each of the financial objectives laid down in the perspective 1988 to 1992 represents an annual expenditure ceiling for the Community. They undertake to observe the different ceilings during the corresponding budgetary procedure.

8. The European Parliament, the Council and the Commission will join in the effort undertaken by the Community gradually to achieve a better balance between the various categories of expenditure.

   They give an undertaking that any revision of the compulsory expenditure figure given in the financial perspective will not cause the amount of non-compulsory expenditure shown in the perspective to be reduced ....

III. BUDGETARY DISCIPLINE FOR COMPULSORY EXPENDITURE

14.   (a) The European Parliament, the Council and the Commission are in agreement on the conclusions of the European Council concerning budgetary discipline for compulsory expenditure in the EAGGF Guarantee Section.

      The three institutions undertake, within this Agreement, to respect these conclusions.

  (b) The European Parliament, the Council and the Commission confirm the principles and the mechanisms for the agricultural guideline and the monetary reserve.

  (c) As regards the other compulsory expenditure, the three institutions undertake to honour the Community's legal obligations in a manner consistent with the financial perspective.

IV. BUDGETARY DISCIPLINE FOR NON-COMPULSORY EXPENDITURE AND IMPROVEMENT OF THE BUDGETARY PROCEDURE

15. The two arms of the budgetary authority agree to accept, for the financial years 1988 to 1992, the maximum rates of increase for non-compulsory expenditure deriving from the budgets established within the ceilings set by the financial perspective.

16. The Commission will present each year, within the limits of the financial perspective, a preliminary draft budget based on the Community's actual financing requirements.

    It will take into account:

    − the capacity for utilizing appropriations, endeavouring to maintain a strict relationship between commitment appropriations and payment appropriations;

    the possibilities for starting up new policies or continuing multiannual operations which are coming to an end, after assessing whether it will be possible to secure a proper legal base.

17. Within the maximum rates of increase for non-compulsory expenditure specified in paragraph 15 of this Agreement, the European Parliament and the Council undertake to respect the allocations of commitment appropriations provided in the financial perspective for the Structural Funds, the Specific Industrial Development Programme for Portugal (PEDIP), the Integrated Mediterranean Programmes (IMPs) and the Research-Technology-Development (RTD) framework programme.

    They also undertake to bear in mind the assessment of the possibilities for executing the budget made by the Commission in its preliminary drafts ....

FINANCIAL PERSPECTIVE

Commitment appropriations

(million ECU at 1988 prices)

	1988	1989	1990	1991	1992
1. EAGGF Guarantee	27 500	27 700	28 400	29 000	29 000
2. Structural operations	7 790	9 200	10 600	12 100	13 450
3. Policies with multiannual allocations (IMPs, research)	1 210	1 650	1 900	2 150	2 400
4. Other policies	2 103	2 385	2 500	2 700	2 800
of which non-compulsory	1 646	1 801	1 860	1 910	1 970
5. Repayments and administration (including financing of stock disposal)	5 700	4 950	4 500	4 000	3 550
	1 240	1 400	1 400	1 400	1 400
6. Monetary reserve	1 000	1 000	1 000	1 000	1 000
TOTAL	45 303	46 885	48 900	50 950	52 800
of which compulsory	33 698	32 607	32 810	32 980	33 400
non-compulsory	11 605	14 278	16 090	17 970	19 400
Payment appropriations required	43 779	45 300	46 900	48 600	50 100
of which compulsory	33 640	32 604	32 740	32 910	33 110
non-compulsory	10 139	12 696	14 160	15 690	16 990
Payment appropriations as % of GNP	1,12	1,14	1,15	1,16	1,17
Margin for unforeseen expenditure	0,03	0,03	0,03	0,03	0,03
Own resources required as % of GNP	1,15	1,17	1,18	1,19	1,20

Source: *Official Journal of the European Communities* L185, 15 July 1988

So as to present a more detailed picture, than is shown in the financial perspective, of particular budget allocations, the main headings of the 1988 budget (the first year in which the financial perspective was applied) are presented in Table 11.1. The most striking feature about the distribution of the funds is the relatively modest sums available in all categories other than that for agricultural price guarantees. So, to take three key areas of non-compulsory expenditure: the European Regional Development Fund (ERDF), which has as its aim the correction of serious disparities in levels of development and prosperity in different regions of the Community, is allocated 8 per cent; the European Social Fund, which is primarily concerned with vocational training and employment promotion activities, especially amongst youth, is allocated 6 per cent; and research activities are allocated 2 per cent. As is explained above, and is apparent from Document 11.1, these potentially very important areas are all scheduled to expand under the financial perspective, but even when they have reached their limits in 1992 the Community's financial capability to effectively act as an agent for tackling pressing problems such as under-investment, technological change, unemployment, and regional imbalances will remain very limited.

Budgetary Decision-making

The Budgetary Process

A timetable and set of procedures for drawing up and approving the annual budget is laid down in Article 203 of the EEC Treaty (as amended in 1970 and 1975). However, in practice, Article 203 gives only an approximate and rather formal guide to what actually happens. It provides a framework which has been fleshed out and adapted over time in response to pressures, necessities, and convenience.

Because variations occur from year to year it is difficult to describe the 'typical' way in which the budget is made. In broad terms, however, and assuming no major problems exist or arise to severely disrupt the process, the pattern is as follows.

Preparation of the Preliminary Draft Budget. The Commission gets down to work on the budget in the late winter/early spring of the year before which it is due to come into effect. In attempting to look this far ahead – almost twelve months to the beginning of the financial year (in January) and twenty-four months to its close – the Commission is necessarily faced with many uncertainties on both the revenue and expenditure sides. Agriculture causes particular difficulties. For example, crop yields cannot be foreseen: a small change in weather conditions might raise production in a particular product from 101 per cent of consumer demand to 102 per cent, thus resulting in a considerable underestimate of the amount of budget support required for that product. Another problem is that agriculture expenditure is highly dependent on world agricultural prices and currency movements which cannot be controlled: a falling dollar can have a drastic effect on Community finances because export subsidies for farm products are linked to dollar-denominated international market prices. (The fall of the dollar in December 1986–January 1987 alone added more than 1 billion Ecu to spending commitments.)

The Commission has, therefore, to make many assumptions, some of which, in the event, may not be realised. If changed situations become apparent during the course of the budgetary cycle corrections can be made fairly easily: by sending rectifying or amending letters to the Council and the Parliament. If, however, the financial situation changes for the worse during the budgetary year itself, that is more serious. In the past, 'temporary' solutions, such as postponement of payments, delays in the introduction of new programmes, and supplementary budgets have been used. Following the 1988 Brussels summit, it is hoped that recourse to such measures will not be necessary in the future. This hope rests on the agreed growth in Community resources, the limits set on expenditure, and stronger management powers which were granted to the Commission so as to enable it to take appropriate action at an early stage if agricultural expenditure rises too rapidly.

The prime responsibility within the Commission for drawing up what is known as the Preliminary Draft Budget (PDB) falls to the Directorate General for Budgets (DGXIX). Inevitably it is subject to pressures from many sides: from other DGs who forward their own estimates and bids; from national representatives – both through the Council and on a direct lobbying basis; from the EP, especially leading figures of its Committee on Budgets; and from sectional interests. The Budget Commissioner and officials from DGXIX have many meetings, of both a formal and informal kind, to enable many of these interested parties to have their say. Naturally, those that have the most chance of achieving some satisfaction are those that carry political weight and/or are already in tune with Commission thinking.

Once DGXIX has its proposals ready they must be presented by the Commissioner to his fellow Commissioners, and all must agree on the package. When they do, the proposals officially become the Preliminary Draft Budget.

In the past, the PDB has disappointed those who have wanted to see the budget used as the motor for change in Community priorities. The Commission did, in the 1980s, make several attempts to use the PDB to effect at least modest shifts in policy emphases – notably by proposing the containment of agricultural expenditure and the expansion of the structural funds – but its manoeuvrability was always severely restricted by existing expenditure commitments, and also by the knowledge that any significant change that it might propose from the *status quo* would be fiercely resisted in the Council. The 1988 Brussels summit agreement and the *Interinstitutional Agreement* have now changed this situation by setting out a framework and a programme for using the budget to effect change. Three interrelated aspects of the 1988 agreements are especially crucial. First, the budget must conform with the principles of the agricultural guideline – which means that the rate of increase in agriculture guarantee expenditure in any one year must not exceed 74 per cent of the annual rate of increase in Community Gross National Product (see Chapter 12 for further details). Second, the budget must be set within the framework of the financial perspective 1988 to 1992. As Document 11.1 shows, the perspective contains a financial programme for altering the balance of Community expenditure. Thirdly, the Commission, the Council, and the EP, are strictly bound to respect the ceilings set out in the financial perspective. (Apart from technical adjustments the financial perspective can be revised only by a joint decision of the Council and the EP, acting on a proposal from the Commission.)

The financial perspective does not, it should be emphasised, totally constrain the Commission when it draws up the PDB. It does have manoeuvrability below the ceilings, and it does have options within expenditure headings. The financial perspective, in other words, is not a straightjacket. But it does place very clear limits on what the Commission can do.

Council First Reading. Assuming there are no major or special problems, the PDB is referred to the Council at the end of May or in early June.

Most of the Council's detailed examination of the budget is undertaken by the Budget Committee, a working group of national officials who, in what are frequently long and exhaustive sessions, examine the PDB chapter by chapter, line by line. As the date of the Ministers' meeting in the Budget Council approaches, the Committee is likely to meet with increasing frequency in order to resolve as many issues as possible. The negotiators are in almost constant contact with their national capitals about what transpires in the Committee, and so they mostly have a prepared view when items come up for discussion. When this produces a rigidity in negotiating positions, much responsibility is thrown on the chairman to find a solution. The Commission can assist him in this task.

From the Committee the draft proceeds to COREPER. The number of unresolved items put before the Permanent Representatives naturally depends on what has happened in the Committee. Normally, much remains to be done, and COREPER attempts, like the Commitee, to clear as many items as possible before the Ministers meet. It is usually most successful with those issues which do not have a potentially conflictual political aspect attached to them.

The Ministers customarily meet in mid-July, although there have been occasions when they have not gathered until September. Before beginning their deliberations they meet a delegation from the EP which is comprised, usually, of the Parliament's President, the chairman of the Committee on Budgets, half a dozen or so Committee members, and perhaps two or three other committee chairmen. The main purpose of this meeting, which is the first of two formal occasions when the Council and the EP meet under budgetary conciliation procedures, is to enable the EP to outline its thinking on the budget and to voice its early reactions to the PDB. The MEPs' observations do not normally have much effect: at this stage the Ministers are primarily concerned with reaching an agreement between themselves.

Prior to the Brussels summit, the Budget Council normally lasted for a couple of days and involved 15 to 20 hours of negotiations in formal sessions, plus extensive informal discussions and manoeuvrings in the wings. Qualified majority voting usually allowed a draft to be eventually agreed, but on controversial proposals a blocking minority sometimes existed. On two occasions the divisions between the states were such that the July meeting was unable to approve a draft, which meant that there had to be a reference back to officials. The officials then produced a new package for the Ministers to consider when they returned in September – by which time the timetable was pressing and an agreement had to be reached.

The reason why the July meeting was often so difficult was that the states differed, both in their views about the balance to be struck between restraint and expansion, and in their perceptions of problems and priorities. What emerged, therefore, was a draft reflecting accommodations and compromises. Almost invariably, however, the general thrust of the draft was, on the one hand, to propose a tighter overall budget than that envisaged in the PDB, and, on the other hand, to propose some shift from non-compulsory expenditure to compulsory expenditure – that is, from items such as regional, social and research expenditure (which were relatively 'soft' because of their non-compulsory character) to agriculture (which was difficult to touch given existing commitments).

The Brussels summit package and the *Interinstitutional Agreement* will almost certainly have two effects on the Council first reading stage. First, they will make the process less divisive and troublesome than in the past. Secondly, they will oblige the Council to produce a first draft that is very similar to the PDB. The reason for these likely outcomes – which did indeed occur in the case of the first two budgets under the new arrangements (the 1988 and 1989 budgets) – is simply that the Council, like the Commission, is now much more constrained in what it can do.

Parliament First Reading. On being approved, the Council's first draft is referred to the Parliament. If the timing is suitable the President of the Budget Council may formally present the draft himself: to the Budget Committee and/or in an address to the plenary.

Although this presentation of the Council's draft marks the first formal point at which the EP becomes involved in the budgetary process, it always, in practice, has been attempting to exert influence for some time: key Parliamentary figures feed views into the Commission and the Council as best they can; the PDB is sent by the Commission to the EP at the same time as it is referred to the Council, and the Committee on Budgets begins its considerations almost immediately; and, as was indicated above, an EP delegation meets the Budget Council before the latter's first reading.

Now, with the Council's draft available, the pace is stepped up. There is a brief debate in plenary session, but the detailed work is given over to committees. The Committee on Budgets naturally has most responsibility. It examines the budget in detail itself, and it also acts as a co-ordinating agency for reports submitted to it by other EP committees which look at the budget to see how their sectors are affected. The Committee on Budgets does not have the power completely to control what goes forward to the plenary – it cannot, for example, stop an amendment that has support elsewhere, especially if it is backed by any of the larger political groups – but its views are usually respected. Its collating of views from other committees, and from other sources within the EP, is therefore very important. But it is an extremely difficult task, for hundreds of proposed changes (500 for the 1989 budget) are put forward, many of which conflict with one another, or are even mutually exclusive. Much, therefore, rests on the liaising, organising, and leadership skills of the Committee chairman and the appointed *rapporteur*.

The intention is normally to hold the plenary session dealing with the budget in October, but if the submission of the Council's draft is delayed it may have to be put off until November. At the plenary MEPs can do three things with the contents of the Council's draft: accept them; propose amendments to non-compulsory expenditure (which requires majority support of members); propose modifications to compulsory expenditure (which requires majority support of votes cast).

As with both the drafting of the PDB and the Council first reading, the EP's first reading will be affected by the Brussels summit and the *Interinstitutional Agreement*. In the past, the customary pattern at this stage was for the EP to propose increases in non-compulsory expenditure (over which, as explained in Chapter 5, it has greater power than it does over compulsory expenditure) and often, also, to raise general points of principle. So, for instance, in 1984 – re the 1985 budget – the Parliament complained about the lack of provision for a projected budget deficit; in 1985 – re the 1986 budget – it criticised the inadequate provision for the accession of Spain and Portugal and for the 'weight of the past'; and in 1986 – re the 1987 budget – it stressed the urgent need to tackle agricultural over-expenditure. The position since the Brussels summit and the *Interinstitutional Agreement* is that there should not be such a gap between the Council and the EP. This is because of the obligations and constraints of the financial perspective which, in addition to partly satisfying some of the EP's policy ambitions – through the changes in projected expenditure patterns – also reduces the significance of the distinction between compulsory and non-compulsory expenditure.

However, it should not be thought that all possible grounds for dispute between the EP and the Council have been removed by the *Interinstitutional Agreement*. One area, for example, where there is considerable room for potential disagreement and conflict is a distinction being insisted on by the Council since the Brussels summit in non-compulsory expenditure between privileged and non-privileged expenditure. The main policy areas in the privileged category are the structural funds, research, and the Integrated Mediterranean Programmes, whilst the non-privileged category includes policy areas such as transport, energy, and fisheries. The importance of the distinction is that the Council is applying a 'maximum rate of increase' to non-privileged expenditure. In doing so it is continuing with a device which, before the *Interinstitutional Agreement*, was applied to all non-compulsory expenditure. A problem, however, is that the EP is refusing to accept the validity of the distinction between privileged and non-privileged expenditure, arguing that there is no basis for it in the Treaties. This means potential conflict in the budgetary process, since the maximum rate feeds into budgetary decision-making at several points: (a) the Commission calculates the rate each year according to a complex formula based on inflation, growth of national budgets, and the overall level of economic growth (the maximum rate for the 1989 budget, announced by the Commission in April 1988, was 5.8 per cent – meaning, as it must every year, much lower levels of increase for non-privileged expenditure as opposed to privileged expenditure); (b) the Council applies – or, at least, has usually done so in the past – half the maximum rate at its first reading of the budget; (c) the EP applies the other half of the maximum rate in the course of its first reading (on several occasions during the 1980s the EP exceeded 'its' half, in the hope that the Council would accept an overall increase in the maximum rate); (d) the Council ensures, at its second reading, that the overall maximum rate is respected; (e) at its second reading, when the budget is supposed to be finally adopted, the EP is under strong pressure to respect the overall maximum rate, because if it does not do so the Council may challenge the legality of the EP's actions – as it did with the 1986 budget which it referred to the Court of Justice, claiming that the EP had exceeded the maximum rate without the Council's assent.

After the EP has debated the draft budget in plenary session, and after all amendments and modifications have been voted upon, a resolution on the budget is adopted by the Parliament.

Council Second Reading. From Parliament the draft goes back to the Council where officials prepare for the ministerial second reading which is usually held in mid to late November. If issues remain to be settled activity can be feverish, and many meetings may be held to try and achieve progress. Amongst such meetings could be one under the

'Tripartite Dialogue' (or Trialogue as it is commonly called), by which the Presidents of the Council, the EP, and the Commission can meet at any time during the budgetary procedure to consider unresolved problems.

At some point, the second formal conciliation meeting with an EP delegation is held. In taking their decisions the Ministers are thus well aware of what is likely to meet with EP approval, and what is likely to produce a full scale row and endanger possible adoption.

In looking at the EP's proposed changes, the Budget Council can, within the financial perspective, take three sorts of decisions:

● Acting by a qualified majority, it can modify amendments to non-compulsory expenditure.

● Acting by a qualified majority, it can reject modifications to compulsory expenditure that do not have the effect of increasing total expenditure. In the absence of decisions to reject them, proposed modifications stand as accepted.

● Acting by a qualified majority, it can accept modifications to compulsory expenditure that have the effect of increasing total expenditure. In the absence of decisions to accept them, proposed modifications are rejected.

Where it is clear that Parliament's views have not been fully met, and particularly where significant funds are involved or possible points of principle are at stake – such as on the classification of a certain type of expenditure – then the Council has to decide whether it wishes to close the door on the matter (and hope for the best at the EP's second reading) or leave it ajar for a possible compromise. In the past this has produced sharp divisions in the Council, raising, as it does, the possibility of budgetary rejection.

Parliament Second Reading. The EP holds its second reading on the budget in December. What happens before, at, and after the plenary depends very much on the extent to which contentious issues remain unresolved.

If the situation is relatively straightforward and most problems have been sorted out, then the normal procedure is for the Committee on Budgets to meet, to reinsert such non-compulsory expenditure as it legally can and, on this basis, to recommend adoption. The plenary then votes, and if the budget is approved the President formally signs it and declares it to be adopted.

But where, as prior to the Brussels summit was frequently the case, major differences between the Council and the EP remain, the two sides are obliged to get down to negotiations. Various procedures can come into play: the President of the Budget Council, accompanied by the Budget Commissioner, may meet with the Committee on Budgets; the President of the Budget Council may make an appeal to the plenary; a Trialogue meeting may be hald; or a special Budget Council may be hurriedly called, perhaps to meet again with an EP delegation, perhaps to give the budget what is, in effect, a third reading. If all efforts to reach a Council–EP agreement fail, the latter can reject the budget by a majority of its members, including two-thirds of the votes cast.

Non-approval of the budget. In five of the first nine years following the introduction of direct elections in 1979, budgets were not approved in time to be implemented at the beginning of the financial year on 1 January. These were the budgets of 1980 and of 1984–8.

If a legal budget is not approved by the EP before 1 January a fall back position applies. This allows for funding to continue, but only on the basis of what are known as 'provisional twelfths', which means that spending is limited to the monthly average expenditure of the previous year. Policies do not therefore collapse, but some payments may have to be suspended, and programmes, especially those that are new, may have to be delayed. A speedy agreement on the budget of what is, by this stage, the current financial year, is thus desirable.

There is no formal procedure or set pattern regarding what happens in the event of non-adoption. The expectation and assumption is that the process is resumed at the point at which it broke down, but practice has shown matters not to be so simple. Developments following non-adoptions have varied considerably, depending principally on the reasons for the non-adoption. So, for example, the 1986 budget was, like those for 1985 and 1988, not approved until halfway through the financial year. The problem with the 1986 budget was not that a budget was not approved by the EP in December 1985, but rather – as noted above – that the Council judged the budget that had been adopted by the EP to be illegal on the grounds that it included more non-compulsory expenditure than was legally permissible. The Council, therefore, asked the Court of Justice for a ruling. On 3 July 1986 the Court eventually delivered its judgement and, in essence, upheld the Council's claim that the budget was illegal. The next week then saw hectic activity, a truncated budgetary procedure and, on 10 July, the adoption of a budget in which creative accountancy and financial ingenuity played prominent parts.

The Brussels summit package and the *Interinstitutional Agreement* remove, or at least blunt the sharpness of, many of the problems that occasioned non-adoption of budgets in the 1980s. In particular, agricultural expenditure is made subject to stronger budgetary discipline, the size of the structural funds is increased, and mechanisms are established to improve the match between income and expenditure. Of course, not all differences or potential problems are removed. But the prospects of budgets normally being adopted at December plenaries are considerably enhanced.

Characteristic Features of the Budgetary Process

Some features of the process that has just been described merit particular comment.

First, the budget, like the annual agricultural price review, is unusual in the Community decision-making context in the sense that it is supposed to operate according to a clear timetable. Legislative proposals can be pushed along if they are strongly supported, but the usual pattern is for them to drag on in the Council until some sort of agreement is reached, and if this proves not to be possible they may be indefinitely postponed or even dropped altogether. With the budget such a relaxed and open-ended approach is not possible, since expenditure and resource decisions have to be made each year. The existence and exigencies of the timetable thus introduce an urgency into budgetary decision-making that is rarely found in other spheres of Community decision-making.

Second, the power balance between the institutions is not the same on the budget as it is elsewhere. Whereas the Council and the Commission are the main decision-makers in most policy sectors, with the EP often struggling to make its voice heard, in respect of the budget the Council and the EP jointly constitute the budgetary authority, and are co-decision-makers. The Commission remains important, but after the presentation of the PDB it is cast in an essentially servicing capacity: responding to what happens in the Council and the Parliament and doing what it can to bring the two sides together. As for the particular nature of the balance between the

Council and the EP, the former is unquestionably the stronger, but, as was noted in Chapter 5, the *Interinstitutional Agreement* does open the way for some tilting in the direction of the EP. It does so by establishing a precedent of all three institutions agreeing to future expenditure patterns, by binding all sides into a relationship which it will be difficult for them to modify without the agreement of the other parties, and by giving the EP a glimpse of shared control over compulsory expenditure.

Third, budgetary decision-making is the only significant decision-making area where Council majority voting has long been common. This has enabled decisions to be made more easily, but it has not necessarily improved their quality. With a blocking minority in the Council needing 23 votes out of 76, and a qualified majority requiring 54, states inevitably have had to look for allies, have had to agree to reciprocal arrangements, and have had to give support in return for support received. This has resulted in budgetary decisions being heavily dependent on the outcome of pushing and pulling between different institutions and interests.

Fourth, many of the arguments and confrontations that have occurred during the budgetary process have been occasioned not so much by the financial sums involved – which have usually been relatively small – but more by a broader institutional struggle, especially between the Council and the EP. With the EP dissatisfied with its overall position in the Community system, it is only natural that it should have sought to use the budget, where it does have real powers, to maximum advantage. There are a number of ways in which it has gone about this. One has been its increased willingness since 1979 to reject the budget. Another has been interpreting the Treaties, along with agreements and understandings about budget-ary decision-making, in ways which are advantageous to itself – as on matters such as the bases for budgetary calculations, and the classification of expenditure in terms of compulsory and non-compulsory. And, a third way has been by attempting to exploit differences within the Council – by, for example, seeking to exert pressure in a particular direction through the indication of preferences in plenary votes or, less formally, in inter-institutional exchanges such as conciliation meetings.

Fifth, certain fundamental budgetary decisions are not taken via the annual budgetary process. As has been shown, decisions on resource ceilings, on 'rebates' for countries making excessive budgetary contributions, and on budgetary discipline, have all been taken by the European Council. (Although, of course, these European Council decisions have had to be given legal form by the Council of Ministers).

Sixth, and finally, the effectiveness of the budgetary process has, like virtually all Community decision-making, tended to be weakened by the absence of a consensus amongst decision-makers as to how the Community should develop, and also by the lack of any single body that has been in a position to impose a framework based on long-term, or even medium-term, priorities. As a result, budgetary outcomes have tended to be incremental in nature, constituting marginal adjustments to the *status quo*, rather than introducing and allowing for significant changes in policy direction. The 1988 agreements, by setting out a programme for altering the balance of spending programmes, allow for some modest changes in this situation. They do not, perhaps, bring 'cohesive' or 'objective' budgetary planning much closer, but they do enable the budget to become the instrument for important – though not radical – reform.

12

Agricultural Policy and Policy Processes: A Detailed Study

Agriculture looms large in the life of the Community. It does so in three main ways. First, it is the most regulated Community policy sector Second, as the major recipient of EC funds, it dominates Community financial deliberations and serves to restrict policy development in non-agricultural spheres. And third, there is a greater institutional presence and activity in the agricultural field than in any other: the Agriculture Ministers meet more frequently than all other Councils except for the Foreign Ministers; uniquely, Agriculture Council meetings are prepared, not by COREPER but by a special body, the Special Committee on Agriculture (SCA); DGVI, the Directorate General responsible for agriculture, is by far the largest of the Commissions twenty-two DG's; and there are far more Council working groups and Commission management and advisory groups in the sphere of agriculture than in any other single policy area.

For its supporters, the CAP is important both in itself – the benefits accruing from joint policy making and common management are seen as far outweighing the disadvantages – and important, too, as a symbol and indicator that real policy integration is possible at Community level. Those who criticise the CAP are thus liable to be attacked, both on technical and efficiency grounds (with the claim that national solutions would be much less satisfactory) and more broadly for being *non communautaire* (with the assertion that the only true Community policy should not be undermined). For opponents of the CAP, economic efficiency is the key issue. Subsidisation of wealthy farmers, high prices for consumers, and production of farm surpluses which nobody wants are the most frequently heard criticisms.

Yet even among those who are most critical of the CAP few seriously challenge the view that there should be a Community agriculture policy of some kind. Certainly no state believes that the agricultural edifice should be uprooted and policy returned to national capitals. The view that there is something special about agriculture, something that distinguishes it from other sectoral activities and merits it receiving advantageous treatment, while not commanding such strong support as in the early days of the Community, still strikes a chord with Community decision-makers.

Why Does Agriculture have a Special Place in the Community?

The attention given to agriculture in the EEC Treaty, and the subsequent creation of the CAP through long and often tortuous negotiations, is often seen as being part of a trade-off between France and Germany. There is something in this view. In exchange for the creation of a common market in industrial goods, which the French feared would be greatly to Germany's advantage, France – with its large, but rather uneconomic, agricultural sector – would benefit from an agricultural system which, though also in the form of a common market, would be based not on free and open market principles, but on foundations which would protect farmers from too much competition.

Important though it was, however, the Franco-German 'deal' provides only part of the explanation for why agriculture, from the earliest days of the Community, was given an elevated policy status. For the fact is that when the CAP was being created in the late 1950s and 1960s, none of the then six member states seriously objected to it in principle, though there were differences on the pace of its construction and the precise nature of its policies. This consensus on the general principle was a result of a shared recognition that agriculture required special treatment.

Today, despite the EC having increased in size from six to twelve, despite the circumstances and conditions of agriculture having dramatically changed, and despite the CAP having caused major difficulties and disruptions to the whole Community system, agriculture is still generally regarded by the national governments as requiring special treatment. Many of the reasons for this are much the same as they were in the EC's early days. Others are more recent. They can be grouped under two general headings: the distinctive nature of agriculture, and political factors.

The Distinctive Nature of Agriculture

For many years, but especially since the Second World War, most governments of the industrialised world have taken the view that agriculture is not like other areas of economic activity. It is special and merits special treatment to encourage, to assist and to protect it. In the Community the main arguments that have been advanced in support of this view have been as follows.

(1) If they are not controlled by public authorities agricultural prices are more subject to fluctuation than are the prices of most other goods. This can result in an extremely undesirable price instability. It is undesirable for two reasons. First, if prices suddenly go up inflation will be immediately fuelled (given that food constitutes around 24 per cent of the budget of the average Community citizen), whilst at the same time low income groups may suffer particular distress since food constitutes a disproportionately high part of their expenditure. Second, if prices fall too low, farmers may not be able to make an adequate living and may be forced off the land. Even those who are able to stay in farming may experience severe difficulties as a result of the high debt loads carried by many farmers on land and capital purchases.

(2) Reliance on imports for vital foodstuffs creates a potential political vulnerability to outside pressures. It is a particular source of weakness during periods of strained international relations.

This factor is not, perhaps, so important now, but in the early years of the EC, when memories of wartime shortages and of the vulnerability and misery this occasioned were fresh, it played an important part in encouraging a drive for greater self-sufficiency.

(3) Because people must have food, insufficient domestic production means that the gap between output and demand has to be met by imports, with potentially damaging consequences for the balance of

payments. Moreover, since the demand for food is fairly inelastic up to necessity levels – as long as income allows it food will still be bought even if prices go up – the economic vulnerability of an importing state is high.

Naturally, as certain vital food products in the Community have moved into surplus – notably dairy produce, cereals, and meat – this self-sufficiency argument for increased farm production has lost much of its force; all the more so since the disposal of the surpluses is expensive owing to world prices being lower than Community prices.

(4) Social reasons for keeping farmers on the land have been increasingly heard in recent years. Sometimes these have an idealistic tone to them, with pleas that a populated countryside is part of the natural fabric, or the suggestion that management of the land is a desirable end in itself. Rather more hard-headed perhaps is the argument that, with rising unemployment in the EC since the early 1970s – to an overall average of around 13 per cent in 1987 – it is both undesirable and potentially dangerous to allow farm incomes to deteriorate to the point that poor farmers and agricultural workers are forced to move to the towns in search of employment that does not exist.

Political Factors

Farmers enjoy political assets that they have been able to translate into influence on Community policy. Three of these assets aré especially important:

(1) At the national decision-making level, Ministries of Agriculture have tended traditionally to be slightly apart from mainstream policy processes, and since 1958 this has been reproduced at the Community level. All policy areas, of course, attempt to use their own expertise, knowledge and information to provide themselves with some insulation from the rest of the decision-making system, but agriculture is particularly well placed to be able to do this. Its supposed special nature, the complexity of much of its subject matter, the customary close relations between agricultural decision makers and producers all make it difficult for 'outside' decision makers to offer an effective challenge or alternative to what is presented to them. At the Community level, this is compounded by the particular strength of DGVI and the fact that co-ordination of policy areas has never been a strong point of either the Commission or the Council of Ministers.

(2) Farmers enjoy considerable electoral weight. Even though their relative numerical importance has declined sharply over the years – in 1958 around 25 per cent of total Community employment was in agriculture, by 1988 it was around 8 per cent – the agricultural vote is still very significant. The significance varies from state to state. The size of the domestic population engaged in agriculture is one important factor: proportions range from around 30 per cent in Greece and 24 per cent in Portugal to 3 per cent in Belgium and the UK. Another consideration is the direction of the vote. On the whole farmers, especially richer farmers, incline to Centre–Right and Right parties, with the consequence that it is they, rather than parties of the Left, which are usually the strongest defenders of agricultural interests in Community forums. But this inclination to the Right does not, in most countries, amount to an exclusive loyalty, so few parties can afford to ignore the farmers altogether: at a minimum they must give the impression of being concerned and solicitous.

(3) Farmers have long had very strong domestic organisations to represent and articulate their views. When it became clear that much agricultural policy and decision-making was to be transferred to Brussels, similar organisations were quickly established at Community level. As early as 1963, some 100 Community-wide agriculture groups had been formed. By the late 1980s, this number had grown to around 150. The most important of these groups is COPA which is an umbrella or peak organisation representing all types of farmers on the basis of affiliation through national farming groups (see Chapter 8). Beyond COPA and a few other over-arching organisations, specialist bodies exist to represent virtually every product that is produced and consumed in the Community, and every stage of the agricultural process – farmers most obviously, but also processors, traders, retailers, etc.

There can be no doubt that this agricultural lobby has been, and remains, a very powerful force in the Community. It is worth setting out the reasons why.

The sheer size of the lobby is formidable. It operates at two levels, the national and the Community.

At the national level, there are considerable variations in the pattern and strength of agricultural representation. But, in all states, there are groups of some kind which have as part of their purpose the utilisation of whatever devices and channels are available to them to influence both national agricultural policy (within the general principles of the CAP, states still enjoy a considerable policy discretion) and Community agricultural policy. Thus, the National Farmers Union for England and Wales employs a full-time professional staff of around 240 at its London headquarters and 600 or so in the regions. Additionally it funds, in conjunction with the NFU of Scotland and the Ulster Farmers Union, a Brussels office, known as the British Office of Agriculture, which has a regular staff of between five and ten who are topped up as required.

At the Community level, the large number of Euro-agric groups means that lobbying activities across the agricultural sector are almost continuous. COPA moves on the broadest front and, with some forty-five full-time officials, is by far the best resourced and staffed organisation. The more specialised groups – the mustard makers (CIMCEE) for example, or the butchers (COBCCEE) – are much more modestly provided for and may have, at best, one full-time member of staff working in an office made available by a national affiliate. But since the interests of these small groups is usually narrowly drawn this may be enough to allow basic lobbying requirements to be fulfilled – meetings and consultations with decision-makers, feeding information through to the Community institutions, preparing policy and briefing documents. If circumstances require it reinforcements are usually available from national and Euro-umbrella associations.

Agricultural interests generally enjoy good contacts with, and access to, decision-makers. Again, this factor operates at both national and Community levels.

At the national level, influence with governments is vital, not only because of their control over nationally determined policies but also because they are the route to the Council of Ministers. Most governments are at least prepared to listen to representations from agricultural interests, and some engage in a virtual automatic consultation on important issues. There are a number of reasons why governments are generally approachable in this way: there may be a pre-existing sympathy for the interests' views; a fuller picture of what is going on in the agricultural world is made possible; policy implementation may be made easier; and political support may be generated by being sympathetic or at least by giving the impression that the government and the interest are as one. If, in the event, the interest is dissatisfied with what is agreed in the Council the government can always try to blame 'the awkward Italians', 'the impossible Greeks', or 'the immovable Germans'.

At the Community level, the Commission is the prime target for agricultural interests. For the most part it is only too willing to listen. Indeed, it has encouraged the establishment of Euro-agric groups and readily makes itself available to them. They are seen as useful channels for a number of purposes, and close Commission-group relations are believed to be of more advantage to the former than to the latter: the interests can contribute their knowledge and their experience which may improve policy; the Commission can explain to the interests why it is engaging in certain actions and thus seek to sensitise them to Commission concerns and aims; face-to-face meetings can help break down barriers and resistance arising from suspicions that 'the bureaucrats in the Berlaymont' do not really understand farming practicalities; and if Euro-groups can do something to aggregate the conflicting national interests and demands that arise in relation to most proposals, they can considerably simplify the Commission's task of developing policies that are acceptable and can also help to legitimate the Commission as a decision-maker in the eyes of the Council and the EP.

The agricultural organisations are not counter-balanced by strong and vigorous groups advancing contrary attitudes and claims. 'Natural' opponents do exist – consumers and environmentalists most notably – but they are weak by contrast. A major reason for their weakness is that whereas farmers constitute a clear section of the population with a readily identifiable common sectoral interest, consumers and environmentalists do not have such a group consciousness, are dispersed, and, in consequence, are just not so easy to mobilise or organise. So, though there are many more consumers than there are farmers in the EC, the largest of the Euro-consumer groups – the Bureau of Consumer Associations (BEUC) – carries a staff of only seven or eight. This is respectable enough when compared with most Euro-groups, but it pales when compared with the massed ranks of the agriculture associations. Moreover, the BEUC has to cover the whole spectrum of relevant Community policies; agriculture takes up only part of its time.

In terms of access to decision-makers the farmers' 'rivals' do not, as a rule, enjoy the 'insider status' granted to the agriculture lobby. They rarely have a 'sponsoring' ministry in the way that agricultural interests do. Nor are they consulted by the Commission as a matter of routine, or automatically called in for discussions when something of importance or potential interest arises. The fact is that they do not have the political and economic power of farmers, they cannot offer trade-offs in the way of co-operation on policy implementation, they are – in some instances – relative latecomers, and a few – notably the more radical 'Greens' – are seen as not quite conforming with established values and the rules of the game. Some of the more respectable of these 'oppositional' groups have their foot in the Community door, but none has quite entered the room.

Agriculture has powerful friends. While farmers and those directly engaged in the agricultural industries have been the most obvious beneficiaries of the CAP, others have gained too, notably the owners of land. Huge profits have been made by investment institutions, financiers, banks, industrial corporations and private landlords from the rising value of land that has been triggered by the CAP. Many of these interests have direct access to decision-makers, indeed are numbered among the decision-makers in some governments, and have sought to use their influence accordingly.

Until the mid-1980s unity was a considerable source of strength. Despite the great range of interests represented, the agriculture lobby was, until the mid-1980s, more or less united in its aims: it pressed for comprehensive market regimes for as much produce as possible, and it sought the largest price increases it could get. In recent years, however, as the first significant steps to bring agriculture spending under proper control have been taken, the unity of the lobby has been subject to increasing strains and its effectiveness has accordingly been weakened a little. Sectors have vied with one another as more careful attention has had to be paid, not only to the size of the cake, but also to the way in which it is cut.

How the Common Agricultural Policy Works

Title II of the EEC Treaty (Articles 38–47) sets out the general principles of the Community's agricultural policy. The objectives are laid down in Article 39:

(a) to increase agricultural productivity by promoting technical progress and by ensuring the rational development of agricultural production and the optimum utilisation of the factors of production, in particular labour;

(b) thus to ensure a fair standard of living for the agricultural community, in particular by increasing the individual earnings of persons engaged in agriculture;

(c) to stabilise markets;

(d) to assure the availability of supplies;

(e) to ensure that supplies reach consumers at reasonable prices.

Many matters are barely touched on in Title II and were deliberately left aside for later consideration by representatives of the states. Among the first fruits of these deliberations was the adoption by the Council of Ministers in December 1960 of the three major operating principles of the CAP. These still apply today:

A Single Internal Market with Common Prices

Agricultural goods are supposed to be able to flow freely across Community borders, unhindered by barriers to trade and unhampered by devices such as subsidies or administrative regulations which might distort or limit competition. However, it is not a free trade system based on pure market principles because common prices are set by the Council for most important products. These prices include a target price, which is the price it is hoped farmers will be able to obtain on the open market, a threshold price, which is the price to which Community imports are raised, and a guaranteed or intervention price, which is the price at which the Commission will take produce off the market by stepping in and buying it up (see Figure 12.1). The amount of support a product is given is a consequence of how high these prices are set, the size of the gap between prices, and the way in which price and currency mechanisms (see below) and intervention practices function.

The price support system, which exists primarily to maintain farm incomes, dominates the CAP. It does so mainly because it is so costly to finance.

There are three principal reasons why it is expensive. First, many goods are produced in amounts that are surplus to Community requirements. Between 1973 and 1984 the Community's level of self-sufficiency increased from 104 per cent to 151 per cent for butter,

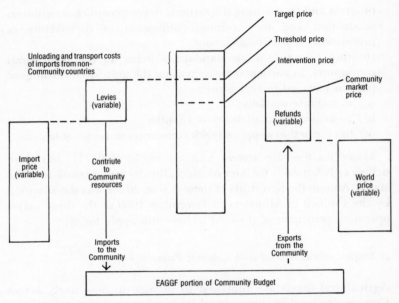

Source: Adapted from *The Common Agricultural Policy and its Reform*, European Documentation, 1987.

FIGURE 12.1
Outline of the different price levels and the levy and refund system for a full market regime product.

from 90 per cent to 105 per cent for cereals, from 90 per cent to 101 per cent for wine, and from 92 per cent to 123 per cent for sugar. High guaranteed prices are the main reason for these surpluses, but improved farming techniques and the concentrated use of fertilisers and additives have also played a part. Second, the range of products protected by a market regime has gradually been extended so that now 94 per cent of all Community produce is covered in some way. Different regimes provide different forms of protection – so that in practice there are several agricultural policies rather than just one – but most (around 70 per cent) are the beneficiaries of support prices, either on an unconditional and open ended basis, or (more commonly, following various Council decisions in the 1980s), subject to restrictions such as quotas and production thresholds. Third, apart from a brief interlude in 1974–5, Community agricultural prices have consistently been above world prices, which has meant that it has not been possible to export surpluses wthout suffering a financial loss: the loss being the difference in price between what the Community has agreed to pay the farmer and what it can sell the product at on world markets. Many devices are used to dispose of the surpluses – exporting and providing a refund (a 'restitution' in Community jargon) to the exporter to ensure he incurs no loss on the transaction, storing until Community prices rise, food aid, converting to animal foodstuffs – but they all have to be financed from the Community budget.

In addition to its cost, another major problem with the agricultural price system is that, apart from a short initial period, it has never been truly based, as intended, on common prices. This stems from the absence of a single European currency. The prices that are agreed annually by the Agriculture Ministers for products that are covered by a market regime are set in European Currency Units (Ecu) – which are based on a 'basket' or weighted average of the national currencies. For payments purposes Ecu are then converted into national currencies. (Following an agreement made in April 1984 support prices are set not in 'standard' Ecu but in a special 'green' Ecu called the agricultural unit of account which is linked to the deutschmark.)

If the exchange rates at which Ecu are converted into national currencies were the same as those which obtain on the open market common agricultural prices would exist. In practice, they are not. This is principally because market rates in the late 1960s and early 1970s became subject to sharp and rapid fluctuations, and this had implications for agriculture which governments were not prepared to accept: farmers' incomes and food prices were affected and trade patterns became distorted. As a result, it was decided to try to stabilise agricultural incomes, prices, and markets by the use of 'green' rates of exchange which would be set by the Agriculture Ministers and which would remain fixed whatever happened to the market rates of exchange. To ensure that differences between market rates and green rates would not distort intra-Community flows in agricultural products a system of border levies and subsidies, known as monetary compensation amounts (MCAs) was also introduced.

As a result of this system, the setting of agriculture prices cannot be viewed in isolation from exchange rates. Trade-offs are common, with, for example, a government that feels pressurised by its farmers, agreeing to low price increases only on the condition of being allowed to devalue its green rate on specified products. (Each currency has not one green rate but several.) The Commission has pressed for the abolition of green rates for some time on the grounds that they undermine common prices, make a claim on the budget, and weaken encouragement to product specialisation. Governments, however, tend to look upon the price-exchange rate linkage as a useful device for protecting their farmers or consumers and for giving themselves a greater flexibility in Council negotiations.

Community Preference

A necessary consequence of the guaranteed price system is that the Community market should be protected from the international market. Since world prices are normally lower than Community prices free access onto the Community markets would clearly destroy the whole CAP system. Community preference is, therefore, required. Whether, however, it is required at quite such preferential levels as in practice apply is a matter of dispute, the balance of judgement depending on the sympathy afforded to farmers on the one side and consumers on the other.

The mechanics of the preference system vary according to the market regime for the product concerned. For the 21 per cent of produce which has a market regime but not one based on guaranteed prices (wines other than table wines, some fruit and vegetables, some cereals, eggs and poultry), external protection takes the form of levies, customs duties, and a combination of the two. For the 70 per cent of produce which does enjoy guaranteed prices (most cereals, dairy produce, milk, beef, lamb) the system is such as to prevent imports entering the Community at prices below the agreed target prices. This exclusion is, as is shown in Figure 12.1, achieved by the threshold price which is calculated at a level to bring the world price up to the Community's target price, minus an allowance for unloading and transport costs. The gap between world prices and the threshold price is bridged by the imposition of a levy, which is adjusted according to variations in Community and world prices. The levies become part of the Community's own resources.

The exclusion procedures just described do not apply to all the imports into the Community from all states. As was explained in Chapter 9, the EC has negotiated arrangements by which a large number of countries, most of them underdeveloped, are given special access to Community markets for at least some of their products, including agricultural products. So, the Community grants 'generalised preferences' to more than 120 developing countries and one effect of this has been the abolition or reduction of levies on about 300 agricultural products intended for processing. Under the Lomé Convention virtually all of the exports of the 66 ACP countries have free access to the Community. (It should perhaps be pointed out here that these 'concessions' do not stem simply from generosity and goodwill. Much of the produce falling under the generalised preferences and Lomé agreements is tropical in nature and not in competition with EC produce.)

Joint Financing

The cost of the CAP is financed jointly by the states through the European Agricultural Guidance and Guarantee Fund (EAGGF) of the Community budget. This is divided into two sections: the Guarantee section which finances markets and prices, and the Guidance section which finances structural policy. The early intention was that the Guarantee section would be larger than the Guidance section by a ratio of two or three to one, but, in practice, this has never been even remotely approached, and the Guidance section hovers somewhere in the region of only 5 per cent of total EAGGF expenditure. The demands on the Guarantee section occasioned by high Community prices is the main reason for this imbalance, but another factor has been that the member states have never given much support to structural policy, mainly because it usually involves contraction or bringing about changes to which agricultural interests are opposed.

But notwithstanding the limited size of the EAGGF Guidance section, there is still a very considerable amount of non-price related agricultural expenditure in the EC. Some of this comes from other Community sources – in particular the Regional Fund, Integrated Mediterranean Programmes, and the European Investment Bank. By far the most of it, however, comes from national exchequers: member states being allowed to assist their farmers in almost whatever way they like as long as they do not – in the judgement of the Commission – distort competition or infringe the principles of the market. In some states national subsidies to agriculture far outstrip those of the Community.

The Impact and Effects of the Common Agricultural Policy

Whether the CAP is to be regarded as a success or not obviously depends on the priorities and interests of those making the judgement. Since, however, the issue raises so much controversy it is worth examining some of the major consequences of the CAP system. This will be done via the five aims that were set out in Article 39 of the EEC Treaty and which were listed above.

Agricultural efficiency has increased enormously as a result of modernisation and rationalisation. Furthermore, despite the popular impression in some places that the CAP is little more than a device to cushion farmers, agriculture, both as a proportion of GNP and as a source of employment, has more than halved among the original six since 1958. That said, it may still be asked whether the over-production of certain products at great cost, and the encouragement that high prices have given to many who would otherwise have left the land to stay, is wholly consistent with 'ensuring the rational development of agricultural production . . . '.

Under the CAP *agricultural incomes have grown roughly in parallel with incomes in other sectors*. However, this overall average masks enormous variations, both between large farmers (who have done very well for the most part) and small farmers, and also between producers of northern temperate products (notably dairy produce, cereals and beef which are the main product beneficiaries of the price support system) and producers of other – mainly Mediterranean – products.

Markets have been stabilised, in the sense that there have been no major food shortages and Community prices have escaped the fluctuations that have occurred in world market prices on some products.

The Community is *now self-sufficient in virtually all of those foodstuffs its climate allows it to raise and grow.* (In 1958 it produced about 85 per cent of its food requirements.) However, in some sectors it is much more than self-sufficient and, because of the high domestic prices, the surpluses can be disposed of only at considerable cost.

The exclusion of cheaper (and often much cheaper) produce from outside the Community means that *the aim of 'reasonable prices' to the consumer has had a low priority*. The undeniable fact is that, within the Community, the principal beneficiaries of CAP's pricing system have been rich farmers, while the main losers have been poor consumers. It might also be added that the exclusion of efficient non-Community producers has had an impact at the international level too – notably in distorting the international division of labour and the rational utilisation of resources, and in fuelling trading hostilities.

Policy and Decision-making Processes

In many respects, policy and decision-making processes for agriculture are much the same as in other policy sectors. However, the importance, the range, and the complexity of the CAP, plus the ever-changing nature of the world's agricultural markets, means that there are significant variations from the 'standard' Community model. The principal variations are as follows.

Commission Initiation and Formulation

Whereas the policy initiation and formulation responsibilites of the Commission in most sectors are much concerned with creating a policy framework, in agriculture they are inevitably directed more towards improving the efficiency of one that already exists.

But, as has been indicated above, there are formidable obstacles in the way of the Commission if it is to come forward with proposals that both go to the heart of the agricultural problem and are also acceptable to the Council. As long ago as 1968 the then Commissioner for Agriculture, Sicco Mansholt, launched a major plan to reduce the size of the agriculture sector and improve the efficiency of what remained, but his proposals had little effect and were not followed up by enough Council legislation. As a result the Commission in the 1970s approached its policy initiation and formulation responsibilities in a very cautious way. It became reluctant to advance wide-ranging schemes aimed at fundamental reform and concentrated more on short-term measures of an essentially reactive nature: reacting, that is, to specific problems in particular market sectors.

In the 1980s, circumstances changed in such a way that they enabled, even obliged, the Commission to bring a longer-term view back onto the agenda and force real and properly integrated reform to be at least seriously discussed. The most important of these circumstances were deteriorating market conditions and increasing surpluses, recurring budgetary problems, international pressures against the EC's high levels of protectionism and subsidisation, and the enlargement of the Community to states which would not do especially well out of the CAP as constituted. It was to this background that in 1985 the Commission launched a consultative Green Paper outlining policy options and the future of agriculture until the end of the century. After wide-ranging discussions with interested parties the Green Paper was followed up with more detailed guidelines in the form of a communication to the Council and the EP entitled 'A future for European agriculture'. At the heart of the Commission's proposals lay an ambitious long-term strategy for a movement to a more market-based and restrictive pricing policy, more flexibility in guarantees and intervention mechanisms, and a greater degree of producer co-responsibility for surpluses. These objectives were re-stated in the Commission's influential 1987 document '*The Single Act: A new frontier for Europe*', and constituted the basis for the important agricultural reforms that the Agriculture Ministers agreed to in December 1986 and the Heads of Government agreed to in February 1988. (Both of these agreements are considered below.)

Council Decision-making

Of all the Councils, the Agriculture Council is the one which is most reliant on issue linkages and package deals for conducting its business.

One reason it *has* to be so reliant is that, whereas in some sectors issues can be allowed to drift almost indefinitely, in agriculture certain decisions, most obviously those taken as part of the annual price review (see below), cannot be continually postponed. They must be resolved, but a resolution is normally possible only if it is based on a recognition of the different interests and priorities of the states: most states, for example, are net exporters of agricultural produce, but a minority are net importers; some have temperate climates, some Mediterranean; some have mainly large and efficient farms, others still carry many small and inefficient family based units; and some have vast tracts of 'less favoured' land, while others have very little.

A major reason the Council is *able* to make use of linkages and packages is that is has available to it a variety of possible policy instruments. By bringing these together in carefully weighted combinations the way can often be opened to agreements in which there is something for everyone.

An example of a package deal is the one which was struck on beef and dairy products in December 1986 when the ministers responded to Commission initiatives (noted above) and Council Presidency (UK) pressure to tackle surplus production. A range of measures were agreed (see Exhibit 12.1), but only after days of negotiations involving ministers and senior officials, after some of the Commission's more radical measures were watered down, and after 'softening' and 'compensating' devices of various kinds were approved. With the agreement still leaving a projected dairy surplus of around 12 per cent above total domestic consumption (even on the

---

EXHIBIT 12.1

Package agreed by Ministers of Agriculture, December 1986*

1) A commitment to achieve a 9½ per cent reduction in milk production over a two year period by a mixture of voluntary and mandatory cuts in quotas. Farmers to be paid compensation. (Some of the measures in this part of the deal – notably the temporary nature of a proportion of the quota cuts and the high level at which compensation was set – were included primarily to pacify the Germans who had an election due. Ireland succeeded in persuading the Council to instruct the Commission to note the 'unique dependence' of Ireland upon the dairy sector, especially in relation to intervention. Unofficial estimates by the Commission put the real size of the reduction at around only 6 per cent.)

2) An agreed 13 per cent reduction in the guaranteed price for beef, and changes in the operation of the beef intervention system. (Ireland threatened to veto the whole package if, as was initially proposed, it was excluded from receiving a new form of compensatory payment for beef producers on the grounds that its farmers were already being adequately supported. A compromise resulted in Ireland receiving a scaled down version of the new funds.)

3) Green rate devaluations: 14.5 per cent on Greek sheepmeat; 4.8 per cent on French beef and veal and 3.185 per cent on sheepmeat; 6 per cent on Portuguese sheepmeat; 3.2 per cent on Spanish sheepmeat; 6 per cent on UK beef and veal and 3.2 per cent on sheepmeat. (The effect of these devaluations would be to boost farmers' incomes in the five countries concerned.)

4) Structural measures. The details of these were left to be worked out at a later stage but it was agreed they would include encouragement for early retirement, provisions for less intensive farming, and the adoption of a flexible attitude towards any government which wished to top up Community funds with contributions of its own.

*Only the four main elements of the package are set out here.

extremely doubtful assumption that the new quotas would be properly applied in all the states), and with the decisions on beef really doing little more than adjusting market support to changes in beef production, the package hardly merited the description of 'historic importance' which some of the participating ministers attached to it. Rather was it a typical Agriculture Council compromise.

What the exhaustive negotiations of December 1986 produced was esssentially a political deal. As with many agreements/pronouncements/resolutions/declarations in the Community, translating the deal into implementing legislation subsequently proved to be very difficult. A particular problem was that some governments, on analysing the implications of the deal in detail and at greater leisure, readjusted their positions. The Danes, the French, the Germans and the Irish – all perhaps influenced by the implications of what was becoming known would be very restrictive Commission price proposals for 1987–8 – decided they had been hard done by. Later Council meetings were thus obliged to debate again issues supposedly resolved at the December meeting.

Management and Implementation of the Common Agricultural Policy

Because of the nature of the CAP, the Community is much more involved in the management and implementation of agriculture than it is in other policy spheres. The Commission, and particularly DGVI, are central in this regard. They oversee the general operation of the whole system, they adjust it as necessary, and, insofar as it is possible, they try to ensure that the national agencies which undertake the front line implementation of policy – Ministries of Agriculture, intervention agencies, and customs and excise authorities – do so in a regular and proper manner.

In exercising these duties the Commission must operate within Community law and Council guidelines. This means that much of what it does in managing the CAP is of an essentially technical nature: adjusting regulators to match ever-changing market conditions. But in some spheres it can do this in ways that amount to rather more than simply applying tightly drawn rules. Many of its decisions – for example on the operation of the intervention and support systems, on refunds, on storage – are taken within margins of manoeuvre that give it at least some flexibility. It is a flexibility that can result in the Commission's choices having important financial implications for producers, traders, processors, and the Community budget.

Where payments and charges have to be adjusted almost daily, and in other instances where quick management decisions have to be taken, the Commission is authorised to act without reference to any other body. However, as was explained in Chapter 3, the Commission's general agricultural management responsibilities are not exercised by Commission officials alone but via management committees. There are over twenty such committees, including one for each product that has a market regime, and the Commission would not normally go ahead with anything important – setting a price on butter sales to the Soviet Union for example – without referring to the appropriate committee, and to the Council if necessary. It is generally accepted that the Commission should determine the direction and set the pace in the committees but, as is intended, their very existence does inevitably mean that the states can exercise a direct influence over all but the fine details of agricultural policy.

The Annual Price Review

A distinguishing feature of agriculture decision-making is that many of the key decisions are made as part of a regular annual process: in the price review. Contrary to what the name suggests, prices are not the only element of this. Many elements get swept up and become components of what is usually a highly complex and interconnected package by the time the final agreement is made. The core of the package usually consists of a range of different product price increases, green currency adjustments, structural measures, and statements of intent about future action.

The price year for most products begins on 1 April and the intention of the Commission is always to have a settlement before this date. To achieve this a timetable exists that is supposed to culminate with the Agriculture Council making decisions in March. In practice, the later parts of the timetable have not been respected in recent years and agreements have been delayed into April, May, and even July in 1987. This has obliged the Council to prolong the previous year's allocations in order to permit payments still to be made.

There is an important sense in which price reviews are a constant part of the work of DGVI, since market situations are subject to constant monitoring, while medium to long-term schemes for agricultural reform have to be implemented, to some extent at least, via reviews. The systematic work on particular reviews, however, is concentrated into the six to seven month period before they are due to come into effect. The main stages are as follows:

(1) In September the directorates and divisions begin to analyse and draw up reports on such matters as quantities, state of stocks, prices, and exports in their market sectors. This is essentially a technical exercise.

(2) During October and November consultations occur between the Commission and interested parties. Some of these are in the structured settings of management and advisory committees, others are more informal exchanges between DGVI officials and representatives of governments and sectional interests.

(3) The first drafts from the various sectors should be ready by mid-November. The process of integrating them necessitates several rounds of meetings involving the Commissioner for Agriculture, members of his *cabinet*, the director general, assistant directors general, directors, and senior officials representing the three main product areas of the review – livestock, crops, wine. In attempting to bring everything together the Commissioner and his advisers have to bear in mind a number of considerations:

● Commission and Council policy preferences drawn from both rolling programmes and continuing commitments.

● The limitations imposed by the agricultural reference framework. Recognising that previous attempts to control agricultural expenditure via budgetary discipline guidelines had not been successful, and faced with growing agricultural surpluses and (another) impending budgetary crisis, the Heads of Government at their February 1988 Brussels summit agreed to a radical new reference framework for agricultural expenditure. The key feature of the framework is that from a reference base of 27.5 billion Ecu EAGGF Guarantee expenditure for 1988, annual growth rates in subsequent years must not exceed 74 per cent of the annual rate of increase in Community Gross National Product. (If the maximum possible EAGGF financing for set-aside schemes is included – that is to say finance made available under the Brussels agreement to encourage farmers to take agricultural land out of production, or out of certain types of production – the 74 per cent rate corresponds to 80 per cent.) It is intended that the reference framework will make a major contribution to significantly decreasing the proportion of the Community budget that is devoted to agriculture (see Document 11.1).

● The likely effect of penalties, some of the more important of which were also agreed at the Brussels summit, for particular products where guarantee production thresholds set for those products are exceeded. Some penalties come into force in the current financial year, and some in the next. So, for example, in the important case of cereals, if the agreed threshold (set at 160 million tonnes up to the 1991/2 marketing year) is exceeded, then a co-responsibility levy of up to 3 per cent is introduced in the next financial year.

● Political factors and the implications proposals may have for states. If, for example, a national election is coming up, a decision may have to be made over whether to draw up the budget early in an attempt to minimise its political impact or deliberately delay it.

(4) On being agreed in DGVI a draft is submitted to the Commissioners for their approval. Ideally this submission is made by mid-December, although often the timetable slips and it may be later.

The Commissioners' deliberations are preceded by meetings of members of their *cabinets* assisted by senior officials from DGVI. If all goes well a general agreement on most key points can be reached at this stage. The Commissioners themselves, however, have to approve the final proposals. Whether this is largely a formality or involves difficult negotiations depends on what has happened at the pre-meetings.

(5) As soon as they are agreed, the Commission's proposals are sent to the Council, and also to the ESC and the EP for Opinions.

The influence of the ESC is very marginal. This reflects its limited role in the Community as a whole, though such potential for exerting influence on the review as it does have is not helped by its customary inability to take a united view on agriculture questions. So, its Opinion on the 1987/8 Commission proposals – which incorporated agreements, disagreements, and agreements subject to conditions – was adopted (at the April plenary because of a timetable slippage) by 94 votes to 53 with 12 abstentions; that is, only half of the ESC's 189 members supported the Opinion.

The EP, by virtue of its greater power and authority, is listened to rather more seriously – or, at least, the Commission and the Council strive harder to give the impression that they are listening. Most MEPs, however, fully realise that they are hardly central actors in the price review exercise. Indeed, largely because of this, the EP has abandoned its former practice of holding a special session on the review and now incorporates its debate and the delivery of its Opinion into the March plenary. (Or, as in 1987 when deliberations were delayed until the May plenary, as soon as is practicable.) The proceedings are conducted on the basis of a report drawn up by the Agriculture Committee in consultation with other interested committees. So, in 1987 three reports were presented and debated in relation to the 1987/8 review – one on agricultural prices and related matters, one on the reform of the oils and fats policy, and one on the olive oil section. Voting resulted in an Opinion comprising over fifty observations/suggestions/complaints to the Commission on the material covered by the first report, nearly thirty on the second, and over thirty on the third.

In the Council, ministers are likely to have an early meeting to give their first reactions to the Commission proposals. All will arrive well armed with briefs and analyses as to how the proposals will affect their farmers, their consumers, their budgetary contributions, their balance of payments, etc. In all probability most will say the proposals are too restrictive, and all twelve will put down markers for future meetings by identifying particular points that are unacceptable as they stand. Subsequent ministerial meetings will be arranged as necessary, by which time new points may have arisen and others may have been resolved as a result of meetings at lower Council levels: most of the agricultural working groups (of which there are around twenty-five, including one for each of the principal commodity regimes) will meet at least twice to consider the Commission's proposals as they affect their areas; and the SCA (see Chapter 4) will try to pull the working groups' reports together and give them an overall coherence.

(6) In the light of views expressed – and quite apart from formal pronouncements by the ESC, the EP, and the Council, intense lobbying campaigns are conducted by national and sectional interests – the Commission makes adjustments to its proposals. These are designed to improve the prospects of a settlement in the Council, while clinging to as much of its own first draft as possible.

(7) Towards the end of March, or later if proceedings have fallen behind schedule, the Agriculture Council meets to try to agree a settlement. Marathon sessions are common, and meetings may have to be reconvened if solutions cannot be found at the first time of asking.

Each minister naturally tries to get the best terms he can and wishes also to be seen to be putting up a vigorous defence of national interests. This makes for extremely difficult negotiations, with much posturing and striking of attitudes on the one hand, and, on the other hand, genuine differences on such matters as price preferences, Community budgetary implications, elimination of surpluses, and commitments to farmers and consumers. Complicated package deals, with many non-price factors being dragged in to increase flexibility, are usually the only means by which a solution can be found. (Exhibit 12.2 is an example of a typical package.) Voting is common, and ministers may well make their vote of approval on one issue dependent on guarantees of support on another. So, minorities on cereal prices may find compensation in green currency adjustments, thus giving all participants something to point to when they leave the negotiating table.

In theory, the final package which constitutes the annual price review should be agreed by the end of March. In practice, it has tended not to be so. In 1987, for example, the timetable fell behind schedule from an early stage when, as a result of differences over cereal prices, green currency devaluations, and a proposed tax on oils and fats, the Commission's draft proposals were delayed. When they were made available, negotiations in the Council, on these same issues, proved to be extremely difficult and it was only after intense diplomatic activity in national capitals, and after the issues were discussed at a European Council meeting at the end of June, that the impasse was eventually broken. The Heads of Government indicated the basis of a deal and the Agriculture Ministers, meeting the very next day, then finalised it. In 1988, the final settlement was also extensively delayed, although for very different reasons to those of the previous year. The principal problem was that the process could not properly begin until the Community's budgetary crisis was resolved at the February Brussels summit. This meant that the Commission was unable to publish its proposals until mid-March. A final settlement was not reached until late June.

The outcome of the Brussels summit – with its clearer and more restrictive guidelines for agricultural expenditure – should have two implications for the price review. First, by placing greater limits on the Council's options, it should make it easier to observe the timetable. (Though there is still plenty of room for disputes – as the 1988 settlement demonstrated when Greece held up for a week the

EXHIBIT 12.2

Major decisions taken as part of the 1986/88 Farm Price Review

		Price Increase* (%)
Wheat	–	
	Target Price	+0.5
	Intervention Price – bread making quality	0.0
Maize	–	
	Intervention Price	0.0
	Feed Quality Grains	−5.0
	except Rye	−5.9
Durum Wheat	–	
	Intervention Price	−4.0
	Aid	+12.3
Olive Oil	–	
	Intervention Price	−5
Rice, Sugar, Rapeseed, Sunflower Seed, Soya, Dried Fodder, Hemp, Cotton, Wine		0
Peas, Field Beans, Lupins		+1.0
Dairy Products, Beef, Sheep, Pigmeat		0
Tobacco		0 to −6

*Spain and Portugal are not due to become full members of the price and aid system until 1996.

Other measures of the 1986/7 'package' to include:

1. All countries except West Germany and the Netherlands to devalue their green currencies.
2. A 3 per cent co-responsibility on cereal production. Member states to be allowed to make various direct payments to farmers to compensate them for this.
3. Higher quality standards to apply on grain bought up for intervention.
4. A 3 per cent cut in milk quotas for all 12 member states spread over three years.

The overall effect of the above settlement was that the Commission's desire for a tight review was broadly satisfied. It did, however, have to make some important concessions, for example, the milk quota reductions were to be spread over three years rather than one, the price of butter was to be frozen rather than cut by 4 per cent, and the green currency devaluations softened the blow of the prices restraint.

Germany – and to a lesser extent Ireland, Luxembourg and Spain – had most reservations about the agreement. A consequence of this was that Germany agreed to compensate its farmers for the real cuts in their income and in May persuaded the Council to allow it to re-classify nearly half of its farm acreage as poor areas, and thus eligible for higher levels of government support. Another consequence was that Germany adopted a very tough position in the 1987–8 negotiations and was openly critical both of the Commission as a whole – which again approved a tight review – and of the President and the two German Commissioners in particular.

package to which the other eleven states had agreed, and insisted on a larger devaluation of its green currency rates.) Second, the traditional pattern, whereby the final agreement is much less restrictive than the original Commission proposals, should be less pronounced. (The 1988 price settlement gave some support to this view – it amounted to a price freeze, with some green currency adjustments.)

Concluding Remarks

The CAP is not quite as common or as integrated as it is often thought to be. On the one hand, at the national level, governments still have the option of making various forms of special assistance available to their farmers. Some of the richer states moreover, especially Germany, have begun to press for such regionalisation to be extended. On the other hand, at the Community level, the supposed common pricing system is distorted by the mechanisms of green currencies and monetary compensation amounts.

None the less, the CAP is, in a number of respects, the most important sectoral policy of the EC. But clearly, as the existence of surpluses demonstrates, the policy does not work completely satisfactorily. A key reason for this is that agriculture is not excluded from, indeed is characterised to an enhanced degree by, the central problem associated with policy and decision-making throughout the Community: competing interests make it very difficult for matters to be decided on a rational basis. Progress and change have thus tended to be circumspect and piecemeal rather than comprehensive and sweeping. But progress and change there have been, as is most obviously seen in the gradual withdrawal since the early 1980s – through the introduction of quotas, production thresholds, and the Brussels summit programme for more modest price increases – of the previously open-ended commitments to high levels of support for farmers. If the more restrictive policies do have their intended effect, it can be anticipated that in the future agriculture will not loom quite so large in the life of the Community, either in terms of finance or political attention.

13

National Influences and Controls on Community Processes

It is generally agreed that the highest price states have to pay for their membership of the Community is a substantial loss of their own law-making powers. In some policy spheres – agriculture and external trade in particular – autonomous national powers have been very largely removed. The reason the states are prepared to countenance this loss of sovereignty and are willing to participate in collective decision-making is that their national decision-makers, supported by large sections of their populations, believe it to be in their national interest to do so. The particular balance of advantages and disadvantages varies from state to state, but each judges that there is more to be gained from being in the Community than being out.

But belonging to the Community is seen to require care and vigilance so as to ensure that national interests are fully articulated and properly defended. Since, however, there are competing views within states about what these interests are, and since too there are a variety of domestic institutions, movements, interests, and parties, which wish to be heard, there are many inputs from each of the states into Community policy and decision-making processes.

The precise nature of these inputs varies from state to state – reflecting such factors as different national political systems, traditions, and cultures – but they can all, in broad terms, be seen as being directed through six principal channels: governments, courts, public opinion, political parties, and interests.

Governments

Governments are naturally in the strongest position to exercise national controls and influence on Community processes. This is most obviously seen in their relationships with the Commission and the Council.

There are many opportunities for governments to bring pressure to bear on the Commission. Formal opportunities include experts groups, management committees, and Council meetings. Informal opportunities can range from a minister ringing up a Commissioner, to a working group representative meeting a Commission official for lunch.

Appointments to the Commission, which all governments watch closely so as to ensure that fellow nationals are well represented and well placed, can also be used to advantage. At the level of the Commissioners themselves, the practice of appointment by national nomination institutionalises national inputs. Below the Commissioners, a similar function is performed by the informal national quota system that exists for senior grades.

This potential for Council influence on the Commission is not to suggest that Commissioners or Commission officials act as governmental representatives. As was shown in Chapter 3, they do, for the most part look to the Community-wide interest and are not open to instructions from national capitals. But they may, quite naturally, be inclined to take a particular interest in the impact of proposals on their own country. And governments looking for sympathetic ears in the Commission may well make fellow nationals their first port of call. (Though not necessarily: competent national officials, especially from the Permanent Representations, cultivate a broad range of contacts in the Commission.)

It should also be recognised that governmental influence on Commission thinking is not necessarily a bad thing. On the contrary, it can be positively helpful, by, for example, improving the prospects for the eventual adoption of proposals for Council legislation. Where, however, it can become unhealthy is when governments try to lean too heavily on their fellow nationals in the Commission, and when clusters of nationals have a disproportionate influence on policy development in a key sector.

The potential for any single government to exercise control over what happens in the Council depends on a number of factors:

The size of the state it represents. No matter what is being discussed the larger countries, such as France and Italy, are always likely to carry more weight than the smaller countries, such as Portugal and Luxembourg.

*The importance of the state to particular negotiations.*On the Common Fisheries Policy, for example, the Spanish government represents many more interests and is likely to be a much more central actor than Belgium.

The desire of the government to play an active role. An illustration of the importance of this factor is seen in the way German governments, until the late 1960s, acted very much as political lightweights, even though their country was clearly an economic heavyweight. This was partly because of Germany's historical legacy and partly because of the delicacies involved in the 'normalisation' of its relations with Eastern Europe and especially the German Democratic Republic. In more recent years, as Germany's position has come to be seen as not so unique or so special, its governments have increasingly asserted themselves across the Community's policy spectrum, and have not been unwilling to adopt 'awkward' and even isolated positions.

The capacity of the government to play an active role. Ministers may be strongly supportive of a particular policy, and wish to play an active role in pressing for it, but be restrained from doing so by domestic political considerations such as a finely balanced coalition government, opposition from key interest groups, or possible electoral damage.

Relations with other governments. Cohesive and fixed alliances *within* the Community between particular governments do not exist. Rather do governments tend to divide and join in different combinations on different issues. However, some governments do make more conscious efforts than others to seek general understandings and co-operation with Community partners, and where they are successful they do appear often to increase their influence as a consequence. The best example of this is the close relationship that has been consciously fostered between most French and German governments since the early 1960s. The so-called Franco-German axis is not so commanding now as it was when there were only six Community members, or when

Chancellor Schmidt and President Giscard d'Estaing worked closely together in the 1970s, but it still plays an important part in helping to shape and set the pace of Community developments.

The procedures applying. Of particular importance is whether majority voting is constitutionally permissible and politically acceptable. If it is, concessions and compromises might be preferable to being outvoted or resorting to the veto. If it is not, any government can cause indefinite delay, though by so doing it may weaken goodwill towards it and so damage its long-term interests.

The competence of governmental negotiators. Given the extensive tactical manoeuvrings involved in Community processes, and given, too, that many negotiations are not about the broad sweep of policy but are about highly technical matters, the competence of individual nego-tiators can be crucial: are they well briefed and able to master details? Can they judge how far their negotiating partners can be pushed? Can they avoid being isolated? Can they build coalitions? Can they time their interventions so as to clinch points? The evidence suggests that variations in such competencies are not so much between states as between individual negotiators.

The arrangements for linking representatives in the Council with national capitals. This point is worth developing in a little detail because there are significant variations in the ways in which governments attempt, and are able, to control their inputs into the Council via their representatives. Two aspects of the control are particularly worth mentioning.

First, some countries – including Belgium, Italy, Luxembourg and the Netherlands – appear generally to allow their representatives to work within a fairly loose framework. That is to say, representatives are often able to negotiate on important policy matters not just at ministerial level but also in working groups and in COREPER. As well as assisting the functioning of the Council as a whole – by reducing the need for awkward issues to be referred upwards – manoeuvrability and flexibility of this kind can be used to the national advantage by competent negotiators. At the same time, however, too much independence for representatives can lead to the necessity for awkward backtracking at a later negotiating stage if a misjudgement is made. By contrast, representatives from other states – including

France, Greece, Ireland and the UK – tend to have less room for manoeuvre in working groups and in COREPER and are generally reluctant to negotiate on policy issues below ministerial level. Whether, as is sometimes claimed, this greater rigidity improves the consistency and effectiveness of a country's negotiating position is doubtful. Undoubtedly, the more that countries lean in this direction, and all do at times, the more negotiations at the Council's lower levels are limited to technical matters and the more the overall Council process is protracted.

At the most senior Council level – ministerial meetings – there is of course, not such a problem of control from national capitals. It is important to ensure that the minister is fully briefed on the national implications of proposals, and is accompanied by national officials who fully understand all aspects of agenda items, but the political weight of the participants usually means that, if the will is there, commitments can be entered into without having to refer back to the relevant ministry for clearance. This is not to say that those in attendance at ministerial meetings can do as they like. At a minimum they are obliged to operate within the general guidelines of their government's policies. They may also be subject to special national constraints: perhaps occasioned by an inability of the minister himself to attend; perhaps linked to domestic political difficulties caused by the existence of a coalition government; or perhaps a consequence of a particular national interest having resulted in the establishment of a rigid governmental position in advance.

Second, the ability of governments to co-ordinate their national position across different sectoral Councils is important. Unless there is some particular advantage, no government wishes its representatives in one policy sphere to be contradicting or undermining the efforts of its representatives in another. All have, therefore, established internal co-ordinating mechanisms of some kind. These work with varying degrees of efficiency, depending largely on the nature of the domestic political and governmental system and the sophistication of the mechanisms that are established.

In the UK, the centralised governmental system and the majority party political system provide a favourable base for effective co-ordinating mechanisms. The mechanisms themselves are formalised, structured, and seemingly well integrated. At the general policy level, the Foreign Office, the Cabinet Office, and the UK Permanent Representation are the key bodies: the Foreign Office has two

Departments: Internal and External; the Cabinet Office contains a European Secretariat which, among other things, runs a weekly interdepartmental meeting of civil servants, attended by representatives from appropriate ministries and by the Permanent Representative; and the Permanent Representation Office acts as the eyes and ears of the UK in Brussels. Taken together, these three attempt to monitor, co-ordinate and control overall Community developments: by giving general consideration to important matters due to come up at forthcoming meetings; by looking at whether a broadly consistent line is being pursued across different policy areas; by trying to ensure that ministries have issued sufficiently clear guidelines for representatives in working parties; and, in the cases of the Foreign Office and the UK Permanent Representation, giving briefings themselves to representatives where appropriate. 'Above' these three bodies, but not involved in such a continuous manner, there is a Cabinet Committtee on the European Community, the Cabinet itself, and the Prime Minister. 'Below' them, each ministry has its own arrangements for examining proposals that fall within its competence and for ensuring that specialist negotiators are well briefed and fully aware of departmental thinking. Where Community matters loom large in a ministry's work special divisions or units exist for co-ordination purposes.

In Germany, by contrast, many factors make effective co-ordination very difficult: the need to satisfy – and not on a consistent basis across policy areas – the different elements of Germany's coalition governments; the relative autonomy of ministers and ministries within the federal government (seen, most notably, in the long running and open disagreement between the Finance Ministry and Agricultural Ministry over the cost of the CAP); the lack of an authoritative co-ordinating centre – the Foreign Office has a rather imprecise responsibility for general integration policy, and the Economics Ministry for routine matters; the strong powers of the federal states – the Länder – in certain policy areas; and strong sectoral specialisation, allied with loyalties to different federal ministries, among the staff of the German Permanent Representation in Brussels. As a result, Germany's European policies are sometimes less than consistent. Fortunately for Germany, its position as the strongest single Community state seemingly enables it to avoid being too seriously damaged by this internal weakness.

Parliaments

Parliaments are much less influential than governments in influencing Community developments. Of course, governments normally reflect the political composition of their national legislatures and must retain their confidence, so, in an indirect sense, governmental activity in relation to the Community could be said to be reflective of parliamentary will. But that is quite different from direct parliamentary control.

One of the major reasons for the relative weakness of national parliaments is that most of the factors that limit parlimentary strength across the domestic policy spectrum apply equally, and in some respects even more so, to Community matters. Thus, much Community legislation is so technical that it is almost incomprehensible to the lay politician. A second source of weakness is that national parliaments have no direct Treaty powers, which means that individual governments choose what to consult their parliaments about. All governments do consult their parliaments on fundmental matters where the Treaties refer to ratification in accordance with 'respective constitutional requirements' (enlargements, Treaty amendments, and the budgetary base carry this provision), but otherwise there are variations between the states. A third source of weakness is the particular difficulties that arise in relation to what might be expected to be the major sphere of influence of national parliaments: advising on Community legislation. The difficulties here are legion: a high proportion of legislation is, or is regarded by governments as being, 'administrative' legislation and not, therefore, within parliamentary competencies; there is virtually no opportunity for considering even the most important legislation at the formative pre-proposal stage; and proposed legislation that is considered is usually well advanced in, and may even be through, the Council system and is consequently very difficult to change.

The position of the Irish Parliament is fairly typical. Following accession in 1973, arrangements were made which were supposed to give Parliament monitoring, advisory, and deliberating responsibilities in respect of Irish participation in the Community. These arrangements were to consist, in particular, of an obligation on the part of the government to present a six-monthly report to Parliament on developments in the Community, and the creation of a new committee – the Joint Committee on Secondary Legislation comprising twenty-six Dail Deputies and Senators – with the brief of examining Community proposals and advising the government on their implications and suitability for Ireland. The evidence indicates that these arrangements have had but a marginal effect. Certainly Irish Community policy is not made, and can hardly be said to be properly examined, by the Dail or the Senate. Rather does it tend to be in the hands of a small, government-dominated, network of politicians and officials who listen to others only as they see fit. So, in the case of agriculture for example, the Minister of Agriculture, senior officials in the Department of Agriculture, and leaders of appropriate organisations – particularly the Irish Farmers' Association – hold the key to decision-making and decision implementation, and they are not unduly inconvenienced by parliamentary probing.

The major exception to the general pattern of legislative weakness is the Danish Folketing. Two principal factors combine to put the Folketing in a rather special position. First, there has been a powerful anti-Community movement and a strong anti-Community popular sentiment in Denmark since accession in 1973. No Danish government has been able to ignore this – especially since all governments have been coalitions or minorities: Social Democratic led between 1973–82, and Centre-Right since 1982. Second, the Folketing has a very strong Market Relations Committee comprised of senior politicians which meets weekly to review the forthcoming business in the Council of Ministers and to hear reports from ministers on their proposed negotiating positions. The committee does not vote or formally grant negotiating mandates, but it does tender advice, and it is necessary that a 'negative' clearance is given to the minister's position in the sense that there is no majority against it. The principal advantage of the Market Relations Committee procedure is that it helps to ensure that agreements reached by Danish ministers in the Council are not subsequently queried or endangered at home. The principal disadvantage is that it can make it difficult for Danish representatives to be flexible in the Council and can result in their being isolated if new solutions to problems are advanced during the course of negotiations.

Courts

National courts might be thought to have a significant role to play as the guarantors and defenders of national rights against Community encroachment. In practice, they do not.

The reason for this, as explained in Chapter 6, is that the principle of the primacy of Community law is now accepted. There were some initial teething problems in this regard, but it is now extremely rare for national courts to question the legality of Community proceedings and decisions. The Treaties, Community legislation, and even case law of the Court of Justice are seen as taking precedence when they clash with national law. The increasing practice of national courts to seek preliminary rulings from the European Court in cases where there is uncertainty over an aspect of Community law is testimony to the general desire of national courts not to be out of step with Community law.

That said, national courts have occasionally sought to assert national rights and interests against the Community. For example, there have been a few instances where national courts have refused to acknowledge the legality of directives that have not been incorporated into national law by the due date, even though the Court of Justice has ruled that in such circumstances they become directly applicable. Constitutional law, especially as applied to individual rights, has been another area where some assertion of national independence has been attempted by national courts, though not so much since the principle of the precedence of Community law over national constitutional law was confirmed in Court of Justice rulings in the early 1970s.

In recent years the most celebrated instance of national court intervention occurred in December 1986 when the Irish Supreme Court by a vote of three to two, found in favour of a Raymond Crotty who challenged the constitutional validity of the Single European Act. The judges ruled that Title III of the Act, which puts foreign policy co-operation on a proper legal basis, could restrict Ireland's sovereignty and might inhibit it from pursuing its traditionally neutral foreign policy. The Act must therefore, they indicated, be endorsed by a referendum. As a result, the SEA was unable to come into effect in any of the twelve EC states on 1 January 1987, as had been intended, and was delayed until the Irish gave their approval in the duly held referendum. The Act eventually entered into force on 1 July 1987.

Public Opinion

National public opinion exercises both a direct and indirect influence on Community decision-making.

The most direct means by which the populace can have their say is in referenda. Six of these have been held on Community-related matters. However, it is hard to sustain a case that they have added very much to the democratic base of the Community: partly because of their rarity, and partly because at least three of the six were not genuine attempts to consult the citizenry but were the consequences of internal politicking. The six to have been held are:

● In 1972 France held a referendum to ratify the enlargement of the Community. In reality it was designed to boost the legitimacy and status of President Pompidou and produce a public split in the Socialist-Communist opposition.

● 1972 Denmark and Ireland held referenda, as they were constitutionally obliged to do, on Community membership following the signing of the Treaty of Accession. (Norway held a 'consultative' referendum after also signing the Treaty. A majority voted against membership and Norway withdrew is application.)

● In 1975 a referendum was held in the UK on continued Community membership following the renegotiation of UK membership terms at the Heads of Government meeting in Dublin. The real purpose of the referendum was to settle a split in the Labour Cabinet on the principle of EC membership.

● In 1986 Denmark held a referendum on the ratification of the SEA. This was brought about after the Left majority in the Folketing had rejected the Act, nominally on the grounds that it undermined national sovereignty, but partly, too, because they thought rejection would force an election they might win. The Conservative Prime Minister, Poul Schlüter, out-manoeuvred them by calling a referendum rather than an election.

● In 1987, in circumstances described above, Ireland held a referendum on the ratification of the Single European Act.

In all of these referenda, with the exception of Norway in 1972, majority votes were cast for the 'pro-Community' side of the question.

By contrast with the only occasional and localised opportunities for participation offered by referenda, the elections to the EP are regular and European-wide (see Chapter 5 for details). For some observers, these elections provide the Community with a democratic base and, through the involvement of political parties and the election of MEPs, serve to link the peoples of the Community with Community processes. This view, however, must be counterbalanced by a recognition of the fact that since the elections are not contested by European parties standing on European issues, they can hardly be regarded as occasions when the populace indicate their European policy preferences. That voter turn out is, in most cases, low by national standards, and that those who are elected to be MEPs have only limited powers, raises further doubts about the participatory and democratic impact of the elections.

National public opinion has an indirect influence upon what happens in the Community through the policies pursued, and the decisions taken, by governments in the Council. (The influence is indirect in the sense that it is exercised at two or three stages removed: national voters elect legislatures, from which governments are formed, which send representatives to Council meetings.)

Where an issue is generally accepted as constituting a national interest, or at least commands strong domestic support, then governments of whatever political persuasion are likely to pursue it in the Council. Even if they themselves do not wish to be too rigid, they may well be forced, by electoral considerations and domestic pressures, to strike postures and make public displays of not being pushed around. So, for example, Irish and French governments invariably favour generous settlements for farmers, Danish and German governments press for strict environmental controls, and Greek and Portuguese governments argue for larger structural funds to enable them to modernise their economies.

Where no very clear national interest is at stake, or national opinion is unformed or divided, then the positions adopted by governments in the Council may be more reflective of domestic partisan divisions. So, for example, from 1974 to 1979 the attitude of the UK government to the Community budget was largely conditioned by Labour objections to the resources devoted to the CAP. After 1979, however, and the election of the Conservatives to power, the attitude came to mirror a more general ideological distaste for high public expenditure.

Political Parties

Political parties normally wish to exercise power which, in liberal democratic states, means they must be able to command popular support. This, in turn, means they must be able to articulate and aggregate national opinions and interests. At the same time, parties are not normally content simply to act as mirror images of the popular will. Drawing on their traditions, and guided by leaders and activists, they also seek to direct society by mobilising support behind preferred ideological/policy positions. Judgements thus have to be made about the balance to be struck between 'reflecting' society and 'leading' it. Those parties which lean too much towards the latter have little chance of winning elections, although in multiparty systems they may well find themselves with strong negotiating hands.

Because, as Figure 13.1 shows, Community membership commands broad, and in most cases majority, support in the member states, it is not surprising to find that the larger national political parties are broadly in favour of their own country's membership. Nor is it surprising that those countries in which there are major political

'Is the fact that your country belongs to the European Community a good or a bad thing?' (as %)*

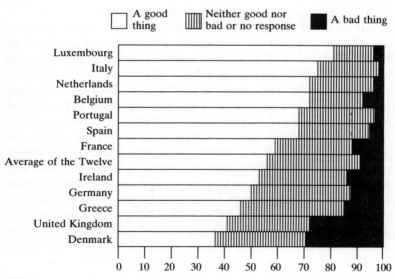

*Replies to the 'Eurobarometer' survey No. 27, organised for the Commission of the European Communities by European Omnibus Survey (11,651 people questioned throughout the Community between 17 March and 8 May 1987).
Source: European File 1–2, 1988.

FIGURE 13.1
Attitudes to Community Membership

parties with significant reservations about Community membership are those countries in which popular opinion has traditionally been least 'European': Denmark, Greece and the UK. Of course, the precise extent to which parties reflect and channel opinions, on the one hand, and shape and determine them, on the other, is impossible to judge. All that can be said is that the processes are two-way and are interlinked. There can, for example, be little doubt that the three main parties with reservations about Community membership – the Danish Social Democrats, the Greek PASOK, and the British Labour Party (all, it should be noted, parties of the Left) – are both responding to, but are also helping to create, public attitudes. These attitudes include: disquiet with the EC's free trade and market-based ethos; dissatisfaction, especially in Greece and the UK, with the apparent encouragement to social and geographical concentrations of wealth; opposition to loss of national sovereignty and to the power of the 'Brussels bureaucrats' (sentiments shared by many on the political Right); and suspicions, especially in Denmark and Greece, that the Community is too much a part of a Western, American-dominated, socioeconomic-political-military system.

But whatever their precise positions on Community membership and Community policies, and whatever the exact balance between their 'reflective' and 'leadership' roles, national political parties clearly do much to affect the attitudinal climate in which Community processes operate. They also feed into Community decision-making in a number of very direct ways. First, they contribute to the ideas of governments and make up most of their leading personnel and thus help to shape national attitudes and priorities in the Council. While it is true that many policy positions are barely altered by changes of government, shifts of emphasis do occur and these can be significant. Second, even when they are in domestic opposition, political parties can influence government behaviour in the Council because governments do not wish to be accused of being weak or not strongly defending national interests. Third, national political parties are the main contestants of the European elections and their successful candidates become the national representatives in the EP.

Interests

Acting either by themselves or through an appropriate Euro-group, national interests have a number of possible avenues available to them to try and influence Community policies and decisions. Some avenues are at the domestic level – such as approaches through fellow national MEPs, government officials and ministers. Others are at the Community level – such as contacts with the Commission, EP officials, or taking a case to the Court of Justice. These avenues were discussed in some detail in Chapter 8.

In very general terms the most successful interests of the sectional or promotional type tend to fulfil at least one of two conditions. Either they are able to persuade their government that there is little distinction between the group's interests and the national interest. Or, they have power resources that persuades at least some Community policy and decision-makers that they ought to be listened to. A major reason why the farmers have been so influential is that both of these conditions have applied to them in some countries. In France, Germany, Ireland, and elsewhere, this has resulted in the Ministers of Agriculture perceiving a major part of their responsibility in the Council being to act virtually as the spokesman for the sectoral lobby.

For regional and local institutional interests, the mark of success is usually their ability to attract allocations from Community funds. This can necessitate lobbying, or at least 'keeping in touch', with key national and Community officials. It also requires, and this is a factor that is not sufficiently recognised, a good knowledge of what is available and how to apply. Even today many important public authorities are not fully aware of what the Community has to offer.

Concluding Remarks

The existence of different, and frequently conflicting, inputs from the states is the major obstacle to the creation of a smooth, efficient and decisive Community policy and decision-making machinery. But that national views and requirements should be able to be articulated, and incorporated into decisions, is vital if the Community is to work at all. For, ultimately, the EC exists to further the interests of the member states. If the citizens of the states and, more particularly, the political elites in governments and in parliaments, were to feel that it was not serving that purpose, then there would be no reason for continued membership. The Community must, therefore, be responsible to its members.

14

Conclusion: Present Realities and Future Prospects

The Community and the Changing Nature of the International System

The Community should not be viewed in too narrow a context. Whilst many of the factors which have influenced its development have applied to it alone, many have not. This is most clearly seen in the ways in which modernisation and interdependence, which have been crucial in the creation of many of the central features of the Community, have produced similar effects elsewhere in the international system – albeit usually to a more modest degree. There has, for example, been a steady increase in the number and variety of international actors, and some corresponding weakening in the dominance of states. An increasing range of methods and channels are used by international actors to pursue their goals. Relationships between governments are no longer so controlled as they used to be by Foreign Offices and Ministries of External Affairs. The range of issues on international agendas has grown with, in particular, traditional 'high' policy issues – those concerned with security and the defence of the state – being joined by an array of 'low' policy issues – those concerned with the wealth and welfare of citizens. And there has been a decline, in the Western industrialised world at least, in the use of physical force as a policy instrument – conflicts over trade imbalances and currency exchange rates are not solved by armed conflict but by bargaining, adjusting, and compromising.

318

The Community must, therefore, be set within the context of the rapid changes that are occurring throughout the international system. It is a system that is becoming, like the Community system itself, increasingly multi-layered and interconnected. Whether the purpose is to regulate international trade, to promote the efficient functioning of the international monetary system, to set international standards on packaging for the transportation of hazardous materials, or to control the hunting and killing of whales, states now come together in many different ways, in many different combinations, for many different purposes, To take just formalised interstate forums and linkages, in Western Europe alone there are now many of these, quite apart from those which occur within the framework of the Community. States, for instance, co-operate with one another in joint projects, such as the European Fighter Aircraft, and EUREKA (the European technology programme). On a more institutionalised basis, Western European organisations include the Council of Europe, The European Free Trade Association, the Western European Union, the European Space Agency, and the European Patent Organisation.

This development of many different types of cross-border relations, in response to the different requirements and propensities of states, has also occurred within the Community. When the 'standard' Community method has been judged to be inappropriate or over-rigid, interstate relations have taken other forms. This is seen, for example, in the development of European Political Co-operation alongside, but outside, the formal Community structure, in the creation of the European Monetary System on a partial membership basis, and in the willingness of the Community to open up some of the programmes it sponsors to non-Community states – Sweden and Switzerland, for example, are associated with the JET (Joint European Torus) nuclear fusion project. As is increasingly the case with interstate relations in the international system as a whole, flexibility and diversity are thus key Community characteristics.

The Uniqueness of the Community

Compared with other international organisations, the Community is in many respects unique. Three aspects of this uniqueness are particularly worth emphasising.

First, the Community has a much more developed and complex

institutional structure than is found in other international bodies. The standard pattern of international organisations – permanent secretariats and attached delegations – is perhaps, a much grander and more elaborated form, replicated in the EC with the Commission and the Permanent Representations, but to these are added many other features. Among the more obvious of such features are the regular and frequent meetings between member governments at the very highest political levels, the constant and many varied forms of contact between national officials, the Court of Justice, and the European Parliament – the only directly elected multi-state assembly in the world.

Second, no other international organisation has anything like the policy responsibilities of the Community. In terms of width, there are now few significant policy areas which have completely escaped the Community's attentions. In terms of depth, the pattern varies, but in many important areas, such as external trade, agriculture, and competition policy, key initiating and decision-making powers have been transferred from the member states to Community authorities.

Third, the Community has progressed far beyond the essentially intergovernmental nature of most international organisations and has incorporated many supranational characteristics into its structure and operation. Since the nature of the balance between intergovernmentalism and supranationalism in the Community is a matter for considerable debate among observers, and since hostility to too much supranationalism – and the loss of sovereignty it is perceived as entailing – is a major reason why governments are often reluctant to permit integrationist developments, some detailed observations on the intergovernmental/supranational question are in order at this point.

In the 1960s, the governments of five of the Community's then six member states were willing to permit – even to encourage – some movement in the direction of supranationalism. President de Gaulle, however, who wished to preserve 'the indivisible sovereignty of the nation state', was not. In order to emphasise this point, and more particularly to prevent certain supranational developments which were due to be introduced, he withdrew France in 1965 from most of the Community's key decision-making forums. The outcome of the crisis which this occasioned was the 1966 Luxembourg Compromise which, though it had no legal force, had as its effect the general imposition of intergovernmentalism on Community decision-making processes: the powers of the Commission and of the European Parliament were contained, and decisions in the Council came customarily to be made, even where the Treaties allowed for majority voting, by unanimous agreements.

The first enlargement of the Community in 1973 reinforced intergovernmentalism, bringing in as it did two countries – Denmark and the UK – where there was strong domestic opposition to Community membership and where supranationalism was viewed with suspicion. The Greek accession in 1981 had a similar effect. The onset of the international economic recession in 1973–4 also encouraged intergovernmentalism, since it made states look rather more critically at the distributive consequences of Community policies, produced a temptation to look for national solutions to pressing problems, and resulted in a greater caution with regard to the transfer of powers to Community institutions.

However, intergovernmental attachments and pressures were never able – and have never been able – completely to stop the development of supranationalism. The Treaties, the ever-changing political and economic environments in which the Community exists, and the logic of the Community itself, have all ensured that in terms of both decision-making processes and decision-making outcomes, national sovereignties have been progressively undermined. Indeed, not only has supranationalism become more embedded in the Community system, but since the mid-1980s it has even been given something of a boost, as states have adopted a slightly more flexible attitude towards its development. They have done so partly because the effects of the delays and the inaction that intergovernmentalism sponsors have become more obvious and more damaging, and partly because it has been recognised that in the larger and more diverse Community of the twelve, over-rigid intergovernmentalism is a greater recipe than ever before for stagnation and sclerosis.

The Community thus displays both intergovernmental and supranational characteristics.

The principal intergovernmental characteristics are as follows:

● In most of the major areas of public policy – including foreign affairs, defence, macro-economic policy, financial and monetary policy, education, health, and law and order – decisions are still mainly taken at the national level. Each state consults and coordinates with its Community partners on aspects of these policies, and is sometimes subject to constraints as a result of Community membership, but usually, in the last analysis, a state can decide for itself what is to be done.

● Virtually all major decisions of the Community are taken by the Council of Ministers, which brings together representatives of the national governments.

● In the Council of Ministers most major decisions are taken on the basis of consensus and unanimity. Where there is constitutional provision for majority voting it is still possible (although it may be politically difficult) for any state, as a result of the Luxembourg Compromise, to veto a proposal if it has a 'vital national interest' at stake.

● The Commission and the Parliament, the two most obvious supranational power rivals to the Council of Ministers, have been tightly restricted by the Council in what they can do, and have had only very limited success in imposing policies on the Council which it did not really want.

● The major institutional innovation since the Community was established has been the European Council, and this is essentially intergovernmental in both its composition (Heads of Government and Foreign Ministers), and its functioning (it almost invariably acts only when a unanimous agreement is reached).

Of the supranational characteristics of the Community, the following are particularly important:

● The Commission may have to defer to the Council of Ministers with respect to the taking of major decisions, but it is an extremely important decision-maker in its own right when it comes to secondary and regulatory decision-making. Indeed, in quantitative terms, most Community legislation is issued in the name of the Commission and not the Council.

● In the Council of Ministers, majority voting has always been an acceptable practice for budgetary decision-making, but, since the mid 1980s, it has come to be increasingly used in other areas too. By extending the spheres in which majority voting is constitutionally permissible – including to the crucial sphere of the internal market – the Single European Act has given a considerable impetus to this growth in the use of majority voting.

● The European Parliament's constitutional powers may be limited, but its role in Community decision-making should not be dismissed altogether: it has important powers over the budget; its ability to discuss – and, if it sees fit, to delay – legislative proposals gives it a potential to influence their content; and, under the SEA, it comes close, in a few policy areas and under certain conditions, to being a co-decision-maker with the Council of Ministers.

● The force and status of decision-making outcomes is crucial to Community supranationalism for, clearly, the Community could hardly be described as supranational at all if its decisions had no binding force. Some, indeed, do not and are merely advisory and exhortive. But many do, and constitute Community law. It is a law that constitutes an increasingly prominent part of the legal systems of all member states. It is a law, too, that takes precedence over national law should the two conflict, and a law that, in the event of a dispute, finds it final authority not in national courts, but in the interpretations of the Community's own Court of Justice.

The three aspects of Community uniqueness which are referred to above – the complex institutional structure, the range of policy responsibilities, and the combination of intergovernmental and supranational characteristics – have combined, and are combining, to produce a system which is quite unique in the extent to which it involves states engaging in *joint* action to formulate *common* policies and to making *binding* decisions. As the words 'joint', 'common', and 'binding' imply, the process of working together is resulting in the Community states becoming ever more intermeshed and interdependent. This is no more clearly seen than in the ratchet-like effect of many aspects of their relationships and their shared activities: ratchet-like in the sense that it will not be possible for them to be reversed without creating major difficulties – and perhaps constitutional, legal, political and economic upheavals – at both Community and national levels.

Clearly a central aspect of the intermeshing and the interdependence, and one of the principal distinguishing characteristics of the Community, is the way in which the member states have voluntarily surrendered some of their national sovereignty and independence to collective institutions. Indeed, in a few policy sectors, such as agriculture and steel, the requirements of the Community system have resulted in the role of the states being relegated almost to that of intermediaries. However, viewed from a broader perspective, the Community is not only the cause of a decline in national powers, but is also a response to decline. This is so because much of the rationale of the Community lies in an attempt – an attempt for which there is no international parallel – on the part of the twleve states to increase their control of, and their strength and influence in, a rapidly changing world. Although all of the states have reservations (and some have fundamental criticisms) about aspects of the Community, each has made the judgement that membership enhances their ability to achieve certain objectives. The precise nature of these objectives varies from state to state but, in virtually all cases, the main priorities are the promotion of economic growth and prosperity, the control of economic financial forces which are not confined to national boundaries, and the strengthening of political influence. Insofar as these objectives are being attained, it may be argued that the diminution in the role of the state and the loss of sovereignty that arises from supranationalism, is counterbalanced by the collective strength of the Community as a whole. Indeed, since international change has resulted in all of the member states experiencing a considerable *de facto*, if not *de jure*, loss of national sovereignty, quite irrespective of the loss which is attributable to Community membership, it can be argued that discussions of national sovereignty, in the classic sense of the term at least, are no longer very meaningful. Rather should it be recognised that the only way in which medium-sized and small states, such as those which make up the membership of the Community, can retain control of their operating environments is by pooling and sharing their power and their sovereignty.

The Future of the Community

Factors Affecting Prospects

The Community has not evolved in quite the way, or as quickly, as was envisaged by many of its early founders. The expectation that policy interests and responsibilities would grow, with achievements in initially selected sectors leading to developments in other sectors, has been partly borne out, but only up to a point, and certainly not consistently – in the 1970s and early 1980s policy development was extremely sluggish. The anticipation that national institutions and political and economic actors would become progressively entwined with one another has been similarly partially realised, but it has also been partially frustrated – not least because of the persisting reluctance of some governments to transfer responsibilities and powers to Community institutions. The assumption that the focus of political activities and attentions would switch from national capitals to Europe has happened to an extent – but in most policy areas the national level is still more important than the Community level. And, finally, the belief that a European spirit would emerge, based on shared perceptions of a common interest, has proved to be over-optimistic.

There has, in short, been no semi-automatic movement in an integrationist direction. But if integration has not inevitably, and of itself, led to more integration, it has certainly stimulated pressures for more integration. It has done so, for example, by creating 'client groups' – of which, in the Community context, Eurocrats are not the least prominent – that have strong vested interests in sustaining and extending integration. Integration has also provided an institutional framework into which integrationist pressures, of many different sorts, have been channelled. Among such pressures on the Community today are: the international trade challenge of the USA, Japan, and the newly-industrialising countries; the increasingly perceived need for monetary stability; the transnational character of problem areas such as the environment and terrorism; and the need to respond to the integration that is occurring outside formal Community processes through developments as diverse as industrial mergers, closer cross-border banking and other financial arrangements, and population movements.

How the Community will respond to these and other pressures will depend on a number of factors, the most important of which are perceptions, support and leadership.

The importance of *perceptions* is seen in the way prospects for progress are considerably enhanced when all of the states perceive an initiative to be broadly desirable, or at least regard the costs of not proceeding as being too high. Very frequently, of course, there is no such common perception, especially where new types of development are envisaged and/or when initiatives have sovereignty or clear distributional implications.

The extent to which actors are motivated to *support* or oppose an initiative is dependent on many things. Perception of merit is obviously central, but this can be offset by other considerations. A government, for example, may fiercely resist a proposal in the Council of Ministers not because it regards it as being innately unsound, but because acceptance would be electorally damaging or would lead to problems with an important domestic pressure group.

A major weakness of the Community is that there is no clear and central focus of creative, consistent, and authoritative *leadership*. The Commission's ability to provide a lead is weakened by the powers of the European Council and the Council of Ministers, while they themselves are normally too internally divided to be able to strike out with bold initiatives or in new directions. When attemps are made to provide leadership – by, perhaps, an informal coalition of states, by an ambitious Council Presidency, or by a forceful Commission President – it almost invariably meets with resistance in at least some quarters.

The three factors are, of course, in constant transition. It is clear, for example, that developments such as the opening up of the internal market, increased international economic competition, technological advances, and changing relations between the superpowers, are helping to produce a climate wherein the Commission is attempting to offer bolder policy leadership. They are also contributing, in governmental circles at least, to an increased perception of the need of, and increased support for, further integration.

But if the internal market and other developments are resulting in a new sense of dynamism being inserted into integration processes, they are far from removing all the obstacles. This is no more clearly seen than in the different public positions taken by governments on the future shape of the Community. On the one hand, there are those which claim they seek a full economic and political union, while on the other hand there are those – of which the UK is the most prominent – which incline towards, or wish to be seen by domestic audiences as inclining towards, preservation of national independence.

In providing some insight into the range of differences which exist on the future of the Community, an interesting public debate occurred in the second half of 1988. It was sparked off by the President of the Commission, Jacques Delors, who, in a speech to the European Parliament, declared: 'We will not be able to take all the decisions that need to be taken between now and 1995 without moves towards a European government of one kind or another . . . In ten years time eighty per cent of economic, and perhaps even fiscal and social, legislation will originate in the Community'.

The British Prime Minister, Mrs Thatcher, was quick to express her opposition to these views stating, in a speech to the College of Europe at Bruges, that:

> . . . willing and active co-operation between independent sovereign states is the best way to build a successful European Community. . . . Europe will be stronger precisely because it has France as France, Spain as Spain, Britain as Britain, each with its own customs, traditions and identity. It would be folly to try to fit them into some sort of identikit European personality. . . . We have not successfully rolled back the frontiers of the state in Britain, only to see them re-imposed at a European level, with a European super-state exercising a new dominance from Brussels.

Mrs Thatcher's hostility to Delors's vision of the future was echoed, and in some respects was taken even further, by the UK Trade and Industry Minister, Lord Young, when he launched a conference on the internal market and 1992. 'We are not', he stated, 'talking about a United States of Europe. We are talking about a trade association with some common rules'.

By contrast with the 'minimalist' UK position, the Belgian Prime Minister, Mr Martens, entered the debate with support for a 'maximalist' position. The Community, he argued, should move from economic to full political union, with 'common sovereignty' covering foreign policy, defence and security, as well as monetary, economic, environmental, and social policy. Martens's views were later given a near full endorsement by the other Christian Democratic Heads of Government of the Community (that is, the Heads of Government of Holland, Luxembourg, West Germany and Italy), who all associated themselves with a declaration avowing their commitment to a full European economic, political, and security union.

Of course, rhetoric is one thing and practical action is another. The statements just referred to do something to capture different ideas about the future of the Community, but they also serve to mask as well as to reveal. So, the UK government, despite the anti-integration rhetoric of Mrs Thatcher and some of her senior ministers, has done much to facilitate integration through such acts as its approval of the SEA, its acceptance of the 1988 Brussels summit package, and its strong support for the dismantling of barriers to the free movement of goods and capital. At the same time, those governments which are highly vocal in their support for integration processes are usually quite prepared to drag their feet and create difficulties when specific proposals do not accord with their own preferences or national interests.

Differences between governments regarding how they react in practice to specific integrative developments are not, therefore, always as great as might be expected from the public statements they make.

Policy Prospects

What the factors identified in the preceding discussion would appear to imply for future policy development in the Community is two things. First, development at a faster pace than occurred in the 1970s and the first half of the 1980s. Second, the overall manner of that development being, as it has been in the past, somewhat sporadic and fitful.

As regards policy content, particular attention can be expected to be given to a number of areas. The 1992 momentum and the much publicised programme of completing the internal market will clearly be given a high priority. Since, however, not all barriers to free movement will in fact be removed by 1992 – decisions, for example, about what is to be taxed and at what rates will continue to be largely determined at national levels – and since, too, there is still far from complete accord between the member states over precisely what needs to be removed and what needs to be harmonised and made common for genuinely free and open competition to exist, the market issue can be expected to remain on the agenda well beyond 1992 itself.

The development of the internal market will strengthen pressures for a rapid movement towards greater financial and economic integration. In the judgement of many, a completely integrated market is impossible without monetary stability and a general consistency in macroeconomic policy. From acceptance of this view it is but a short step – a step which some governments have already made – to perceiving a need for a powerful European Central Bank and common currency.

Paralleling the economic, monetary and market-based integrationist developments and pressures, increasing attention is likely to be paid to what is often referred to as 'the social dimension' of the Community: that is, to areas such as social welfare provision, health and safety at work, and industrial democracy. Awakening interest in social issues has, indeed, already borne some fruit – notably in Commission statements of intent, and in the 1988 Brussels summit decision to double the size of the structural funds. One reason for this increased interest is the ideological preference of some Left-Centre governments, which have increased in number since the late 1970s, for well developed social policies. Another reason, and one that will probably increase in importance in the future, is the desire of the Commission and most governments that certain market consequences – such as excessive regional imbalances – should be softened. And a third reason, and one which is also likely to increasingly make itself felt, is that governments in states where social legislation is well developed are concerned that their industries and businesses should not be placed at a trading disadvantage because they carry costs which do not apply in states where social legislation is poorly developed.

An aspect of future policy development that merits particular comment is external policy and its consequences for the Community's international standing and influence.

It is customary to describe the Community's international position as being one of economic giant and political pygmy. In fact, in important respects, it is not an economic giant at all. This is because most macroeconomic and monetary decisions are not taken at Community level but at national levels. Co-ordination and some joint activity does, of course, occur, as in the context of the European Monetary System, but the Community is very far from being an economic and financial bloc. Community representatives and officials are therefore very restricted in their ability to harness the economic and monetary resources of the twelve for general policy purposes on the international stage.

Where, however, the Community is a bloc, and is an international actor of the first rank, is with respect to trade. The Common Commercial Policy enables the economic weight of the twelve to be harnessed to common goals in many sorts of bilateral and multilateral negotiations. The most important of these goals has been trade liberalisation. Several factors account for this prioritisation, and suggest that the pursuit of free trade will continue to be a key concern in the years to come: as noted in Chapter 9 the Community is the world's largest trader, with its external trade accounting for 19 per cent of world trade, as against 17 per cent for the United States and 10 per cent for Japan: external trade accounts, on average, for around 9.6 per cent of the Gross Domestic Product of the twelve, as compared with 7.2 per cent for the United States and 8.5 per cent for Japan; and there is massive European investment outside the Community, much of it in sectors and activities which are dependent on trade. The spectre, which has been raised in many quarters, of the Community drifting towards protectionism – of, indeed, a 'Fortress Europe' being created to protect the increasingly open internal market from outside penetration – is not, therefore, very convincing. That is not to say that there will not be an increase in protectionist pressures from both domestic and external quarters, or that some protectionist measures will not be taken. Both of these are quite possible, especially if feelings, such as have existed for a long time in relation to Japan, grow that Community exports are being unfairly excluded from foreign markets, or if the Community's trading partners, and especially the United States, decide to act upon their long held resentment with the Community for the exceptions which it makes, notably with agriculture, to its free trade policies. There may, therefore, be difficulties in resisting protectionism. Since, however, any general movement in this direction would appear not to be in the Community's long term interests, free trade seems likely to remain the central plank of external commercial policy unless international circumstances change significantly.

Turning to the Community's international political influence, it is unquestionably slight. This is despite the Community's economic weight, despite the combined population of the member states being larger than that of either the United States or the Soviet Union, despite the defence commitments of the twelve states including the weaponry of two nuclear powers and over two million men under arms, and despite Europe's long history and experience in world affairs. The fact is, that on many issues which have very important implications for Western Europe – including, most notably, arms control and regional conflicts – the United States and the Soviet Union tend to negotiate directly with one another, and Western Europe's voice – even in a consultative capacity with its major ally – counts for little.

If this situation of international political weakness is to be changed it must be via the states acting collectively. Within the Community the anticipated continued development of EPC, especially now that it has been put on a firmer footing by the SEA, will probably facilitate greater foreign policy co-operation and hence promote greater foreign policy effectiveness between the twelve. However, as was shown in Chapter 9, there are still many obstacles preventing the states from adopting common positions, and even more preventing them from engaging in common actions, as a matter of course. Most crucially of all, defence remains outside the Community framework. There are many who would like to see it incorporated in some way, but that would create major difficulties and it is more probable that such progress as may be made in the foreseeable future towards a West European defence identity will be via non-Community, though closely related, groupings. As an indication of what some countries have in mind, comments made in November 1988 by the Spanish Foreign Minister, Francisco Fernandez Ordonez, on the day Spain and Portugal signed the Protocols of Accession to the Western European Union, are worth quoting. He stated that his country had sought membership of the WEU specifically because the organisation recognised that 'the construction of Europe will remain incomplete as long as it does not include security and defence'.

Whatever the mix of pressures for Community policy development and action prove to be in the future, it is quite certain many will be strongly resisted. The reasons for the resistance will be found in the familiar barrage of barriers which explain why so much policy activity is slow, uneven, and uncertain: differences over the merits of proposals, over the costs of proposals, over the distributional consequences of proposals, over whether proposals are appropriate Community business, and over whether or not loss of national controls and sovereignty are acceptable. Conceivably such obstacles to progress may have the effect of causing the states to divide, in certain respects, into fast and slow integration streams. Certainly they will ensure that many initiatives which command a fair measure of support among the states and in Community institutions will nonetheless be put on indefinite hold, will be watered down, or will be diverted away from the making of legislation into relatively harmless liaising and co-ordinating channels.

Institutional Prospects

Finally, something must be said about the prospects for the institutional structure of the Community.

The Community has long been criticised for persisting with a policy and decision-making institutional framework that is slow, inefficient, and insufficiently subject to democratic controls. Many schemes and proposals for reform have been put forward over the years, most of which have focused on two main themes. First, the need for a stronger executive – among specific measures advocated have been a merging of the Commission and the Council of Ministers, a more independent Commission, and more majority voting in the Council of Ministers. Second, the need for a stronger Parliament – measures advocated here have ranged from modest extensions of the EP's consultative rights, to granting the EP real and effective legislative powers.

Clearly the adoption of almost any of these proposed measures would extend political integration in the Community. It is for this very reason that national governments, or at least a sufficient number of them, have been inclined to resist calls for significant institutional reforms. Most governments do not want to see any major departures from the *status quo* and do not want to have to cede any more powers to Community institutions than is necessary. Hence the only very mild dose of institutional reform that was permitted to be incorporated into the SEA.

But institutional reform can occur in many ways. It does not depend wholly on formal political agreements or constitutional amendments. The powers of, and the relationships between, institutions and the actors who are associated with them can change gradually, almost imperceptibly, as adjustments are made to fit evolving circumstances and requirements. So, for example, an increasing use of majority voting in the Council of Ministers, and an increasing role for the EP in the Community system, were both under way before they were given a boost by the SEA. Doubtless shifts of this sort will continue – driven in the 1990s, perhaps, by further enlargements to embrace countries such as Norway, Cyprus and Malta, or by the momentum of the many difficult issues that will need to be resolved if the internal market is to be fully realised and if an economic and monetary union is ever to be even nearly approached.

Chronology of Main Events in the Development of the European Community

1947 March   Belgium, Luxembourg and the Netherlands agree to establish a customs union. Subsequently an economic union is established in October 1947 and a common customs tariff is introduced in January 1948.

March   France and the UK sign a military alliance, the Treaty of Dunkirk.

June   General George Marshall, United States Secretary of State, offers American aid for the economic recovery of Europe.

September   Sixteen nations join the European Recovery Programme.

1948 March   Brussels Treaty concluded between France, the UK and the Benelux states. Aim is to promote collective defence and to improve co-operation in the economic, social and cultural fields.

April   Founding of the Organisation for European Economic Co-operation (OEEC) by sixteen states.

May   A Congress is held in the Hague attended by many leading supporters of European co-operation and integration. It issues a resolution asserting 'that it is the urgent duty of the nations of Europe to create an economic and political union in order to assure security and social progress'.

333

1949   April   Treaty establishing North Atlantic Treaty Organisation (NATO) signed in Washington by twelve states.

        May   Statute of Council of Europe signed in Strasbourg by ten states.

1950   May   Robert Schuman, the French Foreign Minister, puts forward his proposals to place French and German coal and steel under a common authority. He declares 'it is no longer the moment for vain words, but for a bold act — a constructive act'.

        October   René Pleven, the French Prime Minister, proposes a European Defence Community (EDC).

1951   April   European Coal and Steel Community (ECSC) Treaty signed in Paris by six states: Belgium, France, Germany, Italy, Luxembourg and the Netherlands.

1952   May   EDC Treaty signed in Paris by the six ECSC states.

        July   ECSC comes into operation.

1954   August   French National Assembly rejects EDC Treaty.

        October   WEU Treaty signed by the six ECSC states plus the UK.

1955   June   Messina Conference of the Foreign Ministers of the six ECSC states to discuss further European integration. The Spaak Committee established to study ways in which a fresh advance towards the building of Europe could be achieved.

1956   June   Negotiations formally open between the six with a view to creating an Economic Community and an Atomic Energy Community.

1957   March   The Treaties of Rome signed establishing the European Economic Community (EEC) and the European Atomic Energy Community (Euratom).

1958 January   EEC and Euratom come into operation.

1959 January   First EEC tariff cuts and increases in quotas.

1960 January   European Free Trade Association (EFTA) Convention signed at Stockholm by Austria, Denmark, Norway, Portugal, Sweden, Switzerland and UK. EFTA comes into force in May 1960.

       December   Organisation for Economic Co-operation and Development (OECD) Treaty signed in Paris. OECD replaces OEEC and includes Canada and USA.

1961 July   Signing of Association Agreement between Greece and EEC. Comes into effect November 1962.

       July/August Ireland, Denmark and the UK request negotiations with the Community.

1962 January   Basic features of Common Agricultural Policy (CAP) agreed.

       July   Norway requests negotiations on Community membership.

1963 January   General de Gaulle announces his veto on UK membership.

       January   Signing of Franco-German Treaty of Friendship and Co-operation.

       July   A wide ranging association agreement is signed between the Community and 18 underdeveloped countries in Africa – the Yaoundé Convention. The Convention enters into force in June 1964.

1964 May   The GATT Kennedy Round of international tariff negotiations opens in Geneva. The Community states participate as a single delegation.

1965 April   Signing of *Treaty establishing a Single Council and a Single*

Commission of the European Communities (The Merger Treaty).

July   France begins a boycott of Community institutions to register its opposition to various proposed supranational developments.

1966 January   Foreign Ministers agree to the *Luxembourg Compromise*. Normal Community processes are resumed.

1967 May   Denmark, Ireland and UK re-apply for Community membership.

July   1965 'Merger' takes effect.

July   Norway re-applies for Community membership.

December   The Council of Ministers fails to reach agreement on the re-opening of membership negotiations with the applicant states because of continued French opposition to UK membership.

1968 July   The Customs Union is completed. All internal customs duties and quotas are removed and the common external tariff is established.

1969 July   President Pomidou (who succeeds de Gaulle after his resignation in April) announces he does not oppose UK membership in principle.

July   Signing of the second Yaoundé Convention. Enters into force in January 1971.

December   Hague summit agrees on a number of important matters: strengthening the Community institutions; enlargement; establishing an 'economic and monetary union' by 1980; and developing political co-operation (i.e. foreign policy).

1970 April   The financial base of the Community is changed by the *Decision of 21 April 1970 on the replacement of financial contributions from Member States by the Communities' own resources*. The Community's budgetary procedures are regularised and the European Parliament's budgetary powers are increased by the *Treaty amending Certain Budgetary Provisions of the Treaties.*

June   Preferential trade agreement signed between Community and Spain. Comes into effect in October 1970.

June   Community opens membership negotiations with Denmark, Ireland, Norway and UK.

October   The six accept the Davignon report on political co-operation. This provides the basis for co-operation on foreign policy matters.

1972   January   Negotiations between Community and the four applicant countries concluded. Signing of Treaties of Accession.

May   Irish approve Community accession in a referendum.

July   Conclusion of Special Relations Agreeement between Community and EFTA countries.

September   Majority vote against Community accession in a referendum in Norway.

October   Danes approve Community accession in a referendum.

October   Paris summit. Heads of Government set guidelines for the future, including a reaffirmation of the goal of achieving an economic and monetary union by 1980.

1973   January   Accession of Denmark, Ireland and UK to the Community.

January   Preferential trade agreement between Community and most EFTA countries comes into effect. Agreements with other EFTA countries come into force later.

1974   December   Paris summit agrees to the principle of direct elections to the European Parliament and to the details of a European Regional Development Fund (the establishment of which had been agreed at the 1972 Paris and

1973 Copenhagen summits). In addition it is agreed to institutionalise summit meetings by establishing the European Council.

1975	February	Signing of the first Lomé Convention between the Community and 46 underdeveloped countries in Africa, the Caribbean and the Pacific (the ACP states). The Convention replaces and extends the Yaoundé Convention.
	March	First meeting of the European Council at Dublin.
	June	A majority vote in favour of continued Community membership in UK referendum.
	June	Greece applies for Community membership.
	July	Signing of the *Treaty amending Certain Financial Provisions of the Treaties*. This strengthens the European Parliament's budgetary powers and also establishes the Court of Auditors.
1976	July	Opening of negotiations on Greek accession to the Community.
1977	March	Portugal applies for Community membership.
	July	Spain applies for Community membership.
1978	October	Community opens accession negotiations with Portugal.
1979	February	Community opens accession negotiations with Spain.
	March	European Monetary System (which had been the subject of high level negotiations for over a year) comes into operation.
	May	Signing of Accession Treaty between Community and Greece.
	June	First direct elections to the EP.

	October	Signing of the second Lomé Convention between the Community and 58 ACP states.
	December	For the first time the EP does not approve the Community budget. As a result the Community has to operate on the basis of 'one twelfths' from 1 January 1980.
1981	January	Accession of Greece to Community.
	October	Community foreign ministers reach agreement on the 'London Report' which strengthens and extends European Political Co-operation.
1983	January	A Common Fisheries Policy is agreed.
	June	At the Stuttgart European Council meeting approval is given to a 'Solemn Declaration on European Union'.
1984	January	Free trade area between Community and EFTA established.
	February	The European Parliament approves *The Draft Treaty establishing the European Union*.
	June	Second set of direct elections to the EP.
	June	Fontainebleau European Council meeting. Agreement to reduce UK budgetary contributions (which Mrs Thatcher had been demanding since 1979) and agreement also to increase Community resources by raising the VAT percentage from 1 to 1.4 per cent.
	December	Signing of the third Lomé Convention between the Community and 66 ACP countries.
	December	Dublin European Council meeting agrees budgetary discipline measures.
1985	June	Signing of Accession Treaties between the Community and Spain and Portugal.
	June	The Milan European Council establishes an intergovernmental conference to examine various matters

including Treaty reform. For the first time at a summit meeting the decision is taken by a majority vote.

December   Luxembourg European Council meeting agrees the principles of the Single European Act. The Act incorporates Treaty revisions, gives European Political Cooperation legal status, and establishes the completion of the internal market by 1992 as a top priority.

1986 January   Accession of Spain and Portugal to Community.

1987 July   After several months delay caused by ratification problems in Ireland the SEA comes into force.

1988 February   A special European Council meeting at Brussels agrees to increase and widen the Community's budgetary base. Measures are also agreed to significantly reduce expenditure on the CAP and to double expenditure on the regional and social funds.

June   The Community and Comecon (the East European trading bloc) sign an agreement enabling the two organisations to recognise each other. As part of the agreement the Comecon states officially recognise, for the first time, the authority of the Community to negotiate on behalf of its member states.

Selected Further Reading

Reference Sources and Information Guides

A wide variety of reference and information publications are available on the Community. Leaving aside specialist works the following are among the most useful:

Budd, S. A., *The EEC: A Guide to the Maze*, 2nd edn (Kogan Page, 1987).

Directory of Community Legislation in Force (Office for Official Publications of the European Communities, twice yearly).

Documents, (Office for Official Publications of the European Communities, monthly plus cumulated and annual catalogues). Lists Commission Documents, EP Reports and ESC Opinions. *Publications of the European Communities* (issued quarterly and annually) is a companion catalogue listing mongraphs, serials and periodicals issued by the Community institutions.

EC Index, (Office for Official Publications of the European Communities, annual). Provides (a) bibliographic coverage of EC publications; (b) subject and name indexing for the *Official Journal*, Commission documents, EP Reports, ESC Opinions, and Court of Justice judgements; (c) abstracts of documents issued by the Commission, the EP and the ESC.

EEC Update (Eurofi, annual). Provides a summary of Commission policy statements and proposals for legislation.

Hopkins, M., *European Communities Information: Its Use and Users* (Mansell, 1985).

Index to Documents of the Commission of the European Communities (Eurofi, annual). A guide to Commission proposals for Council legislation and to reports presented by the Commission to the Council or the EP.

International Organisations Catalogue (HMSO, annual).

Jefferies, J., *A Guide to Official Publications of the European Communities*, 2nd edn (Mansell, 1981).

Morris, B., and Boehm K., *The European Community: A Practical Directory and Guide for Business, Industry and Trade*, 2nd edn (Macmillan, 1986).

Myles, G., *EEC Brief* (Locksley Press, updated annually). A handbook, in looseleaf form, covering Community institutions, policies and laws.

Overton, D., *Common Market Digest* (Library Association, 1983).

Palmer, D. M., *Sources of Information on the European Communities*. (Mansell, 1979).

Paxton, J., *A Dictionary of the European Communities*, 2nd edn (Macmillan, 1984).

Recent Publications on the European Communities (Office for Official Publications of the European Communities, monthly). Compiled by Commission library. Covers EC publications and documents, books from the commercial and academic presses, and articles from certain periodicals.
SCAD Bulletin (Office for Official Publications of the European Communities, weekly). Catalogues principal Community publications and documents, and presents summaries of articles on the Community taken from a wide range of journals and periodicals.

Official Community Sources

The Community issues a vast amount of material, from brief information leaflets to weighty reports. A good way of attaining a direct acquaintance of what is available is to browse at a European Documentation Centre (EDC). EDCs receive copies of virtually all of the Community's published documents and are located throughout the member states. Usually they are attached to academic libraries.

Clearly a detailed review of Community publications is not possible here. For that readers should refer to the various guides and catalogues that were itemised in the previous section. What follows is merely an outline guide to major publications.

The Treaties Establishing the European Communities should naturally be consulted by all those who wish to understand the nature and functioning of the EC. They have been published in several editions by, amongst others, the Office for Official Publications of the European Communities, HMSO and Sweet and Maxwell.

The Official Journal of the European Communities (OJ) is issued on most week days and provides the authoritative record of decisions and activities of various kinds. It is divided into three series. The 'L' (Legislation) series is the vehicle for the publication of Community legislation. The 'C' (Information and Notices) series contains things such as Ecu rates, appointments to advisory committees, minutes of EP plenary proceedings and resolutions adopted by plenaries, ESC Opinions, Court of Auditors reports, cases referred to the Court of Justice and Court judgements, Commission communications and notices, and Commission proposals for Council legislation. The 'S' (Supplement) series is mainly concerned with public contract and tendering announcements. Debates of the EP are published in annexes to the OJ. An Index to the 'L' and 'C' series of the OJ is available in monthly and annual editions.

The monthly *Bulletin of the European Communities* provides a general account of most significant developments. Some of the information contained amounts to a summary of material included in the OJ (with appropriate references). Much else is additional: there are, for example, reports – albeit rather brief ones – of European Council of Ministers meetings; there are updates on policy developments; there is a monitoring of progress in the annual budgetary cycle; and there is information on initiatives, meetings and agreements in the sphere of external relations.

The *General Report on the Activities of the European Communities* is published annually and provides an excellent summary of both institutional and policy developments. Where necessary it can be supplemented by the annual reports that are also published by most of the institutions.

The most detailed analysis and information about Community policies is usually to be found in documentation produced by the Commission. Leaving aside one-off publications this appears in three main forms. First, in serialised reports which are issued on a regular basis and which cover just about every aspect of Community affairs. As an indication of the sort of reports that are produced three might be mentioned: *European Economy* covers economic trends and proposals and is issued quarterly, with monthly supplements; *Eurobarometer* reports on public opinion in the Community and appears monthly; the *Agricultural Situation in the Community* is an annual report. Second, an enormous volume of information is issued by the Statistical Office: on matters ranging from energy consumption patterns to agricultural prices. It all bears the *Eurostat* logo imprint. Third, there are Commission Documents (COMDOCS) which are made up principally of monitoring reports, policy reviews, and – above all – proposals for Council legislation.

Useful material stemming from other institutions on a regular basis includes: *Reports* (formerly called *Working Documents*), *Dossiers*, and *Research Documents* of the EP; the monthly *Bulletin* of the ESC; and *Reports of Cases Before the Court*.

Finally, it is worth mentioning that a number of Community publications are available without charge. Most of these are rather slight and are intended primarily for those who know very little about the Community, but some do go beyond basics and can be used to build up a useful collection. All of the institutions, for example, produce pamphlets or booklets describing how they are organised and what they do. The *European File* series – which is available from the Office for Official Publications of the European Communities – consists of around twenty pamphlets per year covering a variety of topics. And the *European Documentation* series – which is also available from the Office for Official Publications – consists of four or five quite substantial booklets per year on a range of Community matters.

Other Sources

The governments of the member states produce a considerable volume of documentation on the Community. The precise nature of this material varies from state to state, but mostly it consists of a mixture of 'state of play' reports, reports from relevant parliamentary committees, and information pamphlets/booklets/packs. Because many of the latter are intended to stimulate a greater public awareness about the Community, or are designed to encourage business to take advantage of Community policies, they are often available free of charge.

Several sources contain detailed and regular information abuot the work of the Community. A daily bulletin of events is provided by *Europe* – commonly known as *Agence Europe* – which is published by Agence Internationale D'Information Pour La Presse. *European Report*, which is published by Europe Information Service, also provides a detailed monitoring of events, in its case on a twice-weekly basis. A useful quarterly publication is *European Trends* which is produced by the Economist Intelligence Unit.

In most member states the 'quality' press provides a reasonable review of Community affairs. In the UK the most comprehensive coverage is to be found in the *Financial Times*.

Academic journals include the *Journal of Common Market Studies* (which includes an annual review of activities in the Community), the *Journal of European Integration, Common Market Law Review*, and *European Law Review*.

The number of books published on the Community is now voluminous. Since only a brief indication of what is available can be attempted here, references have been confined to texts in English and preference has tended to be given to recent publications. The titles listed are grouped into broad sections but it must be emphasised that the boundaries between the sections are far from watertight. Comments on books are entered only where particularly distinctive features apply.

(a)   Historical Development

Blacksell, M., *Post-War Europe*, 2nd edn (Hutchinson, 1981).
Hallstein, W., *Europe in the Making* (Allen & Unwin, 1972). Now largely outdated, but useful in capturing the idealism that characterised many of the Community's founders.
Joll, J., *Europe Since 1870*, 3rd edn (Penguin, 1983).
Jones, R. B., *The Making of Contemporary Europe*. (Hodder & Stoughton, 1980).
Milward, A. S., *The Reconstruction of Western Europe*, 1945–51 (Methuen, 1984). An extremely detailed analysis of the early post-war years that challenges some aspects of the interpretations of the 'standard' accounts.
Monnet, J., *Memoirs* (Collins, 1978). The memoirs of the 'father' of West European integration.
Pollard, S., *The Integration of the European Economy Since 1815* (Allen & Unwin, 1981).
Nicholson, F., and East, R., *From the Six to the Twelve: the Enlargement of the European Communities* (Longman, 1987).
Pryce, R., *The Dynamics of European Union* (Croom Helm, 1987).
Urwin, D. W., *Western Europe Since 1945*, 3rd edn (Longman 1981).

(b)   General Books on the Government and Politics of the European Community

Arbuthnott, H., and Edwards G., *A Common Man's Guide to the Common Market*, (Macmillan, 1979).
Butler, M., *Europe: More than a Continent* (Heinemann, 1986). An 'insider' account, by the former UK Permanent Representative.
Daltrop, A., *Politics and the European Community*, 2nd edn (Longman, 1986).
George, S., *Politics and Policy in the European Community* (Clarendon Press, 1985).
Henig, S., *Power and Decision in Europe* (Europotentials, 1980).
Holland, S., *Uncommon Market* (Macmillan, 1980). A critique from the Left.
Kerr, A., *The Common Market and How it Works*, 3rd edn (Pergamon, 1986).

Leonard, D., *Pocket Guide to the European Community* (Blackwell, 1988).
Lodge, J., (ed.), *Institutions and Policies of The European Community* (Frances Pinter, 1983).
Lodge, J., (ed), *The European Community* (Frances Pinter, 1983). A useful discursive review of much of the literature.
Taylor, P., *The Limits of European Integration* (Croom Helm, 1983).
Tugendhat, C., *Making Sense of Europe* (Viking, 1986). Another 'insider' account, this time by the former Budget Commissioner.

(c) Institutions and Actors

Not many books focus exclusively on particular Community institutions and actors. Many of the sources listed in section (b), (d) and (e) do, however, contain relevant chapters and sections.
Barnouin, B., *The European Labour Movement and European Integration* (Frances Pinter, 1986).
Bulmer, S., and Wessels, W., *The European Council* (Macmillan, 1987).
Butt Philip, A., *Pressure Groups in the European Community* (University Association for Contemporary European Studies, Occasional Papers No. 2, 1985).
Kirchner, E., and Schwaiger, K., *The Role of Interest Groups in the European Community* (Gower, 1981).
Nuallain, C. O., (ed.), *The Presidency of the European Council of Ministers, (Croom Helm, 1985)*.
Palmer, M., *The European Parliament* (Pergamon, 1981).
Robinson, A., and Webb, A.,*The European Parliament in the EC Policy Process* (Policy Studies Institute, 1985).

(d) The Court of Justice and Community Law

Brown L. N., and Jacobs, F. G., *The Court of Justice of the European Communities*, 2nd edn (Sweet and Maxwell, 1983).
Olmi, G. et al., *Thirty Years of Community Law* (Office for Official Publications of the European Communities, 1983).
Hartley, T. C., *The Foundations of European Community Law*, (Clarendon 1981).
Lasok, D., and Bridge, J. W., *Law and Institutions of the European Communities*, 4th edn (Butterworths, 1987).
Mathijsen, P. S. M. F., *A Guide to European Community Law* 4th edn. (Sweet and Maxwell, 1985).
Parry, A., and Dinnage, J., *EEC Law* (Sweet and Maxwell, 1981).
Wyatt, D., and Dashwood, A., *The Substantive Law of the EEC*, 2nd edn (Sweet and Maxwell, 1987).

(e) Policy and Policy-Making

Preference has been given in this section to books which examine not only policy content but also policy processes.
El-Agraa, A. M., *The Economics of the European Community* (Philip Allan, 1985).

Harris S. *et al.*, *The Food and Farm Policies of the European Community*, (Wiley, 1983).

Hine, R. C., *The Political Economy of European Trade* (Harvester, 1985).

Holland, M., *The European Community and South Africa* (Pinter, 1988).

Ifestos, P., *European Political Co-operation* (Avebury, 1987).

Leigh, M., *European Integration and the Common Fisheries Policy* (Croom Helm, 1983).

Ludlow, P., *The Making of the European Monetary System* (Butterworths, 1982).

Meny Y. and Wright, V., *The Politics of Steel* (Walter de Gruyter, 1987).

Neville-Rolfe, E., *The Politics of Agriculture in the European Community* (Croom Helm, 1983).

Pearce, J., *The Common Agriculture Policy* (Routledge & Kegan Paul, 1981).

Swann, D., *Competition and Industrial Policy in the European Community*, (Methuen, 1983).

Swann, D., *The Economics of the Common Market*, 6th edn (Penguin, 1988).

Van Ypersele, J., and Koeune, J-C., *The European Monetary System Origins, Operation and Outlook* (Woodhead-Faulkner, 1985).

Wallace, H., Wallace W., and Webb, C., *Policy Making in the European Community*, 2nd edn. (Wiley, 1983).

(f) Member States and the Community

El-Agraa A. M., (ed.). *Britain Within the European Community* (Macmillan, 1983).

Bulmer S. and Paterson, W., *The Federal Republic of Germany and the European Community* (Allen & Unwin, 1987).

Coombes, D., *Ireland and the European Communities* (Gill & Macmillan, 1983).

Gregory, F. E. C., *Dilemmas of Government* (Martin Robertson, 1983).

Hill, C., *National Foreign Policies and European Political Co-operation* (Allen & Unwin, 1983).

Jenkins, R., (ed.), *Britain and the EEC* (Macmillan, 1983).

Simonian, H., *The Privileged Partnership: Franco–German Relations in the European Community 1969–1984* (Oxford University Press, 1985).

Twitchett, C. and K., *Building Europe* (Europa, 1981).

Yanopoulos, G., (ed.), *Greece and the EEC: Integration and Convergence*, (Macmillan, 1986).

Index

347